THE EUROPEAN UNION SERIES

General Editors: Neill Nugent, William E. Paterson

The European Union series provides an authoritative library on the European Union, ranging from general introductory texts to definitive assessments of key institutions and actors, issues, policies and policy processes, and the role of member states.

Books in the series are written by leading scholars in their fields and reflect the most up-to-date research and debate. Particular attention is paid to accessibility and clear presentation for a wide audience of students, practitioners and interested general readers.

The series editors are **Neill Nugent**, Professor of Politics and Jean Monnet Professor of European Integration, Manchester Metropolitan University, and **William E. Paterson**, Honourary Professor in German and European Studies, University of Aston. Their co-editor until his death in July 1999, **Vincent Wright**, was a Fellow of Nuffield College, Oxford University.

Feedback on the series and book proposals are always welcome and should be sent to Steven Kennedy, Palgrave Macmillan, Houndmills, Basingstoke, Hampshire RG21 6XS, UK, or by e-mail to s.kennedy@palgrave.com

General textbooks

Published

Desmond Dinan **Encyclopedia of the European Union**
[Rights: Europe only]

Desmond Dinan **Europe Recast: A History of European Union**
[Rights: Europe only]

Desmond Dinan **Ever Closer Union: An Introduction to European Integration** (4th edn)
[Rights: Europe only]

Mette Eilstrup Sangiovanni (ed.) **Debates on European Integration: A Reader**

Simon Hix and Bjørn Høyland **The Political System of the European Union** (3rd edn)

Paul Magnette **What is the European Union? Nature and Prospects**

John McCormick **Understanding the European Union: A Concise Introduction** (5th edn)

Brent F. Nelsen and Alexander Stubb **The European Union: Readings on the Theory and Practice of European Integration** (3rd edn)
[Rights: Europe only]

Neill Nugent (ed.) **European Union Enlargement**

Neill Nugent **The Government and Politics of the European Union** (7th edn)

John Peterson and Elizabeth Bomberg **Decision-Making in the European Union**

Ben Rosamond **Theories of European Integration**

Esther Versluis, Mendeltje van Keulen and Paul Stephenson **Analyzing the European Union Policy Process**

Forthcoming

Laurie Buonanno and Neill Nugent **Policies and Policy Processes of the European Union**

Dirk Leuffen, Berthold Rittberger and Frank Schimmelfennig **Differentiated Integration**

Sabine Saurugger **Theoretical Approaches to European Integration**

Also Planned

The Political Economy of European Integration

Series Standing Order (outside North America only)
ISBN 0–333–71695–7 hardback
ISBN 0–333–69352–3 paperback
Full details from www.palgrave.com

Visit Palgrave Macmillan's
EU Resource area at
www.palgrave.com/politics/eu/

The major institutions and actors

Published

Renaud Dehousse **The European Court of Justice**
Justin Greenwood **Interest Representation in the European Union** (3rd edn)
Fiona Hayes-Renshaw and Helen Wallace **The Council of Ministers** (2nd edn)
Simon Hix and Christopher Lord **Political Parties in the European Union**
David Judge and David Earnshaw **The European Parliament** (2nd edn)
Neill Nugent **The European Commission**
Anne Stevens with Handley Stevens **Brussels Bureaucrats? The Administration of the European Union**

Forthcoming

Wolfgang Wessels **The European Council**

The main areas of policy

Published

Michele Chang **Monetary Integration in the European Union**
Michelle Cini and Lee McGowan **Competition Policy in the European Union** (2nd edn)
Wyn Grant **The Common Agricultural Policy**
Martin Holland **The European Union and the Third World**
Jolyon Howorth **Security and Defence Policy in the European Union**
Johanna Kantola **Gender and the European Union**
Stephan Keukeleire and Jennifer MacNaughtan **The Foreign Policy of the European Union**
Brigid Laffan **The Finances of the European Union**
Malcolm Levitt and Christopher Lord **The Political Economy of Monetary Union**
Janne Haaland Matláry **Energy Policy in the European Union**
John McCormick **Environmental Policy in the European Union**
John Peterson and Margaret Sharp **Technology Policy in the European Union**
Handley Stevens **Transport Policy in the European Union**

Forthcoming

Karen Anderson **Social Policy in the European Union**
Sieglinde Gstöhl and Dirk de Bievrè **The Trade Policy of the European Union**

Hans Bruyninckx and Tom Delreux **Environmental Policy and Politics in the European Union**
Martin Holland and Matthew Doidge **Development Policy of the European Union**
Jörg Monar **Justice and Home Affairs in the European Union**

Also planned

Political Union
The External Policies of the European Union

The member states and the Union

Published

Carlos Closa and Paul Heywood **Spain and the European Union**
Alain Guyomarch, Howard Machin and Ella Ritchie **France in the European Union**
Brigid Laffan and Jane O'Mahoney **Ireland and the European Union**

Forthcoming

Simon Bulmer and William E. Paterson **Germany and the European Union**
Brigid Laffan **The European Union and its Member States**

Also planned

Britain and the European Union

Issues

Published

Derek Beach **The Dynamics of European Integration: Why and When EU Institutions Matter**
Christina Boswell and Andrew Geddes **Migration and Mobility in the European Union**
Thomas Christiansen and Christine Reh **Constitutionalizing the European Union**
Robert Ladrech **Europeanization and National Politics**
Cécile Leconte **Understanding Euroscepticism**
Steven McGuire and Michael Smith **The European Union and the United States**
Wyn Rees **The US-EU Security Relationship: The Tensions between a European and a Global Agenda**

Interest Representation in the European Union

3rd Edition

Justin Greenwood

First edition 2003
Second edition 2007

This edition published 2011 by
PALGRAVE MACMILLAN

Palgrave Macmillan in the UK is an imprint of Macmillan Publishers Limited, registered in England, company number 785998, of Houndmills, Basingstoke, Hampshire RG21 6XS.

Palgrave Macmillan in the US is a division of St Martin's Press LLC, 175 Fifth Avenue, New York, NY 10010.

Palgrave Macmillan is the global academic imprint of the above companies and has companies and representatives throughout the world.

Palgrave® and Macmillan® are registered trademarks in the United States, the United Kingdom, Europe and other countries

ISBN 978–0–230–27193–7   hardback
ISBN 978–0–230–27194–4   paperback

This book is printed on paper suitable for recycling and made from fully managed and sustained forest sources. Logging, pulping and manufacturing processes are expected to conform to the environmental regulations of the country of origin.

A catalogue record for this book is available from the British Library.

A catalog record for this book is available from the Library of Congress.

10 9 8 7 6 5 4 3 2 1
20 19 18 17 16 15 14 13 12 11

Printed in China

Contents

List of Tables   vii

Preface to the Third Edition   viii

List of Abbreviations   ix

1 Introduction   **1**
The variety of interests in Europe   8
Groups   12
Non-group actors   17
Conclusion   21

2 EU Decision-Making and Channels of Influence   **23**
'Routes' of influence   25
EU interest representation through the
    'national route'   27
EU interest representation through the
    'Brussels route'   31
Conclusion   51

**3 The Regulation of Lobbying and the European
Transparency Register**   **53**
Regulating conduct of those working in
    EU institutions   54
The regulation of lobbyists   56

4 Business and Professional Interests   **65**
Business interest associations   69
Cross-sectoral associations   75
Sector associations and firms   87
Large firms as EU public affairs actors   92
Professional interests   93
Peak associations claiming representation
    of professionals   97
EU sectoral professional interests   100
Conclusion   107

5 **Labour Interests** **109**
Labour and the economic agenda 113
Social Europe through a participative
    labour market model 117
The European organization of labour interests 121
Conclusions 126

6 **Citizen Interests** **128**
The landscape of citizen interest groups 130
The funding of NGOs 136
Historic landmarks in the development of EU citizen
    interest representation 141
Environmental interests 144
Consumer interests 158
Social interests 164
Social movements 171
Conclusion 174

7 **Territorial Interests** **176**
Regional governance in western Europe 178
The organization of territorial public interests at
    the European level 184
The Brussels offices of the regions 185
Territorially based EU collective action organizations 190
Conclusions 196

8 **Organized Civil Society and European Integration** **199**
Organized civil society and the democratic legitimacy
    of the EU 200
Organized civil society and the development
    of EU competencies 226
Conclusions: organized civil society and the EU 231

Bibliography 236

Index 266

List of Tables

1.1	Types and number of interest organizations active in EU public affairs, counted from the 2007 and 2011 editions of commercial public affairs directories	10
4.1	EU business associations employing 25 or more staff	73
4.2	The resources of the cross-sectoral EU business associations	76
6.1	Members of the EU Civil Society Contact Group	131
6.2	Cross-sectoral EU citizen interest associations not in membership of the Contact Group of Civil Society	132
6.3	EU funding of principal EU NGOs	138
6.4	EU NGOs in the Mundo-b building	141
6.5	The 'G10' environmental NGOs and their resources	152
7.1	Degrees of devolved authority in the EU member states	179
7.2	Territorial representation offices in Brussels	186
7.3	Principal sectoral EU trans-regional associations and networks	194

Preface to the Third Edition

Interest Representation in the European Union seeks to meet the needs of researchers, thesis and dissertation writers, postgraduate students on taught courses, commentators, and a range of practitioners in political institutions and civil society organizations. This edition maintains the distinctiveness of its predecessors as the only one with a complete coverage of each of the different segments of organized civil society as business, unions, the professions, citizen interests of all types, and territorial interests, together with all of the wider issues surrounding EU interest representation. It differs from the second (2007) edition in a number of significant ways. Over one third of the bibliographic references in this edition are new, and the concluding chapter offers fresh analysis. There is an entire chapter devoted to the European Transparency Register (ETR) (Chapter 3), and the information resources the ETR yields are used to inform analysis in other chapters. Chapter 5 offers a re-interpretation of the role of the labour movement. In Chapter 6, the emergence of new social movements as actors is considered. Chapter 7 presents analysis from my own recent research on the role of the Brussels offices of territorial representations to the EU. And Chapter 8 expands the assessment of the role of interests in European integration, both in terms of the development of EU competencies and in EU democratic legitimacy, addressing the extent to which the EU system of interest representation is unique by applying tools of comparative politics. Every chapter has been thoroughly revised to incorporate changes in analysis, focus, and substantive events including changes introduced by the Lisbon Treaty. In some cases this yields quite different outcomes to predecessor editions, leading to a new product centred on analysis.

List of Abbreviations

ACE	Architects' Council of Europe
ACEA	Association of European Automobile Constructors
AEBR	Association of European Border Regions
AEMH	European Association of Senior Hospital Physicians
AER	Assembly of European Regions
AMCHAM-EU	EU Committee of the American Chamber of Commerce
AMUE	Association for the Monetary Union of Europe
ANEC	European Association for the Coordination of Consumer Representation in Standardisation
ATTAC	Association for the Taxation of Financial Transactions in aid of the Citizen
BAR	Brussels Automobile Representatives
BEUC	The European Consumers' Organisation (Bureau Européen des Unions de Consommateurs)
CBI	Confederation of British Industry
CCBE	Council of the Bars and Law Societies of the European Union
CCRLA	Consultative Council of Regional and Local Authorities
CEC	Confédération Européenne des Cadres
CEDAG	European Council for Voluntary Organisations
CEE	Central and Eastern European
CEEP	European Centre of Public Enterprises
CEFIC	European Chemical Industry Council
CEMR	Council of European Municipalities and Regions
CEN	Committee for European Normalisation
CENELEC	European Committee for Electrotechnical Standardisation
CEO(s)	Chief Executive Officer(s)
CEPLIS	European Council of the Liberal Professions
CESI	European Confederation of Independent Unions
CGT	Confédération Général du Travail

CIAA	Confederation of Food and Drink Industries of the EU
CLRAE	Congress of Local and Regional Authorities of Europe
COFACE	Confederation of Family Organisations in the European Union
CONCAWE	The Oil Companies European Organisation for Environmental and Health Protection
CONECCS	Consultation, the European Commission, and Civil Society
COREPER	Committee of Permanent Representatives
CPME	Standing Committee of European Doctors
CPMR	Conference of Peripheral Maritime Regions
DG SANCO	Directorate General for Health and Consumer Protection
ECAS	European Citizen Action Service
ECCE	European Council of Civil Engineers
ECJ	European Court of Justice
EEA	European Environmental Agency
EEB	European Environmental Bureau
EEC	European Economic Community
EES	European Employment Strategy
EESC	European Economic and Social Committee
EFM	European Federation of Metalworkers
EFPIA	European Federation of Pharmaceutical Industry Associations
EFSA	European Food Safety Authority
EHF	European Health Forum
EIB	European Investment Bank
EIFs	European Industry Federations
ELISAN	European Local Inclusion and Social Action Network
ELU	European Lawyers' Union
EMU	Economic and Monetary Union
ENSA	European Network of Social Authorities
EP	European Parliament
EPE	European Partners for the Environment
EPFSF	European Parliamentary Financial Services Forum
EPHA	European Public Health Alliance
ERFS	European Roundtable on Financial Services

ERRIN	European Regions Research Innovation Network
ERRT	European Retail Round Table
ERT	European Round Table of Industrialists
ESAN	European Social Action Network
ETI	European Transparency Initiative
ETR	European Transparency Register
ETSI	European Telecommunications Standards Institute
ETUC	European Trade Union Confederation
EU	European Union
EUMF	European Union Migrants' Forum
EUPHF	European Union Public Health Forum
EURADA	European Association of (Regional) Development Agencies
EUREGHA	European Regional and Local Health Authorities
EUROCADRES	Council of European Professional and Managerial Staff
EUROCHAMBRES	Association of European Chambers of Commerce and Industry
EUROCOMMERCE	European Federation of Retailing and Distribution
EUROCOOP	European Community of Consumer Cooperatives
EURODAD	European Network on Debt and Development
EWL	European Women's Lobby
FEANI	Federation Européenne d'Associations Nationales d'Ingénieurs
FEANTSA	European Federation of National Organisations Working with the Homeless
FedEE	European Federation of Employers
FEDESA	European Federation for Animal Health
FGSD	First General Systems Directive
FIEC	European Construction Industry Federation
FIN-USE	Forum of Financial Services Users
FoEE	Friends of the Earth Europe
FSCG	Financial Services Consumer Group
FT	Financial Times

GATS	General Agreement on Tariffs and Services
GATT	General Agreement on Tariffs and Trade
IFN	Friends of Nature International
IGC	Inter Governmental Conference
INTERREG	Cross-border and Inter-regional Cooperation
IRE	Innovating Regions in Europe
IRTUC	Interregional Trade Union Council
ISCO	International Standard Classification Organisation
ISO	International Standards Organisation
IUCN	World Conservation Union
MEP	Member of the European Parliament
METREX	Network of European Metropolitan Regions and Areas
NUTS	Nomenclature of territorial units for statistics
ORGALIME	European Engineering Association
QMV	Qualified Majority Voting
REGLEG	Conference of Regions with Legislative powers
SEA	Single European Act
SEAP	Society of European Affairs Practitioners
SGSD	Second General Systems Directive
SINAPSE	Scientific Information for Policy Support in Europe
SLG	Starting Line Group
SME	small and medium sized enterprise
TABD	Transatlantic Business Dialogue
TACD	Transatlantic Consumer Dialogue
T&E	European Federation for Transport and the Environment
TEU	Treaty on European Union
UAE	Union des Avocats Européens
UEAPME	European Association of Craft, Small and Medium-Sized Enterprises
UEMO	European Union of General Practitioners
UNICE	Confederation of European Business
WHO	World Health Organisation
WPG	White Paper on Governance
WWF	World Wide Fund for Nature
ZdH	Zentralverband des Deutschen Handwerks

Chapter 1

Introduction

'Interest representation' in democratic political systems is channelled through traditional pathways of representative (parliamentary) democracy as well as supplementary systems aimed at participatory democracy. The European Union (EU) is particularly dependent upon a secondary 'participatory' channel because of core weaknesses in the 'representative' channel (most EU citizens do not vote in European Parliament elections or share a sense of common identity) which would otherwise link civil society with political institutions. The absence of popular engagement also means that interest organizations not only dominate input to the EU's participatory channel but also perform surrogate democratic mechanisms, such as acting as agents of accountability. Heavy reliance upon, and institutionalization of, interest organizations in any political system brings to the fore a whole range of issues; centre stage is the extent to which interest organizations can really connect wider civil society with political institutions and vice versa, as well as the types of stakeholders who win and lose from these relationships, and the dimensions and drivers of such outcomes. Thus, long-standing questions about the role of interest organizations in political systems come into particularly sharp relief about the EU because of high systemic dependence, the associated remoteness from civil society, and the impact of a multi-level governance structure. The status of most EU interest groups as associations of associations (and thus with indirect connections to civil society) creates a further point of distinctiveness about the EU system. The task of locating points of difference within an underlying framework of tools which allows comparison of interest representation across political systems is undertaken in Chapter 8.

Most political systems also have a participatory model as secondary to a representative model. Pateman's landmark study (Pateman 1970) noted the incompleteness of democratic systems without participatory channels, recording increasing and diversified

1

forms of political participation alongside traditional representative models. The key issue has always been the type of participatory channels which are feasible. In the EU, the absence of a 'government', a common language, and a 'public space' (e.g. shared media, etc.) are somewhat debilitating to popular participation. While the reliance upon elites has always been a feature of participatory channels (famously noted by, inter alia, Kant, and in the modern era by Pitkin – see the review in Chapter 8), the EU has become unusually dependent upon elite interest groups as intended proxies for wider 'civil society'. While there are established debates as to what the term 'civil society' should mean (and in particular its extent of breadth of embrace), in EU parlance (European Commission 2001a) it is used to denote every type of interest outside of government and the military, and thus 'organized civil society' denotes organizations embracing interests from producers (business, union, etc.) to citizens. Much of what passes for 'dialogue with civil society' at EU level is dialogue with interest groups and related organizations.

The institutionalization of interest groups in the EU system is articulated by the post-Lisbon Treaty. This asserts the primacy of representative democracy, as well as specifying a supplementary participatory democracy stream with a key role for interest organizations. Thus, the first three clauses of Article 11 state that 'the institutions shall: give citizens and representative associations the opportunity to make known and publicly exchange their views in all areas of Union action; maintain an open, transparent and regular dialogue with their representative associations and civil society; carry out broad consultations with parties concerned in order to ensure that Union action is coherent and transparent'.

This dependence upon interest groups therefore arises partly from the lack of popular engagement with the EU. It also arises from the nature of the EU itself. In essence, the EU is a system of pooled sovereignty to enable member states to solve common shared problems, making it primarily oriented towards regulation. In the renowned formulation of Lowi (1964), regulation can concentrate costs and benefits narrowly upon particular stakeholders, often of a highly technical nature, thus making organized interests significant political actors (Wilson 1995). Interest groups are more marginal players in generalized issues involving open public debate, such as the adoption of monetary union ('distributive politics'), and over questions of wealth distribution between social groups which are underpinned by battles between 'rich' and 'poor' as potential winners and losers ('redistributive politics'). The nature of the responsibilities of the European Commission in this regulatory oriented regime (Chapter 2) means that it is at the centre of relationships with interest groups, and that these exchanges are somewhat, but not exclusively, technical in nature. This structures the relationship with interest groups in a number of significant ways (Chapter 2), some of which are paradoxical. It limits the sensitivity of the EU system to pressure from outside interests in that there are limited mechanisms of direct accountability, but the relatively small size of the Commission, with around 38,000 staff (European Commission 2011a) (often compared to a typical medium-sized city administration (Nugent 2010)) may make it overdependent upon outside interests for technical information, raising the potential for 'regulatory capture'.

Such factors reflect that a number of well-recognized challenges arise whenever political institutions work with interest groups. Representative democracy has election results as a means to aggregate popular preferences, whereas there is no equivalent in participatory democracy, leading to the danger that well-organized, knowledgeable, and resourced groups might dominate public policy agendas. Unless these types of issues are addressed, there is a danger that exchanges between political institutions, and interest groups, might detract from, rather than contribute to, popular legitimacy. Some of these can be addressed by measures (summarized in the paragraph below) to ensure that a wide range of interests have the ability to contribute to policymaking and to act as a 'check and balance' upon each other. Whether such pluralistic countervailing forces can really be achieved in highly technical fields, where knowledge 'entry costs' to the political arena are high, remains an open question. One example of this concerns financial services, although even here the European Commission has stimulated consumer organization with the promise of more to come, while a recent initiative launched from within the Parliament has been dedicated to the creation of pluralistic countervailing pressure in financial services (Chapter 6).

Because the EU is so dependent upon its exchanges with interest groups, associated measures to structure them carry significant implications for popular legitimacy. Consequently, a series of mechanisms have emerged from the institutions aimed at addressing these issues. In sum, these are instruments aimed at pluralist 'check and balance' outcomes in which no one type of interest is able to dominate the EU political system, and where interest organizations are enabled to act as agents to exercise accountability pressures upon each other and upon political institutions. These instruments structure exchanges between political institutions and interest groups, and include an extensive system of funding for non-governmental organizations (NGOs), rules for public consultation, and transparency measures including access to documents which equip interest groups to act as accountability agents (Chapters 2, 6, and 8). Even the new 'European Citizens Initiative', ostensibly a direct democracy measure for citizens to bring forward proposals, will ultimately depend upon the professionalized resources of interest organizations to operationalize it given the detail of logistical requirements (Chapter 6).

Such measures raise a variety of related issues. These include: the extent to which the independence of groups is compromised by such extremes of institutionalization, and whether the 'professionalization' of interest organizations matters to attempts to create EU democratic legitimacy(Chapters 6 and 8); and whether formalized rules of exchange between EU institutions and interest organizations are sufficient to overpower the impact of informal policy-oriented relationships or provide EU institutions with a means to help insulate themselves from excesses of pressure politics.

The 'multi-level governance' nature of the EU naturally facilitates institutional insulation and pluralistic outcomes because decision-making is so fragmented. One consequence of this is that no one type of interest would ever be able to 'capture' one of the main decision-making institutions, let alone the entire political system. The Commission has 'services' with entirely different orientations; the Parliament is a multi-party system with no inbuilt majority; and the Council comprises 27 member states. Finding a compromise within just one of these institutions is an achievement in itself, while doing so between the different institutions seems remarkable. Political institutions can use these realities to moderate demands upon them. They can resist pressures by pointing to the need for compromise. They can 'divide and rule' as multiple access points afforded by diversely constituted decision-making institutions invite competitive interest representation. And segments of institutions can also enter into interest alliances with different constituencies of organized civil society, which results in a system of countervailing pressures with unpredictable policy-oriented outcomes. These are the classic conditions for pluralism. A wide-ranging evaluation based on a large number of studies did not find an overall picture of routine business dominance (Kohler-Koch 2008).

The potential satisfaction of its needs by EU political institutions from their exchanges with interest groups is intensive and diverse. Apart from the need for policymaking expertise, and implementation and monitoring capacity, the potential for consolidated collective viewpoint, and the potential to enhance legitimacy, EU institutions also work with organized civil society because the latter has the ability to convey political messages. Most noted among the latter has been the potential for interest organizations to orient member states towards seeking common solutions by ceding sovereignty towards the EU (Haas 1958; see also the examples in Chapters 4–7). For all these reasons, EU political institutions which are most dependent upon engagement with organized interests make themselves highly accessible to them, consistently resisting formalized accreditation schemes on the grounds that it might limit the supply of needed resources. And the ability of groups to convey political messages means that EU institutions lobby interest groups almost as vigorously as the reverse is true, using groups to exert pressure upon the positions of other groups, upon member states, other EU institutions and segments of institutions, and as agents in the international system (Chapter 8). EU institutions, and particularly the European Commission, have therefore been very active in creating and sustaining interest groups of all types constituted at EU level (Chapters 4–7). Because of these factors, and their ability to moderate the demands upon them, some commentators see the EU institutions more a 'master of fate' than a 'victim of pressure' in its exchanges with interest groups (Grande 1996; see also Chapter 8).

The EU's extent of systemic dependence upon organized civil society makes the study of EU interest representation a compelling analytical focus for scholars of European integration and federalism, of comparative public policy, and of interest groups themselves. This degree of dependence is somewhat unique to the EU political system, yet there is also much about EU interest representation which is common to other systems. There are structural features characterizing exchanges between political institutions and organized civil society which arise in any democratic setting (such as resource dependencies), yet there are factors intensively at work in the EU setting (such as deficits among EU institutions of capacity and legitimacy) to make these work out in very specific ways. Thus, particular properties and characteristics of political decision-making systems become drivers of common outcomes, and of differences. Hence, interest representation in consensual decision-making systems (such as the EU) is quite different from those in 'majoritarian' systems of government because the latter has a party of government able to exert its will. In majoritarian systems, government relations are oriented towards a 'winner takes all', whereas in consensual systems, there are rarely outright winners and losers, requiring broadly based alliances to be constructed between civil society interests. And the extent of democratic connections between political institutions and civil society (in particular, accountability mechanisms) significantly structures the ways in which interest organizations behave (Mahoney 2008); at EU level, the lack of these connections may, somewhat paradoxically, help to insulate the system from special interest pressures (Chapter 8).

A complex multi-level system such as the EU intensifies consensual outcomes, and the need for alliances, in the search for solutions of any kind, and information about the potential for solutions. If anything is predictable about the EU system, it is that policy outcomes will be of a consensual nature; until that point, the outcome can be somewhat unpredictable, although the remarkable thing given the sheer number of elements in the decision-making system is that only a handful of proposals out of 900 have ended in a failure to legislate since the introduction of the co-decision-making (now the 'ordinary legislative') procedure (European Commission 2011b). EU interest groups provide the EU institutions with information about the likely chances of success of a legislative proposal. And the extent of the consensual nature of the EU project means that it is not uncommon for an EU 'government relations' manager of a multinational to spend more time in dialogue with NGOs than with EU institutions. Alliances with environmental NGOs, in particular, are influential because of the strength of public interest sentiment towards the environment in Europe, and positioning yourself as 'part of the solution' rather than 'part of the problem' is a recognized goal for 'public affairs' managers. Specific procedures of political institutions also become drivers of interest representation practice, such as where responsibility for policy initiation lies, whether there are default mechanisms to block the passage of legislation, the presence of rules restricting access to justice, and transparency-related infrastructures (Chapters 2, 3, 6, and 8).

While some features of the EU system of interest representation originate in common drivers which produce similar outcomes elsewhere, the feature of particular interest about the EU system to highlight in summary from the review above is the extent of dependence upon interest groups to achieve desired goals, and the corresponding action by political institutions to maintain such groups. For the EU system as a whole, the particularly noteworthy consequences of this lie in the course of development of European integration, both in terms of the expansion of EU competencies and in terms of the potential for impact upon civil society. This is because interest groups have the potential to carry the political messages of the EU institutions to member states and to (and from) wider civil society. This possibility was developed in the earliest works on European integration theory, most notably the 'neo-functionalist' account of European integration of Ernst Haas (1958), but also appeared among the aspirations of the most prominent architects of the initial European Community project, including Jean Monnet. This account highlighted the potential consequences for interest groups to develop the range of EU powers by acting as forces of pressures upon member states to cede competencies to the EU (via treaties), and the potential for socializing participants of EU interest groups (and thereafter the national audiences which they relate to) into seeing European solutions and the consequent identification with Europe. The last of these endeavours has increasingly seemed far-fetched, in that EU interest groups are narrowly focused upon policy advocacy with EU institutions and tend to be staffed by a professionalized cadre who 'know the Brussels scene' (Chapter 8). The first endeavour, however – actions by groups resulting in the development of EU competencies – can be illustrated by a number of examples (Chapters 6 and 8), although it should not be regarded as a universal mechanism, and there are cases where the role of interest groups has been more as supporting agents for action which would have happened anyway, rather than causal agents (see Chapters 4 and 8).

The contribution which interest groups make to European integration depends upon their general alignment with the outlook of the EU institutions. Groups which are generally opposed to the logic of liberal integration of markets effectively find themselves frozen out, and have to re-interpret their core values. Eising (2009) recounts how the main EU electricity association was forsaken by the Commission in favour of a small regionally based organization with more aligned values. Woll (2009) tells the story of how the European textiles organization, EURATEX, had to completely about-turn its demands for a protectionist regime in international trade so as to find the benefits of a liberal regime, and only then did it find an ear for its messages in the European Commission. Bouza finds that the agendas of NGOs are shaped after first checking to see that their general thrust is aligned with those of the Commission (Chapter 6). Once agendas coincide, the contribution which interest groups can make is apparent, whether business or otherwise. Thus, the anti-globalization group Corporate Europe Observatory seemed to became a temporary insider with the Cabinet of Commissioner Kallas in the impetus to create (ultimately successfully) a lobby regulation element of what became the European Transparency Initiative (ETI) because of the coincidence of interests of the two parties during the struggle to establish it, and the configuration of other stakeholders against the initiative (Chapter 3).

The variety of interests in Europe

The variety of interests with a stake in regulation formulated at EU level has a global embrace. Among functional interests, almost every conceivable interest is organized in some way through formal collective entities. Apart from the 'usual suspects', there are interest organizations organized at EU level for mustard seed producers, handwriting analysts, fish pathologists, chimney sweeps, beauticians, fairground hands, aquarium trustees, anti-capitalist/globalization-oriented networks, Muslim women, retired people, and the unemployed. Over 40% of organizations active at EU level are national and sub-national organizations, and over 10% of the active population of interest organizations are those headquartered in non-member states (Wonka et al. 2010).

There is, as yet, no definitive list of the numbers and different types of players active in EU interest representation. This is significant because a teeming 'population ecology' of groups is the basis for a system depending upon interest organizations to perform democratic functions. An emerging source of data is the European Transparency Register (ETR), a publicly accessible web database of entries elected and made by organizations which seek to influence EU public policy, commencing from 2008. While this has attracted around 3500 entries at the time of writing, the register is not yet a reliable means of head-counting the population. The main issue has concerned the absence of governance mechanisms for the scheme. While these have developed with the introduction of a new scheme in 2011, some core problems remain which limit its use for head-count purposes. One is that the database is open to any entity which wishes to be included, resulting in it being used as free advertising space for small- and medium-sized enterprises (SMEs). Conversely, the register is not mandatory, though entries are incentivized, and there remain some organizations which are everyday players in EU interest representation which are not signed up. Organizations can also choose the category they wish to be included under, resulting in miscategorization of a number of organizations, and organizations can also choose to register in Bulgarian or Greek Cyrillic because the reasons for many organizations to make an entry in the database do not appear to be related to the core activities of interest representation (Chapter 3). A predecessor scheme to ETR, the CONECCS database (Consultation, the European Commission, and Civil Society), had much more restrictive entry rules, and was thus confined to less than 750 interest associations organized at EU level, around half the constituency apparent in commercial directories (Table 1.1). A parallel scheme operated by the European Parliament (Chapter 3) is based around individuals but yields just over 1500 organizations to which they are associated (Wonka et al. 2010).

Commercial directories have differing scopes of inclusion (Berkhout and Lowery 2008, 2010), as well as sharing with ETR a degree of quirkiness in the entries. As with the ETR, they are dependent upon consent to an entry, contain organizations which are rather inactive at EU level, and reflect choices made by organizations about the category of interest organization to enter. A thorough-going composite of available directory resources (excluding the ETR, but including CONECCS and the EP register, and commercial directories up to 2007) has been undertaken by Wonka et al., which, after ensuring the removal of duplicate entries, arrived at a total of 3700 interest organizations active at EU level (Wonka et al. 2010). Nonetheless, these authors do not make comprehensive distinctions in the presentation of their data between different types of organizations because doing so requires a judgement to be made about the category of entry for every organization. Their data can be developed by further analysis of entries in commercial directories which have appeared since 2007, allowing for a change of ownership in the principal commercial directory during this period and some differences in data presentation practices. Some cases of miscategorization in commercial directory sources are immediately evident, notably the inclusion of some producer interests (mainly from the professions, and territorial authorities) in 'interest group' categories which seems to inflate the presentation of the population of citizen-related interest organizations presented in commercial directories. Combing through each of the entries in these directories, and making adjustments for miscategorization and for comparability over time, delivers the approximate populations given in Table 1.1 in the different interest segments.

The most important question is whether there are evident gaps in the population of interest organizations; the data in Table 1.1 suggests not. Beyond this, there are dangers in drawing conclusions from the population of categories because apparently high numbers can reflect a landscape of competition between specialist groups, particularly among business interest organizations (Chapter 4). And changes over time in reporting and listing practices within a single directory source means that only indicative temporal comparisons can be made, with apparently small degrees of change discounted. Public policy measures, such as transparency registration pressures,

TABLE 1.1   *Types and number of interest organizations active in EU public affairs, counted from the 2007 and 2011 editions of commercial public affairs directories*

Type	2007	2011
Corporates	295	313
EU trade associations and EU associations of the professions	843	823
National associations based in Brussels		
Trade and professional	122	–
Employers' federations	38	–
Chambers of commerce	40	36
EU and global trade unions	24	23
'Interest groups' – citizen interest associations	350	372
Regions	198	226
Think tanks	72	51
Law firms	115	125
Public affairs consultants	153	200

Data extracted from entries in Landmarks Publications (2007) and Dods (2011).

might be expected to increase the size of some categories. From Table 1.1, a growth in the number of commercial public affairs consultancies is clearly apparent, which seems to be accounted for mainly by new small market entrants. A comparison between Table 1.1 with equivalent figures from the 2001 edition of the same directory (Landmarks Publications 2001) indicates a growth in the number of citizen interest groups during that period, which has since tailed off, reflecting the maturation of this segment. This was also identified in another recent temporal headcount of the population of EU interest organizations from directory sources, where an increasing presence of citizen interest organizations from the mid-1990s was noted, alongside a decline in the population of business and commercially oriented interest organizations since the early 1990s (Berkhout and Lowery 2010).

There is much greater uncertainty about the number of individuals involved in 'EU lobbying'. This endeavour raises definitional issues ('what is a lobbyist?') and methodological issues ('how can a head count of which type of staff be undertaken?') of such magnitude that it is difficult to provide a figure of much value at all. As the issue of EU lobbying has become increasingly politicized, the figures cited tend to suit the purpose. A figure in recent vogue has been 15,000 (Graziano 2010), although the popularity of this seems to relate more to the frequency with which it is cited, most notably in recent times by Commissioner Kallas as part of justification for his new regulatory initiative, than to an authoritative headcount. Notably, its use was not accompanied by a transparent basis or public justification (Kallas 2005), and, when challenged, the Commissioner noticeably backtracked on it as an 'external estimate', without ever revealing the source (EurActiv 2008). Similarly, many references made by commentators to the number of lobbyists are made in passing with no accompanying justification. Another figure, again not without difficulty, is the number of annual passes to its buildings issued by the European Parliament to 'accredited lobbyists', which at the end of 2010 stood at 4695 individuals. This latter source has its limitations in that any one organization is restricted in the number of passes it may have; some organizations do not register, either on purposeful grounds as not wishing to self-present as a 'lobbyist' or for other reasons; some individual researchers from academic institutions with an EU study focus have registered because it provides easier access to the European Parliament library rather than because they seek to represent interests.

Groups

Estimates of the number of groups constituted at EU level have been subject to significant variation. There is no definitively accepted figure, partly because some offerings fail to make clear the basis upon which their count has been undertaken, such as whether it really only does include groups (as opposed to other players such as think tanks), or only groups formally constituted at the EU level. The most popular recent folklore originates from Commissioner Kallas's somewhat ambiguous claim of '2600 groups in Brussels' (Kallas 2005), as part of his justification for a new regulatory transparency initiative in 2005. Because of the apparent authority of the source this figure has been in vogue since, despite the lack of supporting public domain evidence for it. When subsequently challenged, Kallas has backtracked and stressed its basis as an (as yet unknown) 'external estimate' (EurActiv 2008). The figure first appeared as a passing reference to 'about 2600 interest groups had a permanent office in downturn Brussels' in the Executive Summary of a 2003 European Parliament research report (European Parliament 2003a: iii), with no mention of the basis upon which the figure had been arrived at elsewhere in the report. And the somewhat ambiguous wording ('groups in Brussels') would permit the inclusion in the headcount of Belgian national associations and those oriented to the international level (facilitated by a long-standing Belgian legal instrument designed to attract such groups), but has often been misused as a reference point of the number of groups operating on the EU environment.

Most figures in circulation seem to have been drawn from simple category counts in directory listings. All such sources have partial coverage, quirkiness in assigning a particular entry to a category type, and snap judgements about eligibility. Consequently, it is only possible to take impressions from these, such as the extent of growth over time, which refer to more than 100 in existence by 1959 (Eising 2001a); 200–300 in the 1960s (Wessels 1997; Butt Philip and Porter 1997); 400 by 1970 (Watson 2002), rising up to 800 by 1980 (Watson 2002), 1200 by 1997 (Butt Philip and Porter 1997), and to the current vogue. The apparent doubling over the past decade is a somewhat doubtful rate of growth, and can be put into context by the variation evident in other guesstimates, such as one indicating 5000 towards the end of the 1990s (Marks and McAdam 1999). My own composite count from six different directory sources in publication in the year 2000 (Greenwood 2003) indicated a figure of 1450, slightly larger than approximately 1300 EU-level groups apparent from the European Public Affairs Directory data presented in Table 1.1. However, directory sources may have overestimated the population by continuing to include historic entries from defunct or 'post-box' organizations.

The impression provided by directory counts is that of a key growth period dating from the early 1990s. This may be associated with the expansion of the EU following the 1992 Treaty on European Union, and renewed attempts to locate underpinnings of democratic legitimacy since the 2001 White Paper on Governance. The data presented in Table 1.1 presents two striking and related developments over time when compared with my own figures from 2000. The first of these is that around one-third of all associations constituted at EU level are now citizen interest organizations, compared to 20% in 2000. The second is that business interest associations constitute a little more than half of the entire constituency of EU associations, compared to two-thirds in 2000. The general trend of a growth of citizen interest groups relative to the entire constituency of EU level groups is an entirely plausible one, considered further in Chapter 6.

While the geographical distribution of EU level groups is concentrated in Belgium, this only seems to account for around 60% of EU groups (Greenwood 2003). This figure is significant because of the possibility that groups with a base in Brussels may have an advantage through nurturing informal contacts with EU institutions, despite the development of common rules seeking to formalize exchanges with outside groups so as to create the legitimacy which equality of access rules might create. While high-speed trains have made it easier to connect Brussels with France, the UK, Germany, and the Netherlands (the next most popular locations for EU groups, together accounting for one quarter of the total), rushed departures from meetings for train connections limit participation in informal, yet potentially important, network gatherings which follow events. Almost exactly two thirds of the constituency of 'NGOs' listed in the European Public Affairs Directory have a base in Brussels, that is, exceeding the average (60%) for all types of groups. Thus, NGOs do not suffer from a lack of ability to tap into the informal world of Brussels.

In terms of the characteristics of groups established at the EU level, the federated (associations of national associations) format predominates throughout virtually all interest categories.

Significant numbers of direct membership organizations only exist in the business domain where some associations admit companies. In its early days, the Commission operated a policy of dialogue only with European-level groups as an incentive to national groups to form them, as well as the age-old bureaucratic preference for consultation with collective bodies. In practice this proved unworkable because the presence of such groups was patchy, and, where they existed, some were little more than symbolic presences, with enduring collective action problems evident in some as a result of their sheer territorial diversity of membership. Where these proved intractable, the Commission has engaged in dialogue with national groups (Caporaso 1974), or, with large firms and other entities. Bouwen (2002) found that large individual firms had a higher degree of access to the Commission than EU-level associations. While the Commission is open to dialogue with any organization that wishes to engage it, there remains an official policy statement still in force, from the department of the Commission which leads relations with civil society (Secretariat General), which records that 'the Commission tends to favour European (con)federations over representatives of individual or national organizations' (European Commission 1992: 5). While there is variation between and within different Commission services (European Commission 2002), some segments of the Commission reinforce their preference to dialogue with groups when an approach is made by an individual group member. Another mechanism the Commission uses to support EU-level groups is to hand out places on advisory committees through them, a practice which provides a key membership rationale helping to sustain such groups.

Formal groups range in scope from those organizing 'horizontal' interests across a particular constituency (such as confederations of producer interests or citizens), to sectoral type interests, to specialist issue organizations. The large groups representing 'horizontal', or cross-sectoral, interests include Business Europe, a confederation of national business-wide associations; ERT (the European Round Table of Industrialists) and the EU Committee (of the American Chamber of Commerce), both based around large firms; UEAPME (European Association of Craft, Small and Medium-Sized Enterprises), the confederation of national associations representing small and medium sized enterprises (SMEs); EUROCHAMBRES (the Association of European Chambers of Commerce and Industry), representing national associations of Chambers of Commerce;

CEEP (European Centre of Employers and Enterprises providing public services); ETUC (European Trade Union Confederation), the principal organization representing worker interests; and CEPLIS (European Council of the Liberal Professions). Sub-national interests are represented horizontally through the CEMR (Council of European Municipalities and Regions) and the Assembly of European Regions (AER). A notable feature of citizen interest representation is their organization into cognate 'family' networks (such as the 'G10' collection of environmental groups). Citizen interest organization is also marked by a bifurcation between 'representative'-based organizations, whose membership primarily comprises other European associations (such as the Platform of European Social NGOs), and organizations which are based more around advocacy than sector representation, such as the European Citizen Action Service (ECAS).

'Sectoral' organization of interests at EU level follows the tendency for federative structures, that is, most EU interest groups are associations of other associations. The primary unit of membership of almost every citizen group is other organizations; very few have a category of full membership which embraces individuals. For trade unions, the same is true. And for business organization, despite a sizeable presence of associations which have large firms as members (mainly in concentrated sectors), most organizations still remain based around national associations of business. This creates a variety of dynamics which are explored in the individual chapters, but the most important general consequences are those of a distance between elite EU associations and civil society, described earlier, and the concentration of activities upon political representation. Consequently, EU associations are relatively small organizations compared to their national counterparts.

The apparent numerical majority of business interests apparent in Table 1.1 (see also Chapter 4 for a discussion of numbers) should not be equated with 'degrees of influence' because of competition between specialist interests and because of the fragmentation of political authority. The latter makes decision-making 'capture' impossible, as described earlier, but it also affects the way in which interests are organized. A feature of EU business organization is high specialization which makes collective agreement easier, but which creates a landscape of competing organizations (Chapter 4). Thus, the glass industry has separate specialized associations representing the interests of flat glass, container glass, building and automotive glass, crystal glass, domestic glass, and special glass (e.g. fluorescent lighting), as well as a 'peak' cross-sub-sector umbrella association, at EU level; yet finding common agreement across these segments is made more complicated by virtue of their separate organizations. This feature is particularly common at EU level because the multiple-level governance structure of the EU makes it impossible for EU institutions to authoritatively designate organizations as monopoly interlocutors as happens in corporatist settings. Consequently, many EU business associations are marked by continual internal debate as to whether to go for the ease of collective agreement through narrow embrace, at the price of competition, or to contain the scope for competitive lobbying by organizing through breadth, at the price of frustrating 'lowest common denominator' positions. When combined with the natural heterogeneity of business, these factors frequently see rival business factions lined up on different sides of the fence over regulatory proposals which threaten to create narrow groups of 'winners' and losers', with encompassing business associations paralysed by disagreement. And there are only 10 EU business associations with more than 25 staff (Chapter 4). EU business associations are much smaller than national associations because of their specialization upon political representation rather than service provision because their members (national associations, large firms) do not need business services (Chapter 4).

EU funding ensures that resource asymmetries between different types of interests are less extreme than might otherwise be the case. The 'G10' (group of 10) EU Environmental NGOs declare €4–4.5 million of annual funding from EU institutions, comprising around one third of their budgets, and enabling them to fund almost 150 EU staff between them (Chapter 6). These resources exceed the collective resources of the five EU business-wide organizations (Chapter 4). Best resourced among EU environmental NGOs is the World Wide Fund for Nature European Policy Office (WWF-EPO) with a 2009 budget of €4,801,118 (13% funded by EU institutions) and 41 staff. The European Consumers Organisation, BEUC, has an annual budget approaching €4 million. International NGO brands, such as WWF, Greenpeace, Friends of the Earth, and Amnesty International, can supplement the resources of its European policy offices by drawing on resources from offices in other geographic locations, as well as a substantial base of volunteer help. Among European-specific organizations, the European Youth Forum lists 25 staff on its website (European Youth Forum 2010), and its entry in the ETI register reveals that 79% of its total budget of €3,028,122 is derived from the EU institutions in 2008. The Platform of European Social NGOs ('Social Platform'), a leading organization in the citizen field, likewise received 79% of its budget from EU institutions in 2009, and the European Women's Lobby received 84%. The Eurogroup for Animals and Friends of the Countryside each declare a spending on lobbying the EU institutions of more than €1 million each year on their respective entries on the ETR. There are over 50 women's advocacy organizations active at EU level. Purpose-renovated 'NGO eco-houses' from which to network and co-ordinate resources to lobby EU institutions are now appearing in Brussels (Chapter 6). The appealing image of NGOs as small voices drowned out by a chorus of business lobbying ('victimhood') is an effective way of playing upon sensitivities as a means of gaining access to the policy process, but is somewhat removed from reality.

A core question is the extent to which such funding compromises the independence of such organizations, or creates quasi-agencies of EU institutions. Such organizations rarely seem to pull their punches in criticizing EU institutions (see Chapter 6), interpreting their role as the 'unofficial opposition' in the EU political system, and the recipients themselves see it as a means of protection from dependencies on alternative sources of income, such as corporate or individual paymasters. Whether the funding does create psychological boundaries to playing the role of 'opposition' is an open question. There have been, however, new funding donors which have recently appeared on the scene for EU NGOs (Chapter 6).

Non-group actors

There are five categories of players from civil society active at EU level which are not interest groups. These are representations from the regions (Chapter 7), consultancies and law firms providing services on commercial terms, company public affairs offices, think tanks, and activists with a website. Networks with varying degrees of formality have also arisen linking the variety of actors from collective and other sources.

An in-house public affairs capacity is almost exclusively to be found among large firms, and the largest of these can be expected to have a capacity dedicated to the management of EU public affairs because of the potential for regulatory initiatives to impact upon them. However, large firms can also lack the capacity to act rationally and can be notoriously clumsy in the political arena (Hart 2010), and some very large firms have no dedicated capacity to adequately engage with EU public affairs, or only do so after being caught by surprise by a regulatory initiative. The airline sector has a number of examples. A few large firms have set up a public affairs capacity in Brussels only to abandon their office a few years later.

Wonka et al. (2010) identify almost 500 firms who appear in one of the directory sources reviewed earlier. The European Public Affairs Directory lists around 300 companies with public affairs offices which engage the EU level, of which most have a Brussels presence (Table 1.1). The multiple-level architecture of the EU affords access to such players, and the need to participate in and beyond trade associations also contributes to the rationale for establishing such offices. An analysis of the geographical origin (by national headquarters) of those listed in the European Public Affairs Directory in 2003 indicates that around one quarter are American, 17% British, 11% French, and 11% German (Coen 2009). Anglo and American-based firms in particular, familiar with operating in pluralist environments, are used to working outside of groups and with commercial public affairs consultancies, whereas those used to the corporatist traditions of Germanic countries tend to place a greater emphasis upon collective associations. One piece of recent research suggests that the Anglo/Germanic division also works in preferences for the type of commercial sources used, with Anglo/American firms using traditional public affairs consultancies and Germanic firms using law firms (Lahusen 2002). An oft-posed question in the literature is whether national traditions of corporatism or pluralism might influence the ability of organized interests to engage the EU level, and in particular whether the generally pluralist nature of the EU policymaking environment might be disabling for interests with corporatist traditions. However, studies seeking to investigate explanations couched in the 'fit' between national and EU policymaking environments have found contradictory results (for a review, see Eising 2009). There is no evidence that interests from countries with corporatist traditions experience difficulties in engaging with the EU level; rather, the issue is the underdevelopment of organized civil society in the south of Europe, and central/eastern Europe (Greer et al. 2008).

There is very little literature on the organization of organized civil society interests from non-EU member states. Wonka et al. found that over 11% of interest organizations active at EU level had their headquarters in the US (7.8%) and Switzerland (3.3%), and a widely distributed 'tail' of organizations in other locations. Many EU associations already admit organizations from Europe but which are based in countries which are not member states. Beyond this is an issue about the admission of companies from non-EU member states in direct membership business associations, with a mixed picture of practice among associations in the admission of companies based outside Europe. Some take the view that globalization makes it difficult to distinguish between 'European' and 'non-European' companies, with many of the latter holding substantial investments in Europe. Where there is non-admission, multinational firms will inevitably have a presence, and there are isolated cases of national firms with a multinational presence with a Brussels office (e.g. Tequila from Mexico). The ETI currently lists around 150 firms with a head office in third countries who have activities orientated towards influencing public EU policy. While entries from European Free Trade Association (EFTA) countries, candidate countries, and from the US and Japan can be expected, there are entries also from companies based in Brazil, Russia, and India – though not yet China, where corporate interest representation seems to take place through the national representation to the EU, which remains a common pattern.

Large firm EU public affairs capacities in Brussels are often quite small, based around one executive and a personal assistant. A few are much larger, among which the pharmaceutical companies are well represented. The company public affairs official will almost certainly be challenged by the need to reconcile the interests of a variety of product divisions within a company. An example is provided by IBM, where product divisions had a foot in both camps during the course of the proposal for a Directive on Computer Implemented Inventions, which pitted software protection interests against those whose products were based on users of derivative software (Gehlen 2006). Sometimes, companies have little capacity for centralized management of political activities, and any attempt to do so is actively resisted by product divisions which want to preserve their autonomy to participate in technical networks in trade associations, etc. The consequence is that a large firm may have no means to prevent different product divisions taking up contradictory positions on the same issue in different trade associations. Sometimes, there is no central corporate knowledge of the number of trade association affiliations they maintain (Chapter 4).

Large firms are a significant client segment of commercial consultancies, whether those dedicated to a public affairs offering (Lahusen 2003; Mahoney 2008), or law firms who provide public affairs services. Inevitably, law firms have a specialism in offering competition-policy-related services, and this predicts the nature of their clientele. And their pitch for public affairs-related business makes sense as a wider business model because it brings in clients who can be referred to other law-based departments for specialist advice. A further advantage they have developed when compared to dedicated public affairs consultancies is their reluctance to sign up to the ETI register, on the grounds that they are governed by professional codes of conduct in which client confidentiality is sacrosanct. This is likely to attract clients who are reluctant to see their public affairs activities disclosed through the registrations which dedicated public affairs consultancies are asked to make on the ETI register (Chapter 3). The clientele of commercial consultancies are of a much broader spectrum than law firms, and, while based on business from the corporate sector, is much more diverse. They include citizen interest organizations, and public sector organizations, including agencies of central government in, and beyond, the member states. Consultancy services offer a range of services from simple monitoring through to strategic advice. None would claim to substitute for the technical input that their clients would be able to make to issues, which makes them less valuable to policymaking officials than to their clients.

'Think tanks' place information, assessments, and ideas in the public arena and seek to improve the quality of public policies, and democratic debate, accordingly. EU think tanks have come under the spotlight during the recent debates on EU transparency, raising issues about the scope of their activities and their sources of finance. Companies do seek reputational positioning by associating themselves with apparently detached research thinking, and they do make financial contributions to such organizations. Some organizations use think tanks as part of a wider business model in which there is an associated public affairs business, such as 'The Centre', which has positioned itself as Brussels' first 'think-do' tank. But the core of Brussels think tanks are largely independent organizations, funded by a mixture of diverse short-term project work for a wide range of organizations in civil society, together with a pluralism of medium-term stakeholder partners.

At the fringes of EU interest organizations are a range of others, including lone entrepreneurs operating a business model servicing the interest representation community, and website based activists related to wider 'alternatives' social movements with a generally hostile perspective on globalization and liberal capitalism. The latter are of some interest for integration scholars in a variety of ways. Their arrival since the widespread use of the Internet demonstrates the way in which the web has empowered previously marginal voices. Of similar interest is the extent to which such voices have become drawn in to the European public space of debate, and the extent to which any kind of debate ultimately contributes to public engagement with the EU. Another notable feature concerns the progressive institutionalization of some of these interests as policy participants where their aspirations chime with those of a segment of the EU institutions (Chapter 6), and where the balance of their activities turns more towards dialogue with EU institutions and to relationship building than seeking to undermine the system through public messages. The course of establishment of the ETI amply demonstrates some of these aspects (Chapter 3), offering support for pluralistic caricatures of the EU policy process. Their progressive institutionalization is also indicated by tendencies to develop into formalistic organizations with a reasonable level of resources and Brussels office space, and which ultimately come to terms with the label 'lobbyist' (Chapter 6). Of note also is the pluralistic way in which such organization has itself spurned counter-organizations, where self-appointed '… watch' websites themselves become challenged by '… watch.watch' websites, followed by bitter accusations and counter-accusations exchanged between the protagonists (Chapter 6).

Conclusion

There are common drivers of systems of interest representation which the EU possesses, such as the ways in which a consensual decision-making system produces pluralistic outcomes. Distinctive about the EU is the intensity of the dependency of EU institutions upon outside interests as a whole. Organized civil society interests operate in a highly structured environment in which EU political institutions seek to channel their contribution towards systemic input and output legitimacy orientations. Because the EU system is based around regulation, interest groups become significant actors due to the ways in which regulation typically distributes costs and benefits upon, and between, such actors. Conversely, 'high politics' dossiers involving matters of wider interest distributions are driven by different kinds of politics involving forces such as public debate, where member states and political institutions rather than sectional private interests are the drivers. Hence, claims that some of the grand issues of European integration, such as the single market project (Sandholtz and Zysman 1989; Green-Cowles 1995), or European Monetary Union (EMU) (van Apeldoorn 2000), have been driven by sectional interest constituencies should be treated with some a healthy scepticism.

The EU interest group system is essentially pluralist in character. No one type of interest can ever routinely dominate the EU political system because of the high degree of fragmentation of power. Supporting measures to create a pluralistic structure include the funding of NGOs to challenge producer interests, and the empowerment of all types of interests to act as accountability agents on EU institutions, and each other, through transparency-oriented measures. Truly remarkable is the extent of reliance upon interest groups as proxies for civil society. This carries with inherent elite tendencies, which conditions the character of their contribution. Certainly, most EU interest groups are associations of associations, operated by professionalized staff, with a focus more on the 'Brussels circuit' of exchanges rather than on 'communicating Europe'. But democracy has always been dependent upon elites, and the chapters which follow document a wide range of advocacy from every imaginable corner of civil society. Some commentators see in the EU system no more than a structured system of exchanges between interest groups and political institutions which amounts to, at best, no more than 'technocratic lobbying', and at worst the privatization of public policymaking. Certainly, the system of exchange which has been designed in recent years by EU institutions has been created with the purpose that they will at least not detract from public legitimacy, and aspire to a much broader potential for democratic legitimacy from these exchanges. The chapters ahead provide insights into this debate, before returning to it in the conclusions.

Chapter 2

EU Decision-Making and Channels of Influence

Interest representation is conditioned by the nature of the decision-making system in which it is embedded. 'Majoritarian' systems in which a government commands a parliamentary majority can create outright 'winners' and 'losers' in legislative initiatives, whereas 'consensual' systems produce compromised policy initiatives in which there is mostly 'something for everyone'. As was outlined in Chapter 1, the highly fragmented nature of EU decision-making means that no one type of interest can ever routinely dominate it. And without the chance to be an outright winner or loser, civil society constituencies have to find broadly based alliances. Fragmented, multi-level structures of decision-making afford ease of access for a wide range of civil society players but dilute the impact of any given constituency, thus enhancing the prospect of competitive lobbying (such as companies which have lost battles in their trade associations over collective policy positions), whereas centralized structures create difficulties of access but once obtained, the near monopolistic 'insider' status can result in high policy impact (Risse-Kappen 1995).

For EU institutional politics, the complex interplay between subnational, member state, and supranational tiers of authority creates multiple arenas, venues, and points of access. Broadly speaking, intergovernmental arenas tend to lead to more indirect forces involving outside interests in EU public policy, and supranational ones more direct forces. The acquisition of EU competencies involves the socialization of member state preferences for European integration, whereas the operation of EU competencies involves a starting point of the Commission's rights of initiation and of drafting measures. Beyond institutional politics are the means with which some civil society players choose to communicate their messages to a broader audience, and seek to engage political systems with alternative means (Chapter 6).

Over time, the incremental tendency towards community decision-making rules has considerably influenced the character of EU interest representation by focusing it at the supranational level. The shifting of EU decision-making arenas, powers, and procedures according to the issue at stake and the Treaty specifications adds to its complexity, and with greater complexity and venue shifting comes the relative insulation of the system from over-domination by any one particular type of interest. Following the Lisbon Treaty, Qualified Majority Voting (QMV) in the Council, and co-decision-making between the Parliament and the Council, became the 'ordinary legislative procedure'. This has the effect of diluting the power of any one institution, and increasing unpredictability as attempts are made to find resolution between competent institutions. This search for compromise tends to involve settlement by political institutions, progressively excluding outside interests in the process.

The ways in which interests are articulated in institutional politics at the European level can be categorized as a complex series of issues surrounding aggregations of interests, through collective and independent action formats; the routes through which influence is exerted and voiced, discussed below; and the institutional channel and point of entry within the institutional decision-making process. Chapter 1 reviewed the breadth of interdependencies with EU institutions, and particularly the Commission, have with outside interests. The Commission's role in drafting and monitoring legislation, and its representative function for the EU in international affairs, together with seeking to drive forward European integration (Chapter 1), make it the foremost venue for interest representation at the European level. The early stages of the policy process involve the critical ways in which issues are defined and framed by reference to wider criteria, and subsequently shaped. The definition and framing of issues are ideological processes in which civil society players contribute viewpoint, whereas the technical basis of developing policy initiatives into detailed proposals requires of policy participants a corresponding ability to provide technical input. Organized interests which are equipped, and willing, to play this latter role become geared to playing the game of institutionalized politics.

Second in importance to the European Commission as an institutional venue is the Parliament, arising again from its role as the representative outlet of civil society, and from its ability to amend and, where Treaty provisions stipulate, to co-decide upon proposed legislation. An exception to this is social legislation arising from the social partners, outlined later in this chapter, where policymaking procedures completely by-pass the Parliament. On the whole, the democratic credentials of the Parliament and its openness as an arena make it a natural venue for citizen interests to engage where actors recognize the secondary status of participatory democracy models to that of representative democracy. Nonetheless, there are signs that the increasing legislative powers of the EP are changing its needs, and therefore the structure of interactions it has with interest organizations (Chapter 6). As is described below, the Parliament has become the most unpredictable of all the EU institutions. The next most important venue is the Council of Ministers, with its full decision-making powers at the end of the policymaking process, although the Council itself has been somewhat reluctant to accept that it is a venue for EU interest representation, initially choosing to exclude itself from inter-institutional discussions on a common European Transparency Register on the grounds that such activities were directed at other EU institutions. At the later stages in the decision-making cycle, it becomes more difficult for those outside the EU institutions to make interventions because the institutions become involved in an inward-looking dialogue oriented towards finding common agreement between them.

After the passage of legislation, a different balance of policy forces arises. Much legislation depends upon national administrations for its implementation, and some have used producer self-regulation as a preferred mechanism of implementation. These roles, together with the monitoring of implementation, create opportunity structures for participation by organized civil society.

'Routes' of influence

The multi-level character of the European policy process means that actors seeking to participate in European public affairs therefore have a number of so-called 'routes' of communication. At its most simple level, the 'national route' refers to the use of other national structures to engage EU decision-making, whereas the 'Brussels route' involves representation to the European institutions themselves, whether alone or through collective channels organized at EU level. Thus, an entity using a national organization to engage the EU uses the 'national route', whereas a direct approach to EU institutions constitutes the 'Brussels route'. These two routes, the institutions and political players which come under their umbrella, and variations between them in courses of decision-making governed by the Treaties provide the organizing device for the rest of the chapter. The extent to which sub-national domains are both a participant in and a route of European-level interest representation calls for a separate chapter on the territorial domain (Chapter 7).

While the routes are not mutually exclusive, a long-standing debate in the literature has been the extent to which the balance of EU interest representation occurs through the 'national route' or the 'Brussels strategy'. A very early pattern proposed by Lindberg was that those interests in search of European integration would take the 'Brussels strategy', whereas those with defensive postures would take the national route (Lindberg 1963). Some empirical verification can be found for this plausible distinction, not least because of the need for the agendas of civil society actors to chime with those of the European Commission (Chapter 1). Woll (2009) notes how interests proposing pan-European solutions in international trade policy (whether pro-liberalization or aimed at restrictions) can work closely with the European Commission, whereas protectionist-oriented lobbying based around national divergences involves, through necessity, the use of the national route.

Unsurprisingly, the balance of views expressed pre-Single European Act tended to emphasize the 'national route' (see, for instance, Averyt 1977), with the development and extension of EU competencies and of community decision-making rules tipping the balance for the better resourced, organized and networked types of civil society interests towards the 'Brussels route'. A recent large-scale survey of 100 UK trade associations, in which 70% of the sample comprised small- and medium-sized associations, found that EU legislation had exceeded UK legislation as the principal source of their representation work, with some 80% of the sample citing an ability to achieve access to senior Commission staff (Trade Association Forum 2006). Lehmkuhl compared the impact of the Common Transport Policy upon associations in the Netherlands and Germany. Liberalization and subsequent national deregulatory policies led to a much stronger struggle for legitimacy among associations in Germany because deregulation rendered the political raison d'être of transport associations in Germany unnecessary. These had worked to preserve the existing regulatory framework so as to guarantee protection from domestic and foreign competition, and after deregulation the membership incentive had gone, resulting in a dramatic loss of resources to German transport associations.

In the Netherlands, the situation was different because liberalization was seen as providing the possibility to expand internationally, making it a factor to strengthen the relationship between the association and their membership constituency (Lehmkuhl 2000).

Most interests, in recognition that they are significantly affected by EU policy, develop channels of political communication at both national and European levels. The 'routes' concept is complicated by the idea that member states and the supranational institutions are both objects and subjects of interest representation, that is, they are participants as well as channels. There appears to be significant variations in the permutation of channels of influence used, depending upon a variety of circumstances, including the nature of the issue concerned, the type of interest affected, and the prevailing context, including the prerogatives of political institutions (Mahoney 2008). These are reviewed in the sections below.

EU interest representation through the 'national route'

The use of the 'national route' for interest representation at the European level is conditioned by the role of member states in EU decision-making, the nature of the positions being taken, and by the extent to which it provides a convenient and familiar point of access for interests.

Intergovernmental influences are at their strongest during Treaty negotiations between the member states and strategy direction through the European Council. These are 'high politics' venues involving inter-state negotiations, and therefore civil society interests are not in the forefront, although significant interests at the national level become national interests in EU politics. But the progressive democratization of the process of drafting Treaties through Conventions has led to the design of some parallel space for organized civil society. The presidents of the principal social partner (a mechanism described later in this chapter) organizations, Business Europe, CEEP, and ETUC were allocated observer status at the 2003/4 Convention drafting the Treaty establishing a constitution for Europe, taking advantage of the opportunity to draft a Treaty clause aimed at continued institutionalization of social dialogue, now established in the Lisbon Treaty. At the convention, a parallel 'Forum of Civil Society', in which the designated lead organization was the Social Platform, enabled organized interests to channel proposals for draft Treaty amendments through sympathetic convention members. A key clause introducing a 'Citizen's Initiative' provision to EU policymaking found its way into the draft Treaty in this way (Kaufmann, Lamassoure and Meyer 2004), and which ultimately became included in the Lisbon Treaty.

The 'social partners' are the civil society players which have achieved most access to intergovernmental EU decision-making. They are participants in the 'macroeconomic dialogue' alongside representatives of the Council, as well as the Commission, and the European Central Bank. They participate in social summits held on the eve of European Councils, and the 'Tripartite Social Summit for Growth and Employment' with Council Presidencies. Together with the Social Platform, they have also been included in the informal preliminaries of the Employment and Social Affairs Council of the Council of the European Union. Environmental NGOs are privy to a similar type of arrangement preceding Environment Council meetings (Hayes-Renshaw 2009). Hayes-Renshaw sounds a note of caution in that the importance of such access arrangements should not be exaggerated, in that they occur at an advanced stage in the Council decision-making cycle (ibid.).

The priority (and back-burner) European Council agenda themes chosen by each member state are often the subject of advance input by civil society interests, while during the 6 month period of office meetings it is now relatively common for the Presidency to meet with interests within the priority theme arenas. Both Business Europe and ETUC have made a point of contacting the Presidency with their carefully agreed internal agendas around 24 months in advance of its office while it is still preparing its programme, in co-ordination with the national federation concerned. Meetings with the Presidency during their term of office tend to be more geared towards publicity than operational public affairs. The rapid turnover of the office bearer, together with the contrasting variations in culture and agendas of each Presidency, mean that the possibilities introduced by these relationships fluctuate considerably. Post Lisbon, both organizations maintain their engagement with the European Council and the rotating presidencies of the Council of Ministers.

Interest representation in the Council of Ministers machinery is only beginning to emerge. One interpretation is that the Council is not lobbied as such, just its members (Nicoll and Salmon 1990):

> The Council portrays itself as an institution where no lobbying takes place; the secretariat keeps no listing of lobbyists and

takes the position that 'all contact with lobbyists and NGOs is handled with the European Commission'. (Friends of the Earth Europe 2006)

It has been ambivalent about participating in inter-institutional discussions on the lobby regulation element of the European Transparency Initiative, and for some time refused to do so on the grounds that 'lobbying' was something which happened to the other institutions (Commission, Parliament). For these reasons, Hayes-Renshaw suggests that indirect lobbying of the Council, that is, through member states, 'has become the route of choice for lobbyists because of the difficulties associated with lobbying the Council as a body' (Hayes-Renshaw 2009:78), and concludes that 'there is little direct evidence of overt lobbying of Secretariat officials in their own right' (ibid.:83), and, whenever received, 'in listening mode only' (ibid.:84):

> [the] Secretariat tend to refuse on principle to circulate position papers from interest groups, or to provide them with mailing lists of working party or committee members. (Hayes-Renshaw 2009:84)

Bouwen's data that national-level interest groups appear to have the most degree of access compared to other interest aggregations (e.g. those organized at EU level) of organized civil society (Bouwen 2002) suggests that the nature of interest representation with the Council is different, rather than absent. Interactions with civil society tend to be unstructured and thus lack the formalization through procedures which has recently emerged from the European Commission. There is some anecdotal evidence of interaction through Council working groups, either with organized interests constituted at EU level (Hayes-Renshaw and Wallace 1997) or through contact between interests and the national civil servants who serve on the working groups (Pointer 2002). Indirect lobbying arises through contacts with national ministry members of Council working groups (Hayes-Renshaw 2009), and – where access is possible – at ministerial level. Pointer recounts the tale of how her employer, the CBI (formerly the Confederation of British Industry), was alerted to a proposal drawn up in an ad hoc Council Justice and Home Affairs working group which had very significant implications for the conduct of electronic commerce. Nonetheless, despite following the issue through subsequent Council stages, the organization could do no better than damage limitation (Pointer 2002). Beyond working groups, intriguing issues are always likely to be raised by the significance of Committee of Permanent Representatives (COREPER) as a venue for Council of Ministers decision-making. Available research on this topic is limited. Saurugger usefully distinguishes different types of national co-ordination mechanisms for EU policy considerations. Where national ministries are lead bodies, such as Germany, civil society organizations which approach permanent representations are referred back to the national ministries; whereas the French permanent representation, with a more 'horizontal' co-ordination mechanism, can be more accommodating (Saurugger 2010).

By the time an issue has reached ministerial level, the scope for intervention is diminished, but nonetheless dramatic interventions do arise. The dossier of decision-making over the End of Life Vehicle Directive (1997–2000), for instance, involved an intervention from German Chancellor Gerhard Schröder, inspired by the Chief Executive of Volkswagen, Ferdinand Piëch. Piëch used Schröder's position as a former board member of the company, and as head of the country then holding the EU Presidency, to his advantage, to buy time on the dossier when Schröder instructed his Environment Minister to postpone the item from an Environment Council agenda, and subsequently to acquire sufficient votes for a temporary blocking minority. Subsequently, some aspects of the original proposal were watered down, although the end result was not entirely to the liking of the automobile constructors (Tenbücken 2002). Like many other dossiers, the End of Life Vehicles (ELV) case involved 'horse trading' between member states, and, while increasing transparency is likely to reduce the scope for this, decision-making in the Council continues in practice to be the least transparent element of EU decision-making. The consequence is that it is an unpredictable venue for civil society interests focused upon the detail of a legislative proposal. The reality of Council decision-making in an EU of 27 member states is intergovernmental negotiation and consensus. The search for common ground among so many elements in finalizing legislation will continue to make the Council a secondary venue for EU interest representation.

While the limited number of dossiers prescribed by unanimity decision have reduced the attraction of the 'national route', it has historically represented the 'tried and tested' ground for many interests, where established policy networks and dependency relationships operate which can equally well be used for the purposes of EU representation as they can for the governance of domestic affairs. The resources available to small firms has always meant that any single firm needing to engage with EU decision-making is likely to use domestic contacts first, with federated representation available through national association membership of EU business associations. Civil society interests in southern and central/eastern European countries have few direct channels of representation in Brussels and consequently have been notable individual users of the national route when EU representation is required. A range of internet-based procedures developed by EU institutions to make it easy for civil society interests to engage with them, described later in this chapter, now make it possible to do so from a base in the member states. These mechanisms have undoubtedly resulted in a shift from reliance upon national intermediary structures to engage with the EU, to more direct mechanisms.

EU interest representation through the 'Brussels route'

The development of procedural rules of engagement for civil society actors to engage with EU institutions, together with Treaty changes resulting in progressively more powers being vested in supranational mechanisms of decision-making, has shifted the modus operandi over time to the 'Brussels route'. A related question is whether relying on engaging directly with Brussels from a base in the member states results in disadvantage, and whether the balance of power remains in engagement via a Brussels base. Despite the development of formalized channels for communication, asymmetries will always accrue in favour of those able to be 'on the spot'. The simplest of these are advantages arising from direct contacts or from participating in networks of varying degrees of formality, ranging from access to information through to interaction. The worst excesses of these asymmetrical disadvantages constitute threats to democratic legitimacy, giving rise to the proceduralization of these exchanges, and to the use of mechanisms designed to present monopolistic influence. The broad impetus to create these arose from the broad consensus following the Treaty on European Union to find democratic mechanisms which did not simply rely upon the participation of nationally elected governments together with Members of the European Parliament (MEPs). To this was added the need for administrative reform, following the crisis surrounding the resignation of the

European Commission in 1999. But a key landmark was the 2001 White Paper on Governance, which asserted its intention to

> reduce the risk of policy-makers just listening to one side of the argument or of particular groups getting privileged access. (European Commission 2001:17)

The broad thrust has been to create a pluralistic design of 'checks and balances', where any one interest is challenged by another, and where interests are empowered through procedures to do so, and to keep EU institutions accountable. The foundation stones of these are regimes of transparency, and participative measures, including the funding of citizen interest groups (Chapter 6), and detailed rules for consultation. Some of these have been applied on an inter-institutional basis, while some are specific to individual institutions, and the context in which they operate. These are described in further detail for the purpose of their evaluation in Chapters 3 and 8.

Inter-institutional mechanisms for engagement with organized civil society

In overview, the most important inter-institutional procedural mechanisms structuring exchanges between EU institutions and civil society involve transparency-related measures. One is the 2001 Regulation on Access to Documents (1049/2001), which provides for rights of access to most documents, supported by open access internet-searchable document registers, and by facilitation mechanisms and vigorous enforcement procedures. While there are safeguards in place for restrictions of access on various grounds, it has been implemented zealously as a result of retroactive application, an activist ombudsman who has championed rights granted by the measure through assertive interventions, and rulings by the Court of First Instance which have favoured release by favouring public interest transparency over personal privacy (Chapter 8). The measure has become increasingly used, with around two thirds of requests granted, and the remaining cases comprising the single most numerous category of cases taken up by the ombudsman (European Ombudsman 2010a). This measure has changed the landscape of EU interest intermediation, empowering civil society organizations vis-à-vis the EU institutions and each other. The Access to Documents Regulation has also altered the modus operandi of the ways in which civil society organizations communicate with EU institutions, resulting from the stipulation that access also applies to documents received by the Commission which originate with third parties. This changes behaviour through the recognition among staff of civil society organizations that the communications they send to EU institutions can be observed, either by their members (Naurin 2007) or by other interested stakeholders.

The European Commission and interest representation

The interests, and roles, of the European Commission make organized civil society its natural constituency. It has seen interest groups formed at EU level, comprising interests with substantial recognition at member state level, as key political allies in its quest to stimulate further European integration (Chapter 1). Its powers to initiate and draft legislation, in policing European legislation, and in external representation (Chapter 1), make for regular interactions with civil society organizations, in 'every-day policymaking'. This creates a series of issues with implications for democratic legitimacy (Chapter 1), particularly where technical dependencies arise, and consequently the Commission has developed a series of procedures to facilitate, and govern, its exchanges with civil society as a whole. These largely emerged from the 2001 White Paper on Governance, with its search for the means to achieve democratic legitimacy, and were therefore aimed at embracing its interactions with, but deliberately going beyond, interest groups. Pointedly, the European Commission now maintains separate web page portals for 'The European Commission and Civil Society', and 'The European Commission and Interest Representatives', though each maintain links to public consultations. The most important of its specific procedures for engaging with civil society concern those aimed at making civil society aware of its intentions to undertake policy initiatives, and to facilitate engagement with them. The guiding principles behind these are pluralization and transparency, although there are some deficiencies of implementation in detail.

The stages are

- the announcement of all legislative initiatives in advance in an annual programme of work;
- each measure is accompanied by the publication of a comprehensive consultation plan, specifying the goals and means of

consultation. At the choice of the Commission services, the latter can be an open public consultation, or focused through, expert advisory groups, workshops and forums, through which a wide range of stakeholder organizations are represented, providing for pluralism of the advice process;

- the consultation plan forms part of a wider impact assessment which accompanies legislative proposals, which makes transparent the basis of evidence used to arrive at the proposal. This is a key stage, in that the evidence becomes the subject of public debate involving detailed scrutiny by interested participants, who are primarily EU level interest groups acting in the general absence of civil society mobilization (Chapter 1). Frequently, organizations issue their own impact assessments. In this process, evidence is subject to challenge, and counter-challenge, and the key concepts used for the detail of legislative proposals become crystallized;

- a Green Paper is a 'thinking aloud' consultation instrument about the need to legislate. Once completed, a White Paper consults over the detail of the policy options;

- minimum standards of consultation apply, embracing the information in consultation documents, and measures to ensure that relevant parties have an opportunity to express their opinion;

- frequently, the consultation is placed on an open web portal inviting responses from anyone inclined to do so, and individual responses made to consultations are often published;

- More focused consultations with stakeholders may be conducted as an additional, or alternative, route, through the expert groups, workshops, and forums described above, including e-forum structures. Instruments of the latter include a European Business Test Panel, a database of (currently, 3600; European Commission 2011c) companies, with a structure of specialized panels, through which viewpoint is obtained via e-questionnaires, and accompanied by a website with details of participants and summary consultation results. A similar type of tool is the SINAPSE e-network (Scientific Information for Policy Support in Europe) through which scientific opinion for policy purposes is elicited from individuals (currently around 11,000 are registered), scientific, and stakeholder organizations (around 1300 registered). These instruments are covered by transparency provisions, although more informal and irregular structures will always be less visible;

- the final legislative proposal from the Commission contains a statement identifying the consultation procedures undertaken, together with a presentation of what the responses advised. It is also supposed to include the Commission's own response to these, identifying why a particular course of recommended action was taken or rejected, although there are significant deficiencies in the implementation of this (Quittkat 2011; see also Chapter 8). There is, however, some degree of oversight, with a well-placed MEP secretariat commenting that the EP 'often requests the Commission to present more detailed information on who is consulted when and how such consultations have been carried out' (Lehmann 2009:48).

While Treaty Article 11 provides the legal basis for consultation, the procedural formats adopted are not enforceable in law, instead forming part of a package known as 'Better Regulation'. Similar schemes, with the same nomenclature, also exist in the UK and in Ireland, embracing procedural practice aimed at participation and consultation, ranging from access through to probity, and at providing a baseline of wider legitimacy for the ways in which policy outcomes are reached. At EU level, given the extent of dependence upon organized civil society, such measures carry particular importance, both because of the need to broaden out policy participation and because of the potential for 'negative externalities' which engagement with interest groups can bring (Chapter 1). Citizen interests in civil society organizations have generally responded positively to these attempts to open up and broaden the basis of policymaking, seeing them as a baseline for further development. Friends of the Earth declared that 'the general principles and minimum standards for consultations ... are a good start' (Friends of the Earth Europe 2006). The European Citizen Action Service and the Social Platform have been at the centre of attempts to develop them, seeking to upgrade their status. Their calls for such procedures to be underpinned by a legal basis, enabling instances of deficiencies to be remedied through the Courts, has met with predictable resistance by EU institutions unwilling to see their hands tied in such a way. A long-standing alternative has been the pursuit by 'NGOs' of a 'Compact', modelled on arrangements in a number of member states, whereby participants in consultation sign up to a series of commitments (Chapter 8), although this has made little headway with EU institutions to date.

The key institutional figure within the Commission in the preparation of policy proposals and the associated interaction with interested parties is the rapporteur. A 'rapporteur' is a middle-ranking
official within a division with functional responsibility for a dossier,
who is given responsibility for preparing the draft, operating within
the broad parameters of EU policy, and to any political and technical parameters for the measure already set. Acting in this capacity to
develop a policy proposal is regarded as a major career opportunity
and challenge for the responsible individual. Cini comments:

> [T]he rapporteur's job is to explore ways in which these prior
> considerations are pre-requisites can be taken into account, whilst
> avoiding many of the potential loopholes and unintended conse-
> quences as possible ... the involvement of interests is vital for
> the rapporteur at this initial stage. The responsible official will
> normally consult widely with interest groups of all types. (Cini
> 1996:147)

The internal Commission deliberation process has been further illu-
minated by Gillies. During the drafting stage, other departments of
the Commission affected by the proposals will be given the broad
outlines and asked for comments, and one person allocated in each
of these to follow the proposal's progress. Discussions are also held
at this stage with the member states' permanent representations,
Council officials and technical advisors, and extensive informal
consultations are held before a proposal is drawn up. Once a full
first draft of the proposed legislation is drawn up and circulated to
all Commissioners and their Cabinets (described below), interested
departments, and the Commission Legal Service. Changes may be
suggested at this stage by any one of these actors. The drafting process can take several years, and a number of drafts produced before a
proposal is agreed and adopted as a Commission formal proposal.
Once the Director Generals of the Commission services have nearly
agreed on the text for a proposal, it then goes to Cabinets and to
the College of Commissioners for approval. Once approved, it is
published in the Official Journal (Gillies 1998).

Once drafts are passed upwards through the Commission and
on to Cabinets of Commissioners, their private office of around
six advisory staff (12 in the case of the President), usually hand-
picked individuals who the Commissioner concerned has chosen to
work with. Commissioners are often dependent upon the assistance

provided to them by their 'Cabinet'. Some are functional experts, while others might have a more wide-ranging role in keeping a Commissioner briefed on wider developments inside and outside the Commission. Eventually, a draft reaches the level of 'Chef (head) de Cabinet. The heads of each of the different Cabinets meet once a week and prepare the agenda for the weekly meeting of Commissioners on Wednesdays. Relatively uncontentious proposals are agreed at Chef de Cabinet level and passed on up to the College of Commissioners for rubber-stamping. Proposals which are more contentious are left for debate at the College, where the different perspectives of differing Commission departments come to the fore. In general, the higher a proposal goes within the Commission, the more reduced is the capacity for interest representation because of the mechanics of seeking change, the increasing politicization of measures, and the trade-offs that form part of reaching agreement. After a measure has left the College, the responsibility for following it through other legislative stages falls back to the permanent staff within a division of the Directorate (Cini 1996).

Collins has suggested that 'a Commissioner, like a king, can be a lonely figure, adrift from executive personnel, cut off from domestic politics, having no popular constituency to provide a real power base. Their ability to exercise authority stems to a large degree from the force of their personalities' (Collins 1993:53). These factors make them particularly dependent upon their Cabinet, and to their own domestic links, often inter-related through Cabinet members. Members of a Cabinet will help the Commissioner to achieve his or her goals through alliances with civil society organizations that share the same policy thrusts, whether business- or NGO-oriented. Kauto tells the story of how Nokia worked with the Cabinet of the Finnish Commissioner to good effect (Kautto 2009). Chapter 3 tells the story of how the Deputy Head of Cabinet for a Commissioner developed a productive working relationship with a key figure from an 'outsider' NGO, based on broadly shared political lean-ings, as a means to build impetus and support behind a new policy proposal, and to tackle opposition to it in public fora. Otherwise, there is support in the literature for the quirkiness evident in the reading from Collins, with the head of the European Policy Office of WWF (and a key participant in the 'G10' group of environ-mental NGOs outlined in Chapter 1) recounting the story of how 'one former Commissioner had the habit of participating in G10 meetings without any formal invitation' (Long and Lörinczi 2010), and of Commissioners helping an animal welfare NGO draft a proposal for a Directive (Harlow and Rawlings 1992). Public focus on the relations between Commissioners and civil society interests is mainly set on the issue of 'revolving doors' of taking up positions with outside organizations on leaving office, and the potential for conflicts of interest which it might create. There were four cases where Commissioners demitting office from the 2004–9 Commission took up positions in companies. Current rules involve seeking clearance from an ethical committee for taking up positions within a year of taking office, although the regulatory framework is presently under review (Public Affairs News 2010).

The consultation procedures cover the process of using expert advice, including a code of practice for those who provide and use it, which, inter alia, seek to make the evidence basis transparent (European Commission 2002). The two main types of bodies providing such input are expert groups and comitology committees. Expert groups provide non-binding advice to the Commission throughout the policy process, although much of the significant input arises during the policy development phase. These groups are (primarily) constituted by the Commission, with members nominated by representatives of national authorities in the member states, and civil society. In practice, the latter category arises mainly from nominations from interest groups constituted at EU level, a 'gatekeeper' role which helps sustain their membership. These are considered further in Chapter 8. More formalized are the (around 250; European Commission 2011d) 'comitology' committees appointed by the legislator (Council; Parliament), which issue opinions on Commission proposals for implementing measures, and, comprising representatives of the member states. While the role of these in oversight of implementation makes them less of a venue for interest representation than committees involved in the preparation of legislation, some authors have seen in them civil society interest politics on 'low politics' (technical) issues (Buitendijk and van Schendelen 1995; see also van Schendelen 1998). More startlingly, some have seen evidence of discursive practice in comitology committees with democratic potential (Joerges and Neyer 1997), although this is somewhat disputed (Rhinard 2002). A new set of procedures surrounding comitology seem to tilt further power surrounding their use towards the Commission (Georgiev 2011), but more detailed evaluation is required once the new procedures become firmly embedded in practice.

The procedures described above have sought to provide some baseline standards for the ways in which the Commission engages with outside interests, addressed to democratic legitimacy through working to principles such as pluralism, equality of access, and transparency. Beyond this baseline, there is inevitably diversity to be found among the Commission services in the character and formats of engagement. Some of the Commission services have highly developed 'dialogues with civil society', most notably DG Development (the longest established), DG Trade (dating from 1999), and DG SANCO, forming extensive and proceduralized frameworks of participation. These are described in more detail in Chapters 6 and 8, though noteworthy are the number and diversity of organizations they embrace. Inevitably, there are differing aspirations of the outcome of these dialogues from civil society, and EU institutions, summed up in the evaluation of one as 'a voice, not a vote' (ECORYS 2007). The institutionalized dialogues of DG Trade, and SANCO, were designed by the same individual during the passage of his career from a Director in DG Trade to the Director General of DG SANCO. Both dialogues are noteworthy for fostering understanding among participants of the need for compromise by bringing together a range of participants from diverse parts of civil society whose competing demands are then apparent. DG SANCO's dialogue is noteworthy for the public commitments to problem solving which participants are expected to make (Jarman 2011), such as contributions from the food industry towards tackling obesity. Beyond these dialogues are more informal, but seemingly permanent, regularized, exchange fora, such as those between DG Environment and the G10 network of environmental interest groups.

Some Commission services have their own specialized structures which are much more than consultation mechanisms. Notable here are the 'Technology Platforms' from DG Research, which are stakeholder-led forums used to provide strategic advice to the Commission on ways to develop technology-led industries which are critical to Europe's future wealth creation capacities. From these have emerged the design of the funding support programmes for Research and Development; thus, some of the key funding instruments were designed and proposed by many of the organizations likely to source financial support from them in the EU Research Framework Programmes. Some of these platforms have developed into more formalized Joint Technology Initiatives (JTI), which undertake collaborative (public/private) research aimed at creating future dedicated projects. While participation in Technology Platforms is in principle open, members of JTIs are appointed by the Council of Ministers in an official process notified in the Official Journal.

The European Parliament and interest representation

The absence of an inbuilt majority to the European Parliament makes it highly oriented towards coalition building and consensus, as well as unpredictable. It is a place where proposed legislation is decisively amended (Nugent 2010). Each majority is built afresh, with different tendencies towards the left and the right on different types of issues. Nonetheless, it has an orientation towards the defence of diffuse interests (Young 2010), although there is some evidence that this may be changing given its increasing needs for expert knowledge as its powers have increased (Chapter 6). These factors make it an intense venue of interest representation across all segments of organized civil society.

Proposals from the Commission, and initiatives from the EP itself, are considered first in the standing committees of the Parliament. Each committee has a secretariat of around five officials, who provide regular support to the work of the committee, and can therefore be sources of information for outside interests. Technical input through the committee system can make a considerable impact. In the first stage, a proposal is passed to a lead committee, which then appoints a rapporteur from among its members to prepare a draft report on the proposal. Like the Commission rapporteur, this individual becomes a natural focus for interest representation. As well as using the committee secretariat for help, rapporteurs may also draw upon the resources of their own political group, who can therefore also be a target for lobbying. Other committees may also be asked for an opinion and will work independently (Gillies 1998), as will a shadow rapporteur who is appointed by each political group to monitor the process on behalf of the interests of that party. Gillies comments:

> The rapporteur exerts an important influence on amendments; they have an assistant who carries out the research and produces a draft report including a draft resolution and amendments, an explanation of the proposal, and a report of the views of other committees. The rapporteur then presents the draft report, which is discussed by each of the political groups who receive

advice from shadow rapporteurs appointed by the political group to advise them. During the committee stage, any member can propose amendments to it – thus this is a good time to contact MEPs and their assistants. (Gillies 1998:181)

Different committees have predictably differing degrees of receptivity towards different types of civil society interests. The Committee on the Environment, Public Health and Consumer Protection, for instance, is a sympathetic venue for NGOs (Smith 2008). Once a committee has finished its deliberations, amendments are more difficult because the report is discussed by the Parliament in the full plenary. The process can be unpredictable, and it is not unusual for the plenary to adopt a different position from that proposed by the lead committee (see, for instance, the proposed Directive on Computer Implemented Inventions – Gehlen 2006). All these factors result in substantial lobbying. Lehmann gives the example of the roaming telecoms charges file, where the chair of the Industry Committee reported receiving around 50 requests for appointments each day from stakeholder organizations (Lehmann 2009). Almost all cases with notable outcomes generate complaints of excessive intensity of lobbying, and the above two are no exception. Something similar applies in the cases of the Takeover Directive, and the Directive on Computer Implemented Inventions. These latter cases demonstrate the highly unpredictable nature of the Parliament. The first of these resulted in the proposal being defeated on the casting vote of the Chair of the EP, while the second involved the plenary of the Parliament completely unstitching the proposals of the lead committee, and ultimately its defeat (Gehlen 2006). All of these examples have involved mobilization by a range of interests with highly polarized positions.

Most lobbying activity is directed at the Parliament until the first reading has been taken because intervention becomes progressively more difficult as inter-institutional discussions intensify in a search to find common ground. Progressively less lobbying does occur at later stages, with reduced scope for impact. Some recent research suggests that both 'friends and foes' are lobbied, although there is a disproportionate focus upon the larger parties (Marshall 2010).

Intergroups of the European Parliament are cross-party, cross-committee groupings of individual MEPs clustered around subjects on which members have particular interests, with open public meetings acting as an informal forum for discussion as well as a means to link politicians with various civil society stakeholders. They have no formal role in the policy process and are explicitly required to act in a way which does not create confusion with 'official' activities of the Parliament, though this implies they have become progressively institutionalized over time by rules of establishment and disclosure. Recognition of their establishment arises from agreement at a meeting of Secretaries General of the political parties, which enables such groups to use the facilities of the EP and logistical support of the parties, and requires compliance with rules of disclosure of sources of external support. In 2009, the establishment of some 27 intergroups was agreed, ranging from those with a citizen orientation, such as groups on anti-racism, youth issues, families and children, urban affairs, disability, animal welfare, and lesbian and gay rights, to those with a producer orientation, such as trade unions, SMEs, and the Social Economy, those with mixed impact, such as water, seas, and climate change, those on regional issues, such as Tibet and Baltic Europe, as well as groups on topics such as the media and public services. Beyond this, Corbett et al. suggest the presence of a 'twilight' world of non-registered de facto intergroups, whose response to new rules requiring regulation for those wishing to use EP facilities was to meet off-site. These groups may however have since disbanded or opted for an institutional existence (Corbett et al. 2007).

Corbett et al. have suggested that the scale of intergroup activity has had a considerable effect on the working methods of the EP, and in particular during the plenary sessions in Strasbourg, where intergroup meetings are normally held:

> [intergroups] permit members to focus on a particular set of issues of specific national, constituency or personal concern. They enable them to specialise, make contacts with outside interest groups on a more informal basis than in committee meetings, and make political contacts outside their own political groups. Intergroups thus not only help to form cross-group coalitions on specific issues, but to forge wider political friendships which can be useful in other circumstances, and can help to build that wider consensus which is essential in the European Parliament. (Corbett et al. 2005:177)

This view on the importance of intergroups is in part shared by Cullen, who has suggested that they represent one of the main avenues for citizen interest groups lacking access to other institutional structures (Cullen 1999). However, some MEPs seem to take a view that their importance has been exaggerated, the concept has gone stale, and that those who attend are few in number and tend towards the converted. One earlier account has suggested that MEPs use them for symbolic purposes to demonstrate to their constituents an interest, arranging for their name to be signed in the attendance register even when they were unable to attend (Harlow 1992).

Citizen interest groups have traditionally found their strongest home among Parliaments because of their democratic foundations, while for producer interests the openness of these arenas can make them unfamiliar and unpredictable territory, resulting in a legacy of clumsy interventions, and the engagement of professionalized public affairs services or the engagement of dedicated parliamentary liaison staff. Lehmann summarizes it as a

> heteroclite and multipolar institution ... with multiple veto points and opportunities for horse trading institution with multiple veto points at the centre of the rise of European party politics and media attention. Effective interest representation in the Parliament therefore requires wider coalitions, better networking, and non-technical approaches, combined with an acute sense for regional or even local political priorities. (2010:40)

The European Court of Justice and interest representation

Judgements delivered by the European Court of Justice have had a major impact on the course of European integration, and a significant number of these have centrally involved civil society interests. The *Defrenne* cases (Cases 455 (1976) ECR and 1365 (1978) ECR in the European Court of Justice) were among the earliest; Harlow records that

> The *Defrenne* case was the start of a steady flow of equality litigation to the ECJ. A conscious decision by the Commissioners to capitalise wherever possible on the favourable jurisprudence of the European Court lay behind this, and the ability to disseminate knowledge of these cases through information networks built up by the women's movement with Commission support has meant that they have received wide publicity. (Harlow 1992:347)

Individuals can invoke EU law (which has higher standing than national law) on their behalf in national courts. Where this raises issues of applicability, cases are referred to the European Court of Justice (ECJ) via the 'preliminary reference' mechanism (McGown 2009). This is the primary means through which organized interests access the EU legal system because of restriction of legal standing on the type of entity able to bring a case to those upon whom a measure has 'direct effect'. While the Lisbon Treaty softened restrictions by removing another long-standing principle, that of individual concern, the ability of third parties to bring cases remains restricted by direct effect. Thus, interest groups resort to 'plaintiff stacking' (Harlow and Rawlings 1992), finding the right case to develop a legal principle through case law, and an individual willing for their case to be put forward. A systematic investigation of the role of civil society with the ECJ system concludes that it has been a significant 'opportunity structure' for citizen-oriented civil society interests, enhancing democracy, and stimulating collective action (Cichowski 2008). The UK has a legal system which facilitates group litigation (McGown 2009) and provides one well-recognized route. Thus, a dedicated organization, the Women's Legal Defence Fund, was set up to take cases to the Court as a means of advancing their cause, using a grant by the Nuffield Foundation. Although this collapsed through lack of funding in 1991 (Harlow and Rawlings 1992), the UK Equal Opportunities Commission has maintained a policy of funding cases likely to extend or clarify legal principles of entitlement (Dorey 2005). As with the account of European integration in Chapter 1, the European Commission not infrequently plays the role of 'agent provocateur', encouraging groups to challenge or establish principles which will have the effect of expanding the frontiers of European integration. The Ombudsman can also use the existence of this route as a means to gain leverage, with a legacy of favourable transparency-oriented rulings on the Access to Documents dossier where the office has been highly active (see, for instance, the 'Bavarian Lager' Case T-309/97).

McGown charts attempts by organized interests to establish legal foundations by building up a legacy of case law and by bringing forward test cases. While this is expensive,

> win or lose, any decision will give the litigant useful information about the viability of pursuing an issue through the judiciary and the worth of a more elaborate litigation strategy. A positive response will potentially open a floodgate of cases from them and other parties, putting pressure on Member States and EU

institutions to change national practice or even provide more EU legislation in the area. (McGown 2010:96)

In the event of a favourable ruling, litigants can develop principles by bringing other cases designed to lock in the case law established by the earlier ruling. Another strategy is to bring simultaneous cases as a means of applying pressure and disseminating rulings through national courts. McGown documents recent use of these types of strategies by business interests to challenge member states in the field of taxation law and cites an advertisement placed by PricewaterhouseCoopers in which companies are asked:

> Are you familiar with the consequences of the latest develop-ments in EU case law? Are you aware of the fact that in many EU member states tax regulations are in breach of Community law, which has primacy over national law? Do you know the poten-tial risks and opportunities resulting from EU law for your own company? PwC can assist you all the way. (McGown 2010:100)

Interest representation viz. other institutions

Of the other venues which provide an arena and access point for EU interest representation, the European Economic and Social Committee (EESC) is the most closely built around the concept of organized civil society. Separate groups bring together interest cate-gories of employers (Group 1), employees (Group 2), and 'other' interests (Group 3), and in doing so replicates similar types of public governance institutions to be found in some of the original European Economic Community (EEC) member states, in particular Belgium and the Netherlands. As the European Union has developed, the EESC has become more challenged as an institution by the acces-sion of new members in which such traditions do not exist. Another anachronism is the constitution of group 3, which does not embrace the full range of citizen interests which can be found in direct organi-zations at EU level, but which contains a diverse range of mainly producer (e.g. agricultural, SMEs, the professions) interests. There are, however, nominees linked to some of the mainstream citizen interests, such as those concerned with the environment, consumer affairs, and disabilities. In order to address these issues, the EESC developed a 'Liaison Group' comprised of a selection of EU citizen-related civil society organizations. While this brought together some of the mainstream organizations identified in Chapter 6, some leading EU civil society 'family' organizations are somewhat reticent about being marginalized from mainstream EU institutional politics as a result of being 'parked' at the EESC and do not participate in the Liaison Group (including, notably, the Social Platform, the 'G10' network and the 'Human Rights and Democracy Network' – see also Chapter 6). Nonetheless, the Liaison Group has been the source of some interesting thinking and debate, particularly on the concept of 'representativeness' criteria for civil society organizations, which includes the need to have members in at least half of the member states. The concept of group 'representativeness' is considered further in Chapters 3, 6, and 8. Beyond the Liaison Group, EESC has spawned lots of interesting events and 'think pieces' about the role of organized civil society in an EU version of participatory democracy.

While the EESC acts in an advisory capacity only (similar to the Committee of the Regions – Chapter 7), its right to issue opinions on matters for which it has not been consulted is a factor which enhances the significance of it for the interests who participate in it. Another niche of the EESC is that members are appointed by member state nomination to the Council, which means that the EESC has links to national civil society in a way in which no other organization does. This helps to distinguish it also from EU-level organized civil society, who have no formal role in the EESC other than the somewhat tenuous 'liaison group' linkage. Nonetheless, these range of factors have helped sustain and develop an institution which would otherwise have been something of an anachronism, although its advisory powers always make for a marginal position among EU institutions.

The European Investment Bank (EIB) has increasingly found itself a target of interest representation activities in recent years through its role in providing loans and guarantees to co-finance investment in industry and infrastructure. Increasingly, environmental interest groups have been active in pressing the EIB, together with the European Bank for Reconstruction and Development (EBRD) to ensure compliance with strict environmental criteria for work involving large-scale projects, with Friends of the Earth Europe spawning a separate organization, 'CEE Bank Watch', comprised of organizations in Central and East European Countries, to monitor the activities of international financial institutions in the region. A number of other EU-related political institutions have become venues for interest representation through the use of procedures to pursue interests. The Court of Auditors and a number of the EU agencies have been used in this way.

EU agencies perform various roles which respond to the need for scientific, technical, and legal capacity in governance, independent from political decision-making. An example concerns a decision in 2010 by the Commission to give final approval for an application (originally generated by BASF) for commercial cultivation of Amflora, a genetically modified potato. Because member states had not been able to make a decision for or against the proposal, the matter referred back to the Commission. The Commission's approval drew heavily upon a preceding judgement reached by the European Food Safety Authority (EFSA) which considered it to be safe, and in particular following an investigation into concerns about the presence of antibiotic-resistant marker genes. There is a debate about the extent to which such agencies are best insulated from popular pressures in the interests of achieving efficient policy outcomes (Majone 1996) or require elements of democratic architecture for participative-based legitimacy. While those established at an early stage perform monitoring roles, more recent agencies perform regulatory roles which raise significant legitimacy-oriented issues about procedures and outcomes, particularly as the work of these are funded primarily from fees paid by users seeking regulatory clearance. Such agencies have developed governance procedures based on essentially pluralist principles and the avoidance of capture, relating to participation, conflicts of interests, and transparency. These tend to steer a mid-way course between 'insulation' and 'participation', with the emphasis upon avoiding suspicion of third-party capture, and public confidence in the outcome of decisions (Williams 2005; Gehring and Krapohl 2007; Borrás et al. 2007).

Interest representation in other EU-related structures

The technical work of European standardization committees extensively involve, and impact considerably upon, civil society interests. These are established within the framework of CEN, the Comité Européen de la Normalisation; CENELEC, for electrical products; and ETSI, the European Telecommunications Standards Institute. Although these are formally independent organizations, they are structures used for EU objectives of removing non-tariff barriers to integration through harmonization of technical standards. Members of technical committees include around 25,000 participants drawn from industry, science, trade unions, and consumer interests, who, together with local and central government departments, resolve the details involved in standardization issues among themselves (Egan 2001). Some companies play a key agenda-setting role and invest considerable resources and time to them because of the benefits at stake (Egan 2001). A number of trade associations at both EU and national levels devote a considerable amount of time to helping their members with the technical issues involved in standardization. For instance, a study of 135 UK trade associations found that 71% had live contact with a European standards body (Compass Partnership 1997). Some of the extreme specialization in the landscape of EU trade associations can partly be explained by their alignment with technical standards committees. The rather bewildering structure of specialized associations in the European glass industry, for instance, partly results from European standards institute-oriented work.

Because membership of each committee is not constitutionally determined by a general structure, complaints have arisen that some committees are over-dominated by particular sectional interests, that they have been used to advantage some at the expense of others in the writing of technical standards, and that some have acted as a cartel. Key cleavages include those between large and small firms, between European firms and others, German firms and others, and between producer and non-producer interests, with complaints by ETUC and BEUC that standardization committees are over-dominated by industry (Egan 2001). Both these organizations have received Commission funding to help them participate in the standards bodies, and BEUC then spawned a substantial offshoot, ANEC, the European Association for the Coordination of Consumer Representation in Standardisation, which is dedicated to this task (Chapter 6). Environmental organizations, too, have developed a specialist offshoot to enable them to participate in the technical business of standard setting, the European Environmental Citizens Organisation for Standardisation, which also attracts funding from the European Commission. This has resulted in some committees (such as those concerned with automobiles) being venues for considerable contention, but the net result is to enhance the governability of the EU (Eichener and Voelzkow, in Eising 2009).

Other policymaking procedures: social dialogue

Social dialogue between EU employer and trade union organizations arose in the mid-1980s as part of a drive by Commission President Delors to build a social aspect to the European single market. The macroeconomic dialogue with public authorities, described earlier in this chapter, is one part of the social dialogue; another is the dialogue between the social partners themselves. In return for the promise to stem the tide of social legislation, Delors asked employer and trade union organizations to engage in labour market dialogue as 'social partners', and a number of agreements between them have arisen from their 'social dialogue', including a small number with legislative effect.

At cross-sectoral level, there are six participating organizations, three for employers and three trade unions, although the key organizations are Business Europe and UEAPME (for business), CEEP (for public sector employers), and ETUC (for labour) (Chapter 1). Employers participated because they anticipated that 1992 would bring a UK Labour government and with it remove the last obstacle to a veto on QMV in the social policy arena. Business Europe reasoned that they would be better placed if they were in a position to influence legislation, and acceded to long-standing Commission requests that they enter into an arrangement, together with CEEP and ETUC for formalized social partnership with a legal basis in the EU Treaties. These powers give the social partners the opportunity to write EU employment measures by mutual agreement, either by-passing the Parliament directly to the Council for legislative endorsement or through binding agreement between themselves for implementation in the member states.

The first of these mechanisms, through Council legislation, is driven by a 'negotiate or we'll legislate' dynamic from the Commission, in that where employers fail to do so, the Commission has the option of initiating a standard Directive, depending upon an assessment of its chances in the other EU political institutions (Branch and Greenwood 2001; Smismans 2008). These factors introduce substantial politics into the equation, and as a result most negotiations under this route stalled or broke down, with just three legislative cross-sectoral agreements of no more than moderate significance resulted, the last of which being in January 1999. On more occasions, agreements broke down or employers refused to enter into negotiation, and those agreements that have been reached have not added to social protection for workers in a number of member states, who already enjoyed superior domestic legislation. The 1996 agreement on parental leave is estimated (by former ETUC Deputy General Secretary Jean Lapeyre) to have benefited workers (relative to conditions in their own member states) from 5 of the (then) 12 member states, the 1997 agreement on part-time work to bring benefit to no more than 4–5 million workers, and the 1999 agreement on fixed-term contracts to improve the position for workers in 6 of the 15 member states. Notwithstanding three agreements reached at sectoral level in different transport domains, the difficulties involved in finding agreement between the parties at a significant level meant that this latter measure was the last through Council legislation to be negotiated through agreement between the principal representative employer and union organizations. While the Treaty provisions remain, the mechanism has now passed into disuse, and this historic experiment in social partnership entered a new phase.

The second route of formal social partnership agreements, through binding agreement between the parties involved for implementation at national level, became the de facto successor modus operandi. There have been four such binding agreements at 'horizontal' level, on telework (2002), work-related stress (2004), harassment and violence at work, and inclusive labour markets (2010), as well as two 'frameworks of actions' on lifelong training (2002) and gender equality (2005). Sectoral social dialogue has had limited impact (Bieler 2005), and, while the mechanisms are there with over 30 such committees established, agreements are dependent upon action taken by the member organizations of signatories at national level (Ales et al. 2006). There are two binding directives, each on working time, in the civil aviation and maritime sectors (Erne 2008). Beyond these lie a vast number of less formalized joint statements between social partners at both horizontal and sectoral levels on relatively uncontentious issues, and some agreed codes of good practice, together with the Council-related arrangements for dialogue with horizontal social partners described earlier. Taken together, EU social dialogue arrangements are procedurally significant, both as legislative arrangements and for the organizations endowed with elevated status from them, but in terms of outcomes should not be overstated. The significance of this for the trade union movement is considered in Chapter 5.

A noteworthy feature of EU social dialogue has been the attempts to establish criteria for the representativeness of organizations as a pre-condition for their participation. At cross-sectoral level at the outset there were independent detailed studies commissioned of candidate organizations. This resulted in 'tiers' of participation status, the contentiousness of which ultimately resulted in a significant legal challenge to the Court of First Instance by UEAPME seeking annulment of one of the agreements concluded, and which was resolved by Business Europe incorporating UEAPME into the employer delegation. At sectoral level, employer and union organizations need to file a joint application to the Commission, and to demonstrate that they are organized at EU sectoral level with adequate structures for effective participation. They must also demonstrate that they

> consist of organisations which are themselves an integral and recognised part of Member State's social partner structures, and have the capacity to negotiate agreements, and which are representative of several Member States. (European Commission 2011e)

This focus upon geographic representativeness has spilled over from producer organizations to NGOs (Chapter 6), with consequences for democratic legitimacy by the potential to exclude 'what' groups whose existence is not based around representing members, but advocating for a cause for whom representativeness is irrelevant, such as animal welfare and the environment. This is considered further in Chapters 3, 6, and 8.

Conclusion

The starting point for this chapter was that characteristics of political systems and their structures of power and decision-making greatly influence the nature of interest representation. Whereas majoritarian regimes concentrate power, fragmented and multi-level decision-making structures disperse it, resulting in the dilution of impact for any one type of interest constituency. Multiple-level opportunity structures thus have a pluralistic effect, limiting the potential of some to dominate, creating venues for competitive lobbying, strengthening the hand of political institutions and their insulation from outside pressures, and empowering others by opening up venues. Civil society interests therefore have to align their agendas with those of the Commission, rather than vice versa. The institutions are the drivers, with a variety of inter-institutional procedures, and those specific to individual institutions, which are designed to empower civil society organizations and facilitate their participation. Some of the Commission departments, and the natural receptiveness of the European Parliament towards civil society concerns, creates a variety of such venues for citizen-oriented interests. Recent literature has highlighted the way in which the European Court of Justice system has been a significant empowering force for civil society organizations. Together, there are a plethora of political opportunity structures for organized civil society, but never in such a way as to upset the driving balance of power away from the institutions.

Chapter 3

The Regulation of Lobbying and the European Transparency Register

'Lobbying' raises similar types of issues for most democratic political systems which leads to some degree of regulation. The core issue involves public assurance as to the probity of these exchanges. This is particularly important in the EU political system because of the high degree of reliance upon organized civil society to undertake core democratic mechanisms (Chapter 1).

'Lobby regulation' can embrace a variety of goals, on a spectrum ranging from limited aims of avoiding corrupt practice through to contributing to more complex regulation of access to political institutions, and exchanges between them and outside organizations aimed at ensuring pluralistic democratic outcomes. The EU's systemic reliance upon organized civil society means that it has all of these features. Chapter 8 considers the range of procedures which regulate exchanges with organized civil society aimed at democratic outcomes, while this chapter focuses more narrowly upon the EU's lobby regulation schemes, although it does consider the contribution of these schemes to, and implications for, achieving democratic goals.

The focus of lobby regulation schemes can be bifurcated between the behaviours of public officials and 'lobbyists'. The former is easier to achieve because the target constituency is easier to identify and regulate within organizational confines, and the latter involves definitional complexities. For instance, the Green Paper setting out the principles of the European Transparency Initiative offers a definition of lobbying as

all activities carried out with the objective of influencing the policy formulation and decision-making processes of the European institutions. (European Commission 2006a:5)

53

This raises problematic issues of embrace, in that it would seem to include routine mechanisms of participation and representation, from citizen activities, such as petition signing, letter writing, or attending a demonstration, through to the activities of member states in the EU political system. The attempt to further clarify this in the Green Paper by defining a 'lobbyist' only serves to illustrate the problem:

> [P]ersons carrying out such activities, working in a variety of organisations such as public affairs consultancies, law firms, NGOs, think-tanks, corporate lobby units ('in-house representatives') or trade associations. (Ibid.)

Thus, the 'definition' involves providing 'such as' examples, later refined further with the exclusion of public authorities. In essence, the 'definition' involves subjective generalized notions based around a loose concept of 'you know the type of player we mean'. This is a somewhat problematic foundation for a regulatory system seeking water-tight legal standards, and explains why regulation has usually commenced with the easier task of developing formalized codes of conduct for the behaviour of officials (permanent and elected) working in political institutions, with sanctions attached to them which can easily be enforced. Over time, these have been supplemented with encouragement to 'lobbyists' to develop self-regulatory codes of good practice, usually directed first at caricatures of such players, the commercial public affairs providers, followed by those working for business entities. The difficulties of operationalizing these to satisfy regulatory goals, together with entrepreneurial activities of politicians seeking popular agendas, often lead to the later development of more formalized regulatory schemes for 'interest representatives' hosted by political institutions.

Regulating conduct of those working in EU institutions

The *Staff Regulations for Officials of the European Communities* (Europa 2011a) provide for a variety of general principles with regulatory effects within the scope of this chapter. Thus, there are clauses which prohibit taking or seeking instructions from any organization or person outside of their institution; the acceptance of any honour, decoration, gift, payment, or favour; acting in circumstances which give rise to a conflict of personal interest; engaging in outside activity without permission; the unauthorized disclosure of information; and 'any action or behaviour which might reflect adversely upon his position' (Article 12). They also impose a duty of whistle-blowing where illegal activity is suspected, including fraud or corruption.

The Rules of Procedure of the European Parliament (European Parliament 2010a) have a chapter specifically directed at elected members, in which an Article specifies principles concerning members' financial interests, standards of conduct, and access to Parliament. An annex to one of these (Title 1, Article 9.1, Annex 1) specifies conduct relating to transparency and members' financial interests. This requires electronic public disclosure of interests, including professional activities, and any financial or material support from (named) third parties, and of assets as per the legislation in force in the member state in which they are elected. Assistants to MEPs also have to make a written declaration of their professional activities and any other remunerated functions or activities (Annex X, Article 2.1). MEPs are required to refrain from accepting any other gift or benefit in the performance of their duties. Chairs of any groupings in the Parliament are also required to disclose donations of support in cash or kind (including secretarial assistance) to those entities. This latter provision has a particular effect upon the regulation of intergroups, where civil society organizations have often undertaken secretariat roles (Chapter 2).

In essence, the above rules are centred upon transparency, supplemented by prohibition of excess, as well as general 'catch-all' provisions ('reflect adversely ...'). There are separate rules governing organizational transparency of business (Chapter 8; see also Chapters 1 and 2 on Access to Documents). The European Commission's Code of Good Administrative Behaviour also embraces principles of lawfulness, but extends beyond this in specifying principles of non-discrimination and equal treatment, proportionality and consistency, objectivity and impartiality, and respect for the protection of personal data and confidential information. The Code further states a series of procedural norms for engaging with the public (such as times for responding to communications) (European Commission 2000a).

These provisions have regulatory effect upon the behaviour of those in EU institutions when engaging with outsiders, with the potential to impact upon 'lobbying scenarios'. Beyond this are measures aimed at 'lobbyists'.

The regulation of lobbyists

Definitional complexities leading to loopholes have oriented schemes aimed at regulating lobbyists towards incentives upon such actors to participate in regulatory schemes. One version of this is to encourage self-regulation, backed by perceived or explicit disapproval for non-participants, which can extend to degrees of access to political institutions. As with many producer self-regulatory schemes, the main point of criticism concerns the absence of real sanctions and of structural independence from the industry, leading to an inability to satisfy regulatory demands. Another version of regulation involves a scheme hosted by political institutions in which incentives attach varying degrees of difficulty for 'lobbyists' who do not engage with the scheme, including access to political institutions. Another version again would involve a formal accreditation scheme for access linked to explicit organizational criteria, such as those operated by the United Nations and the Council of Europe. The EU has the first two of these schemes but has rejected de jure accreditation schemes, although there are arguments that its incentive schemes bear elements of de facto accreditation schemes (Greenwood and Halpin 2007).

The first self-regulatory scheme in the EU was operated by commercial public affairs practitioners from 1994, and has its origins in gentle pressure applied by the Secretariat General of the European Commission, then anxious to protect its access to the resources which outside interests bring by anticipating emerging pressures for regulation (McLaughlin and Greenwood 1995). This organization of 'Public Affairs Practitioners' (PAP) evolved into the present European Public Affairs Consultancy Association (EPACA), with a code whose progressive development reflects the strength of demand for regulation, but which has failed to forestall regulation by political institutions. Watchdog organizations have tested out EPACA's code and adjudication mechanisms by filing a small number of allegations of contravention. Another organization has a wider embrace of membership, extending to business associations and to 'in-house' company public affairs managers, the Society of European Affairs Practitioners (SEAP), which also operates a self-regulatory code dating from the second part of the 1990s. They have developed slightly different policy positions about the detail of the European Commission's European Transparency Initiative (ETI) lobby regulatory scheme, the European Transparency Register (ETR), operational from 2008. While the schemes of both EPACA and SEAP remain in place, the principal regulatory instruments are now operated by EU institutions.

PAP's code of practice was more notable for agenda-setting future regulatory standards within EU institutions than for its use by other stakeholders, and in 1996 the Parliament adopted these standards in the launch of its incentive-based regulatory scheme. The incentive for registration was that those who wanted ease of access to European Parliament buildings would sign up to the code of conduct in exchange for a 1-year permit (instead of needing an invitation from a member and queuing for a day pass), and entry as an individual (with affiliated organization listed) in a public register. The EP code itself is somewhat unremarkable in content (European Parliament 2010b) though it has extended over the years to cover relationships with assistants, former members, and former officials. 'Watchdog' organizations have filed a very small number of allegation complaints relating to the rule about (non)disclosure of the interest represented. There have also been issues about the number of individuals from a particular organization (with a maximum of six permitted), and individuals signing up to the register who are not 'lobbyists' but who wanted easy access to the Parliament library, resulting in the number of entrants (currently a shade under 5000 – see Chapter 1) on the register not being a reliable 'headcount' of lobbyists. There was also a brief controversy about the way in which the Parliament's security service was (mis)interpreting a rule, resulting in the temporary exclusion of organizations without a Brussels base, with obvious democratic implications, until the problem was fixed. The Parliament's scheme commenced linkage to the European Commission scheme in 2008, with progressively greater degrees of collaboration.

The depth of the buildings access incentive is highlighted by proposals linking it to a regulatory scheme with the European Commission as a means of strengthening its range and depth of incentives to actors to participate. Like the Parliament scheme, the European Commission's version is an incentivized non-mandatory scheme. The Commission's first two incentives to participate are relatively shallow. One involved automatic early consultation alerts for nominated interest areas, which has little impact because intentions to legislate are publicly announced, and routine monitoring functions mean that professional lobbyists will be informed. Nonetheless, a small number of organizations have signed up for this reason alone. The second was that the consultation responses of non-participants to the scheme would be treated with the same weight as that of a private individual, which seems impossible to operationalize in practice. The third incentive is pressure from the European Commission, with advice circulated within the Commission that meetings with non-registered organizations should commence with an invitation to join the register. Such an invite also appears prominently at the start of the page on the Commission's portal for open public consultations. While 'pleasing the Commission' is an incentive to sign up, there are a (dwindling number of) notable absentees, particularly among banks and financial service providers. The fourth incentive, currently awaiting formal inter-institutional agreement, is making the availability of the EP's 1-year pass conditional upon signing up to the register. This will change the incentive structure considerably.

The basis of the present Commission scheme involves registration to a 'European Transparency Register' public web database with disclosure for organizations (other than public authorities), rather than individuals, which seek to influence public policy. The key transparency components involve disclosure elements surrounding organizational contact and other details; interest categorization; who is represented; mission/interest areas; spending on interest representation; and, for NGOs and think tanks, budget and sources of funding. Entry is conditional upon signing up to an associated code of conduct, whose contents reflect its heritage from the code first devised by PAP, but which also contains an interesting clause which develops the accountability of civil society organizations to wider civil society, considered later in this chapter.

The emergence of the Commission European Transparency Register

The announcement of the Commission lobby regulation scheme in February 2005 seemed to follow a long line of procedural initiatives aimed at strengthening EU participatory democracy which originated most directly from the 2001 White Paper on Governance (Chapter 1). The scheme was developed from a co-incidence of interests between two key agents: an anti-globalization/capitalist activist organization, the Corporate Europe Observatory (CEO), seeking regulation of business lobbying, and a new Commissioner seeking to develop his agendas early in his term of office. A key individual in CEO, Erik Wesselius, took the opportunity apparently presented by a new Commission in the autumn of 2004 (Corporate Europe Observatory 2004) to write to the European Commission President advocating a comprehensive lobby regulation scheme similar to that in the USA. The reply he received from the responsible Commission service was not encouraging; the (Secretariat General of the) Commission saw no need to change the existing arrangements. He re-sent a similar advocacy letter to the Commission Vice Presidents in January 2005, which drew interest from a new Commissioner, Siim Kallas, whose portfolio embraced 'administrative affairs' and 'anti-fraud' (Cini 2008). Kallas invited Wesselius to a meeting prior to the surprise announcement of a 'European Transparency Initiative' in a speech in March 2005. Chabanet records that

> the speech ... basically used the ... demands, concerns and alarm-ist, not to say vehement, tone of the campaigners. (Chabanet 2007: 33)

Wesselius was among the first off the mark in the media in respond-ing to the speech as 'good news for democracy' (Kirk 2005), which followed closely the discourse Kallas had used. In July 2005, Kallas attended the launch event of a broader NGO advocacy alliance in which Wesselius played a leading role in establishing, the Alliance on Lobbying Transparency and Ethics Review (ALTER-EU), sitting alongside him at the event. Kallas gave the lead ETI support task to his Deputy Head of Cabinet, Kristian Schmidt, who developed a work-ing relationship with Wesselius and other figures in the ALTER-EU alliance to help with the political establishment of the scheme.

A trail of emails between these parties confirms this interpreta-tion. These appeared in the public domain between 2008 until they were archived on *Europa* sometime in the spring of 2010, via a link from Kallas's ETI website to 'Correspondence relating to the Commission's register of interest representatives'. This made avail-able 172 separate items of correspondence between Cabinet/Kallas and outside correspondents, written between 2007 and the spring of 2008, and concluding with the formal 'Access to Documents' request filed by Wesselius to see all such documentation. This latter action seems to have marked the end of the close working relation-ship; the request seems to have been perceived as hostile by Cabinet

Kallas, in that they responded by making the documentation thus released generally available through the ETI website. The differences between these two parties on the operational issues surrounding the registration scheme became apparent thereafter. Nonetheless, during the key period of their close working relationship, the list of correspondence reveals that the most frequent outside correspondent with Cabinet Kallas was Wesselius himself. In sum, the items of correspondence include mutual supply of, and request for, materials ahead of speeches by Commissioner Kallas; briefings and advice seeking on the positions of other stakeholders; holiday tales, and the exchange of 'smiley' emoticons denoting shared understandings between correspondents on first name terms; reassurance of support; and an 'in-confidence' notation where the two exchange behind the scenes information about a nomination to CEOs 'worst lobby' award.

The operation of the ETR

Once the scheme was launched, a key issue became the number of registrations it would attract. In announcing the scheme in 2005, Kallas had placed particular emphasis that 'around 2600 interest groups have a permanent office in the capital of Europe' (Kallas 2005:5), and the achievement of this number of registrations became the key performance indicator of the scheme by various media. Rather less attention was given to the type of organizations signing up to it, of which a significant number are of interests not organized at EU level, nor primarily addressed to the EU level. In the most populated category, 'professional associations', embracing business/trade associations as well as the professions, just over one third of entries at the time of writing (310/850) are of associations organized at EU level, with most entries constituted by national, and sub-national, associations. In other categories can also be found individuals, including would-be politicians, and small service enterprises in suburban locations far from political decision centres all taking the opportunity of free advertising space, as well as organizations from third countries with highly tenuous links to EU interest representation. Historically, there have been organizations registering because they believed that their chances of grant funding would be increased, and entries of non-existent organizations claiming an annual lobbying spend of €250 million, attributed to the work of a 'prankster' (Phillips 2009).

The quirkiness of entries belies the low level of resourcing by the Commission to monitoring entries. At first this amounted to seemingly none at all, but when some dubious entries began to attract media attention, the Commission allocated part of the time of one person to scrutinizing the worst excesses. However, less prominent infractions, such as the failure to enter information on funding, and the obvious mis-categorization of entries have gone without apparent intervention. Rather, the database has relied on the principle of checks and balances, supplemented by a limited resource within the Secretariat General service of the Commission. CEO scrutinizes the detail of new entries, and together with its key alliance partners launches strategic complaints. A formal complaint lodged by Friends of the Earth Europe, concerned the low lobbying spend entry for the European Chemical Industry Association (CEFIC) (EurActiv 2009a). CEFIC's entry of €50,000 followed a template of many early registrants, resulting from a lack of detailed guidance for how the expenditure should be calculated. The declarations of annual expenditure for representing interests to the EU institutions consequently range from zero to €2 million, while some organizations claim to be spending more on lobbying than the entire organizational budget they declare. Some registered organizations do not answer the question about spending on interest representation to EU institutions. However, there has been a noticeable improvement in both the number and extent of data entries, recently, enabling greater use of the register as a research tool (see, for example, Tables 4.2 and 6.5).

There has been a stream of adverse comment from the outset about lack of attention to detail in the scheme, with Cabinet Kallas extremely reluctant to become drawn into detailed questions of operationalization. Thus, the advice from Schmidt to requests for clarification as to how the expenditure on lobbying the EU institutions should be calculated was to make a 'good faith estimate' (Hood 2009), resulting in large variations in declaration. Now that the scheme has met its 'headline' quota of 2500 entries, there has been a progressive extension of detail, and monitoring. The key point is that Kallas and his Cabinet were, at the outset, less interested in operational questions than in the establishment of the scheme, assessed most importantly for them in the number of registrations attracted. For one commentator, Kallas had been seeking to 'maximize his legacy and reputation' before changing his portfolio of responsibilities in between the Barroso 1 and 2 Commissions

(EurActiv 2009b). Kallas and his Cabinet devoted their efforts to pockets of poor registration rates, such as law firms and think tanks, and 'naming and shaming' high-profile absentees when Schmidt and Kallas made speeches.

Kallas was transferred to other portfolios in the new 'Barroso II' Commission at the end of 2009, with responsibility for the dossier passing to Commissioner Šefčovič. While the drive to increase participation rates in the register continued, the focus became one of trying to find common ground between the institutions for a register, and some increased attention to the quality of data entries. For a while, the Council refused to participate (Chapter 2), and when it did so it complicated the discussions between the Parliament and Commission, particularly over the link to the EP pass incentive. The Parliament continues to prefer a mandatory scheme, while the Commission prefers a voluntary one. Nonetheless, the High Level Working Group composed of representatives from the two institutions have been able to reach significant agreement on a new scheme, starting with the name, the 'European Transparency Register'. There is an expansion of the sub-categories of entries to embrace a wider set of organizations, including academic and research institutions, and an expectation for the first time that representative offices linked to territorial public authorities should register. Also new are an articulated set of governance arrangements, including an inter-institutional secretariat operating under the patronage of the Secretary General, an established complaints procedure, a tariff of sanctions, and a code of conduct expanded to cover the employment of former members of EU institutions. The tariffs have a limit of penalties which are the same as at present, that is, up to expulsion from the code (highly damaging for a commercial public affairs company through the potential for negative publicity leading to the loss of business from clients) and the withdrawal of access passes to the EP.

Links to democratic mechanisms

The European Transparency Initiative contains three strands, of which lobby regulation is one. The common theme is the protection and advancement of public legitimacy through transparency. With lobby regulation, the rhetoric from the announcement of the initiative onwards (Kallas 2005) was that a system of transparency was needed in order to safeguard public legitimacy, particularly given the extent of dependence by the EU system upon its exchanges with organized civil society. Transparency has always been the driving concept in the justificatory rhetoric, from which other desired 'benefits' for democratic legitimacy would supposedly flow, such as exposure to public scrutiny of the degree of representativeness of NGOs.

The information sought from registrants to the ETR differs for different categories of entrants. NGOs, in particular, are asked to provide information about the number of members they have, and (in the current version of the scheme) their geographic spread. This follows a tradition inherited from a predecessor database, CONECCS (Consultation, the European Commission and Civil Society), in which access to the public internet database was conditional upon declaring that the organization had members in at least three member, or candidate member, states (Chapter 8). The transition from CONECCS to the ETR seems to have softened the position on both geographic and constituency representativeness. This has been further softened by the new scheme with the requirement to list only the number of members, rather than also the countries where members are. The more subdued focus in the ETR is upon using transparency as an exposure device as a means to address the issues. NGOs are asked to list their members, a requirement which is not made of other categories of entrants such as business associations, who are apparently assumed to have the desired quality of representativeness.

One clause contained in the Code of Conduct linked to registration is set apart in terms of significance from the otherwise anodyne content. Clause 4 of the code states that

> interest representatives shall always ensure that, to the best of their knowledge, information which they provide is unbiased, up-to-date, complete and not misleading. (European Commission 2011f)

This carries overtones of public accountability, recognizing that stakeholders who become institutionalized policy participants (rather than simple public advocates) carry wider responsibilities. This principle is apparently accepted by NGOs themselves, in that it is included in the International NGO Accountability Charter (INGO 2011) and in some of the 'Compact' codes to be found at member state-level setting standards for, and agreed by, the consultative partners. The emphasis upon accountability for information placed in the public domain carries deliberative overtones, in that deliberation places emphasis upon public reasoning. This reasoning finds an outlet through debate over the 'impact assessment' of proposed legislative measures produced by the European Commission (Chapter 8), in that stakeholders produce their own impact assessments for public consumption. Thus, claims are required to be evidence-based, and hence the emphasis upon standards of information has deliberative overtones (Chapter 8).

Beyond this, another key point of wider significance to have emerged from the ETR story is the extent to which an anti-globalization activist organization achieved apparent insider status with Cabinet Kallas during the political battle to establish the European Transparency Register. This demonstrates a key point which contributes to the conclusions of this volume: that the impact of any interest depends more upon the extent to which its goals coincide with those of the Commission at critical junctures, rather than the type of interest represented.

Chapter 4

Business and Professional Interests

Business interests and the professions are key components of producer interests. The extent to which some branches of the professions are engaged in economic activity – accountants, architects, dentists, lawyers, engineers, etc. – makes analytical consideration possible in one chapter alongside business interests, albeit in a different section. While the professions are diversely constituted, even where most members of a particular profession perform their activities in the public sector, there is a mixed model of private and public sector contracting, and as private operatives.

The first phase of the EU was driven by a search for economic prosperity and global competitiveness. Creating one single Europe-wide home market and replacing protected national markets with open borders has been based, inter alia, on enhancing competition and the capability of European business to compete in the global economy of the twenty-first century, and reducing transaction costs of market exchange. The mechanics of achieving this liberal vision has meant that business-related issues have been at the forefront of European integration and its everyday policymaking. An overwhelming proportion of economic measures passing through member state legislatures have a 'made in Brussels' stamp on them. Yet the multiple-level architecture of the EU prevents any one interest from routinely dominating, as well as creating tendencies of fragmented collective action of business interests, while the EU's democratic deficit has recently created a favourable environment for other types of interests to operate in.

Some literature has followed the assertion by Karl Marx in the Communist Manifesto that 'the state is but a committee for managing the common affairs of the whole bourgeoisie'. However, market power does not automatically translate to political power, as analyses of collective action among business interests below demonstrate.

Beyond this lies a simple observation that capitalists frequently complain about lots of things that governments do which seem to be inimical to their interests, and in particular the burden of 'red tape'. The traditional Marxist objection to this is that either capitalists cannot always see what their long-term interests may be or capital has to be seen to be losing the odd battle in order to preserve popular legitimacy in government. Marxist analysis has however never been able to satisfactorily address the point that government officials have an entirely different power base to that of capital – that of administrative control (which produces 'red tape') – and thus the capability to be independent of capital. Political systems have constructed regimes which restrict the ability of capital to play one country off against another (such as 'regime shopping' to the most favourable cost base) by constructing common cross-border rules, of which the Single European Market is one. And the threat of capital mobility tends to be limited once it has been invested in production infrastructure. At the EU level, a wide-ranging evaluation based on a large number of studies did not find an overall picture of routine business dominance (Kohler-Koch 2008). In Chapter 1, the work of Lowi was recited to demonstrate how regulatory policies distribute costs and benefits to different types of interest constituencies, resulting in contested interest group politics (Lowi 1964). In this scenario, different domains of business engage in competitive politics, seeking to shift the costs involved in regulatory proposals to other constituencies, and maximize benefits for themselves. As a regulatory-based regime, the EU fits this scenario entirely.

Vogel's seminal essay on business/governmental relations draws attention to the ways in which government receptivity to business concerns is highly variable across issues, political settings, and economic circumstance (Vogel 1996). Issues such as monetary union are matters of 'high politics' of open public debate in which no one type of interest can assert monopolistic influence. Additionally, the potential impact of such initiatives creates considerable uncertainty, which makes it difficult for business interests to accurately assess costs and benefits, and therefore to come out strongly on one side or the other of the argument (Leblond 2008). There are also the inevitable difficulties of reaching common positions across sectors which have different interests. On such issues, the contribution of business is therefore restricted to muted and qualified endorsements through public statements, rather than cartoon caricatures of effortlessly pulling strings 'behind the scenes' in public policy.

The thesis of routine business dominance is also challenged by literature examining variations within capital itself, challenging assumptions of 'homogenous capital'. Firms vary considerably, as do industries, in their capacity to engage in political action, and have greatly competing interests and positions. At the simplest level in European single-market terms, multinational firms in a sector may seek access to markets across borders, while domestically oriented firms may want to adopt defensive postures to the threat of increased competition by protecting their domestic markets from intensified competition. And multinational firms themselves carry significant diversity, creating problems in reaching common positions, and co-ordinating across product divisions. Energy firms, for instance, may have interests in fossil fuels and in alternative sources of energy, resulting in different public policy orientations. And firms have differing degrees of centralization, with some product divisions operating as quasi-autonomous entities which resist attempts at centralized control. At worst, differences between product divisions are unknown, and there is no mechanism of co-ordination or resolving differences, with limited knowledge of the number of membership subscriptions to business associations across companies. And the preferences of firms are themselves variable. Levy and Prakash note how

> [t]he preferences and power of MNCs vary across issues and sectors, and from one negotiating forum to another, accounting for the uneven and fragmented nature of the resulting system. (Levy and Prakash 2003:131)

They draw attention to a divergence of preferences towards free market or regulatory-oriented solutions across and within business actors, as well as issues, and negotiating forums. When these changing preferences are mixed with multiple sources of power, including state authority and NGOs, the result is indeterminate outcomes upon international governance.

This range of factors resonates with perspectives drawing upon management studies literature. In a review article published in the *Journal of Management*, Hillman et al. (2004) list four categories which have emerged as leading explanatory variables which condition corporate political activity. They focus on the firm itself, the types of industry, the issue at stake, and institutional factors. The 'behavioural theory of the firm', which casts doubt upon the perspective that firms are coherent actors, well appraised of their actions and consequences, and fully equipped with capacities to act in the political arena. Managing information and calculating all the factors relevant to the interests of a firm is significant. Routine, inertia, accident, and drift, explains much of what happens in organizations. Firms which are proven actors in the market can be extremely clumsy in the political arena, lacking the skill sets and capacity to know what to do. Thus, resources are not the factor of dependency, as Microsoft's clumsy and ineffective interventions in both Washington DC and Brussels in facing anti-trust actions initiated by regulatory authorities bear testimony (Hart 2010).

The degree of presence and incorporation of NGOs in policy-making is also a factor conditioning business influence. At the EU level, where the accommodation of NGOs is much sought after in pursuit of a participatory democracy model (Chapters 1, 3, 6, and 8), a European public affairs manager of one multinational consumer brand firm reported spending half of his time seeking to make common cause with NGOs. This recognizes the reality that policy outcomes in a multi-level governance system are consensus-oriented (Chapter 1), and therefore stakeholder actors need to spend time constructing alliances. And intra-business alliances may be more difficult to achieve than they are among relatively cognate NGOs. The Director of the European Policy Office of the World Wide Fund for Nature (EEF-EPO) recently reflected that

> NGOs might have an advantage over business groups in that NGOs find it easier to construct and maintain broad cross-national coalitions than do business interests who are essentially in competition with each other and who are differentially affected by EU regulation. (Long and Lörinczi 2009:177)

Where collective action is possible, business interest associations can help firms reduce 'transaction costs' through pooling resources. Assessing the potential impact of a regulatory measure is inherently problematic for a firm, and the costs of their intelligence gathering efforts designed to do so can be reduced through participation in collective fora. At the very least, checking an interpretation of an issue against the perspective of peers is the least a company will need to do. While associations differ in their effectiveness, as a general rule where there are common shared problems within an industry, associations work well. Even when these conditions are not present, the norm is towards participation in business associations for a variety of reasons reviewed below, not least because participants need to retain some influence over the positions which associations adopt. There are limits to what associations can do; as primarily political representation bodies, they cannot be expected to have the same intimate knowledge of markets which companies do from their day-to-day involvement. As one large EU business association manager put it, 'EU officials know when they talk to us that we are industrial civil servants'.

Business interest associations

Previous headcounts composited from Directory sources have identified that around 1000 formally constituted associations are organized at, and addressed to, the EU level, accounting for approximately two thirds of all EU groups (Greenwood 2002a). Available indicators suggest that their numbers have reached a plateau since the mid-1990s, and that the proportion in Brussels, at just under two thirds of their total, is also relatively stable. Despite the ambiguity of Commissioner Kallas's 'guesstimated' Brussels total interest group population of 2600 groups, the European Transparency Initiative Lobby Regulation Database included entries 2 years after its commencement for 310 'professional associations' organized at EU level, embracing primarily business/trade associations (the largest category), and also the professions. This either means that groups are not signing up to the database in significant numbers or that previous headcounts have overestimated the number of associations in some way, perhaps by including defunct or 'post-box number' organizations. Something between the two of these seems plausible. The variety to be found among directory and database entries is astonishing. At one end of the spectrum can be found the ERT, an exclusive club of the chief executive officers of European-based multinationals geared to creating the macro-environment within public policy in which business can flourish. At the other end of the spectrum lies specialist interest organizations such as the European Federation of Chimney Sweeps (ESCHFOE), with a German-based secretariat supplemented by a Brussels post box in the Belgian association.

EU business associations are quite different from those to be found in domestic politics. The main differentiating factors are that EU business associations are mainly federated (i.e. associations in which other associations are members), and have functions restricted primarily to political representation. Associations including other associations as members continue to account for the vast majority of all EU business interest associations. Together, these factors generally result in tendencies towards narrow specialization, high membership densities, low collective action problems, and a low level of resourcing and autonomy, considered further below.

Chapter 1 outlined the interests of the European Commission in developing the landscape and capacities of interest groups, and its activism in doing so. While the balance of recent Commission intervention has been towards citizen interest groups, there is an historic legacy of activism in the landscape of business groups so as to create capable partners able to supply support to policymaking and ambitions to expand European integration. This factor has been observed in some of the earliest evaluations of EU interest politics (Neunreither's 1968 analysis is cited by Grande 1996), and came to prominence in the 1980s. The most familiar of these concerns the initial phase of formation of the ERT, with Commissioner Davignon reportedly recruiting most of the members of the original group (Sandholtz and Zysman 1989; Fielder 2000). At the sectoral level, notable examples were provided in the 1980s in the biotechnology (Greenwood and Ronit 1994) and retail domains (Sargent 1987), and a decade or so later in the eco-friendly energy domain (Bartle 1999), and the European Services Forum (ESF), established by UNICE (Union of Industrial and Employers' Confederations of Europe) at the prompting of the European Commission (and launched by its then Vice President Sir Leon Brittan) to provide them with assistance throughout the present General Agreement on Tariffs and Services (GATS) negotiations process. Woll (2009) tells the story of how the European textiles organization, EURATEX, had to completely about-turn its demands for a protectionist regime in international trade so as to find the benefits of a liberal regime, and only then did it find an ear for its messages in the European Commission. Eising (2009) tells a story with a similar message in the case of EURELECTRIC, the main EU electricity association. The positions which groups take up are therefore highly conditioned by its principal institutional interlocutor. Bouza Garcia (2010) reaches a similar conclusion in the case of NGOs (Chapter 6), where organizations seek to align their position with the general thrust of where the Commission is heading, before working out the detail of their policy position. In effect, organizations are limiting their scope to the broader agendas set by EU institutions and seeking to work within that, but the message is clear: the extent of impact of a group depends partly on the co-incidence of its message with EU institutions.

This message resonates with a wider literature which sees lobbying as the exchange of information between well-informed interest groups and understaffed decision-makers (Chalmers 2011). Sending information with the aim of changing minds is likely to bring limited results (Lowery 2007), and the limited resources of associations – particularly relevant in an EU context – are better directed to those most likely to support their cause (Crombez 2002). The goal of lobbying is thus to 'subsidize' the work of those who already do (Hall and Deardorff 2006; for a review, see Chalmers 2011).

Key features

While the reasons for specialization were provided in Chapter 1, some of the consequences have been reserved for description in this chapter. Apart from chimney sweeps, there are, for instance, specialist associations dedicated to the producers of heat pumps, autoclaved aerated concrete, and six different types of glass products (each with their own associations). While many specialisms can be explained around divisions in the product chain, others reflect 'issues' rather than sectoral clusters. Some of these did not start life as representative associations at all, but as 'issue niche' organizations created by an entrepreneur 'selling' a 'winnable' issue in order to create a flourishing member organization (Browne 1990), or as technology clusters in EU research framework programmes.

The best available information suggests that around three fifths of all EU associations are pure federations (i.e. those which have only national associations as members), a quarter embrace both national associations and firms, and around one sixth have only companies as members (Greenwood 2002a). These latter organizations are almost exclusively large firm clubs. The mixed types of member group are usually associations drawn from sectors with a significant large firm population. These typically started life as federations, and sought to embrace the best of both worlds by attracting the resources, status, and expertise that large firms bring, while retaining their claim to comprehensive representation. They also respond to the realities of being 'by-passed' by multinationals in their domain which are active in Brussels. Of greatest significance is, however, that the membership base of national associations and large firms results in a very low degree of Olsonian type 'collective action problems'. Olson challenged the basis of interest group analysis by questioning whether like-minded interests would automatically associate. Using behavioural principles derived from economics, Olson used the concept of rational pursuit of interests on the part of the potential member to show how membership would not arise if benefit could be derived without bearing the cost of membership. That is, if the benefit of interest group activity could be obtained without joining, the most logical behaviour would be to 'free ride' the benefit. Free riding would particularly arise in the political representation work of interest groups, in that any benefits negotiated with state authorities would apply universally (such as industry regulation or deregulation), rather than be restricted to interest group members only. In consequence, Olson argued, interest groups would need to develop special incentives that were only accessible through membership (Olson 1965).

Olsonian-type 'collective action problems' tend to be less significant to the constituency of EU business interest associations when compared to national associations. This is because, unlike national associations, they draw their membership constituency primarily from those who are already politically active, and who have sought avenues to express this political activity in Brussels. Hence, it makes little sense not to join, and even less to leave. The members of European business associations are national associations and large companies, neither of which require an elaborate structure of membership incentives of the type commonly to be found among national business interest associations where a wide variety of companies are members, such as low-cost financial services, employment law and taxation advice, and training. Large companies and national associations instead look to EU associations for political representation, and consequently EU business associations are focused on this task. Their resource base reflects this relatively narrow specialization, often with fewer staff than five. While there has been a modest incremental uplift in the secretariat sizes of EU associations over the past decade, in 2010, only 10 EU business associations employed 25 or more staff (Table 4.1). A recent survey of 101 UK trade associations indicated a median subscription to an EU association of around €20,000 each year, representing less than 1% of average total income (Trade Association Forum 2006). For companies who hold membership of EU and national associations, the affiliation fees for EU associations are likewise comparatively small. An annual subscription to AMCHAM-EU costs €12,500 a small sum for an American multinational to pay.

TABLE 4.1 *EU business associations employing 25 or more staff*

Name	Acronym	Secretariat size
European Chemicals Industry Association 'family'	CEFIC	160
Committee of Agricultural Organisations in the EU/ General Committee of Agricultural Cooperation in the EU	COPA/COGECA	50
European Federation of Pharmaceutical Industry Associations	EFPIA	46
Business Europe		45
Association of European Insurers	CEA	44
EURELECTRIC – Union of the Electricity Industry	EURELECTRIC	32
European Association of Craft, Small and Medium Sized Enterprises	UEAPME	32
European Confederation of Iron and Steel Industries	EUROFER	30
European Cement Industry Association	CEMBUREAU	29
European Association of Chambers of Commerce and Industry	EUROCHAMBRES	27

Data from: Association websites, September 2010.

Some larger members are willing to pay higher fees than other members in an association as a way of achieving a higher degree of influence over the work of an association. The tendency in some large firm sectors in the 1990s to create direct company membership as a route to more exclusive collective action also acknowledges the presence of calculation and a membership decision. But some may not even undertake this. For some large firms, membership became a 'habit', and, even if the original membership decision once constituted a calculated decision, their continued affiliation may not have required any thought or action. In sectors where there is a high degree of similarity in the issues facing members, association membership is never seriously questioned. In industries where the case for collective action is less apparent, the cost of non-membership may be a higher consideration than the benefits of membership. These costs can include the loss of ability to influence the positions of an association, the loss of access to a dialogue channel with EU political institutions, and the perceived potential for loss of information. Consequently, membership density of EU associations tends to be higher, and member turnover lower, than those of national associations. This latter scenario presents a decision calculus with a membership incentive, and beyond this there have been some recent signs of a growth in significance of membership evaluation among large firms, accompanied by attempts to achieve greater internal co-ordination of public affairs activities. A number of large companies now hold periodic internal review events bringing together personnel responsible for working in European and national associations, resulting in an additional constituency of member-driven pressure upon associations.

A consequence of the specialization of EU business associations upon political representation is their total dependence upon subscription income from their members, rather than having independent resource streams of their own from service provision. The greater the dependence of an association among its members, the lower is its autonomy from them. Associations with a low degree of autonomy from their members have a reduced capacity to bring long-term value to them because it becomes a mouthpiece for their short-term demands (Coleman 1988). Associations bring value to their members by identifying and representing their long-term interests rather than their more or less shaky opinions (Burnheim, in Phillips 1995), in that the latter may be based on a lack of knowledge, insight, or capability for overview. That is, associations bring value to their members by helping them, during their participation under the umbrella of the association, construct a sense of what their interests are.

Cross-sectoral associations

The distinguishing feature of business-wide organizations is that their interventions are geared to those which affect the main breadth of their constituency, and where they take a position on a sectoral issue they have to do so with care as there may be issues of inter-sectoral competition. The main business-wide associations all have their own 'niche', each with very different structures. This is not accidental, in that new groups emerge to operate in unfilled niches (Salisbury 1969; Browne 1990). Where they fish in different pools for members there is no need to compete, and there is a good degree of collaboration where there is no overlapping representation constituency. The main degree of overlap for EU associations only arises in the representation of SMEs, where a number of associations have rival claims, although even these have substantially distinct niches which differentiate them from each other. Of the constituency of business-wide associations as a whole, it is striking that two, Business Europe and the ERT, have mirror-image strengths and weaknesses, and properties which are both a strength and a weakness to each. Thus, as is evident from the descriptions below, the strength and weakness of Business Europe lies with its breadth of membership, whereas the strength and weakness of ERT is its selective membership constituency. Their different niches are also covered by their respective functions, in that Business Europe does 'everyday lobbying', while ERT does 'strategic issues'. It is therefore not difficult for these organizations to work together where necessary.

This feature of 'mutual accommodation', where organizations are deliberately designed to differentiate themselves and to limit competition between them, allows organizations to co-exist. While the group of business-wide associations are far from being a common set of actors and have differences in policy positions on individual files, it also means that where the issue is one in common they do participate in alliances together, and combinations of them sometimes issue joint statements. Business Europe, as the lead cross-sectoral association, brokers a number of alliances with cross-sectoral, and sectoral, associations. Thus, the Alliance for a Competitive European Industry, created in 2004, provides a common platform where required, bringing together 11 of the major sectoral EU business associations with. The Alliance periodically issues a 'manifesto', where strategic priorities for global competitiveness of the major European industries are identified, contributing to agenda-setting public policy needs. Business Europe also participates in the European Services Forum, bringing together the major European stakeholder companies and associations for services-related issues.

The five principal EU cross-sectoral business associations, described below, have a total staff complement of 134 and a declared annual expenditure on lobbying EU institutions of approaching €4 million (Table 4.2). The organizations are described in detail below.

Business Europe

Formed in 1958, Business Europe (formerly UNICE) now has 40 full members, these being national associations of business from 34 countries, spanning EU-27, accession and aspirant, and EFTA, countries. With the debatable exception of Austria, these associations represent the most significant business-wide organizations in each of these countries, spanning the breadth of the business community.

TABLE 4.2   *The resources of the cross-sectoral EU*
             business associations

Organization	Budget declared on ETR	Expenditure on lobbying EU institutions declared on ETR	Total number of staff listed on website
AMCHAM-EU	€2,217,000	€400,000–450,000	23
Business Europe	Undisclosed	€550,000–600,000	45
ERT	Undisclosed	€300,000–350,000	7
EUROCHAMBRES	Undisclosed	≥€1,000,000	27
UEAPME	€1,643,200	€1,561,000	32
Total		€3,811,000	134

This breadth of membership helps to prevent the association from over-domination by one particular constituency, although larger members pay a higher pro rata share of Business Europe income. Further income is supplied by a Corporate 'Advisory and Support Group' of (currently, 38) large firms, although these play no formal role in decision-making other than through access to working groups which then report upwards to committees.

The overwhelming majority of Business Europe members have offices in Brussels, including many in the same building complex. These are key to understanding the way in which Business Europe functions. They supplement the work of 45 staff members of the association, help it to address national points of influence in EU decision-making, and widen its network of access to information. They help to build internal consensus through personal relationships, links to their own national association offices, and through informal caucuses between groups of them, although their ability to monitor the work of the association places some restrictions upon its autonomy. They also undertake their own independent political activities, and it is not uncommon for them to give a different message to EU institutions than those of Business Europe.

Because any organization with such a wide membership constituency will by nature have some difficulties in reaching common positions, it is something of a cheap point to be critical of it on the basis of a tendency towards lowest common denominator positions. A former General Secretary presents the other side of this equation, referring instead to the 'miracle' of its cohesiveness under the circumstances of its breadth of membership constituency (Tyszkiewicz 2001). The 'miracle' interpretation offers an alternative to a view presented by an unnamed 'former senior EU official' in a *Financial Times* (*FT*) article, who is quoted as saying that

> Unice's problem is that it consists of a federation of confederations. It is a heavily bureaucratic system, even though it is the only recognised body that represents formally the whole of European industry. In short, it is a reactive institution whereas the ERT with its minimal bureaucracy is proactive. (Betts 2001)

While there is a degree of plausibility to some of this, the quote should not be taken out of context. Business Europe operates in a completely different niche to ERT, in that it seeks to defend the broad interests of the entire constituency of European business across the spectrum of EU politics, based around national representative business-wide associations. The ERT was created to draw from a strictly selected membership of Chief Executive Officers (CEOs) from large companies, and performs a 'strategic issue think tank' role in which members pick and choose their issues. These niches have helped to differentiate the respective organizations and restrict competition between them.

The breadth of interests Business Europe embraces is therefore its core strength and weakness. It allows the organization to speak with unrivalled authority based on its position as the representative organization for the entire constituency of business. This means that its decision-making is by nature lengthy as members need to consult with their own extensive memberships. Its breadth of membership means that its orientation towards consensus is evident throughout the culture of the organization, with provisions for QMV seldom used. Policy Committees meet approximately three times a year, and this greatly regulates the speed of decision-taking within Business Europe. Membership of working groups can be much sought after by organizations seeking the authority and endorsement of the association, or by those wishing to prevent the association from taking up a damaging position for them.

AMCHAM-EU

The American Chamber of Commerce–European Union (AMCHAM-EU) speaks for 'American Business committed to Europe' (AMCHAM-EU 2011). Its origins lie within Amcham Belgium, though it has operated largely independently since the mid-1980s, and completely since 2004 (AMCHAM-EU 2009a). Virtually all of its 140 member companies have their own public affairs presence in Brussels, and the size and quality of this network provides the essence of the organization. It is notable for the high degree of member participation, resulting in a service-based, though proactive, secretariat. It has a long-standing reputation on the Brussels circuit for strategic-level transatlantic business bridge-building, for advocacy on cross-sectoral regulatory issues, and for its publications and information. Hayes-Renshaw's recent claim that it is 'widely regarded as one of the most successful interest groups in Brussels' (Hayes-Renshaw 2009:82) builds on a legacy of similar summation (Green-Cowles 1996). In 2009, it received an industry award for 'trade association of the year' (AMCHAM-EU 2009b).

The organization has historically helped socialize American member companies in the more diplomatic orientation of Brussels public affairs compared to Washington (for an example, see Thomas and Boyer 2001) (Gardner 1991). It has moved on from being 'the American outsider' as a result of a number of factors, stressing the way in which many firms of American origin have such extensive investments and operations in Europe, often highly devolved from company headquarters in the US, such that their prosperity has become a European issue. This positioning is supported by the employment of European staff in AMCHAM-EU. These factors have contributed to a long-standing legitimacy of the organization with EU institutions, with its work finding recognition within services of the European Commission, where some see it as a supportive ally in its quest to develop European integration. This European profile of AMCHAM-EU has brought a view of it in US domestic politics that it has somewhat gone native (Calingaert 1993).

The Executive Council of AMCHAM-EU (until 2006 the European-American Industrial Council) comprises a group of CEOs responsible for the European operations of US multinationals (supported by public affairs heads), providing a forum for business leaders of EU Committee members at the highest level to engage EU politicians at the highest level. An example of the work which the Executive Council has undertaken is a study on the impact of globalization in Europe at the behest of President Barroso (AMCHAM-EU 2008).

The ERT

The ERT is a selective forum of around 45 industrial leaders (at CEO, or President, level) of multinational firms headquartered in Europe, of which many are among the largest transnational corporations in the world. A unique niche is that membership is thus personal rather than corporate, and by invitation only. This membership means that it is not geared to address the everyday issues of operational public policymaking, but a strategy- and vision-oriented outfit aimed at inserting 'big issues' into the EU policy agenda.

The organization was stimulated by the promptings of European Commissioner Etienne Davignon, seeking a high-level business interlocutor capable of supporting the push for Europe's global competitiveness, and the organization emerged in 1983 under the Chairmanship of Volvo's CEO, Pierre Gyllenhammer. Davignon then attended part of the founding meeting of the ERT (ERT 2010). An *FT* article (Betts 2001) recites a familiar story of how policymakers, analysts, and critics alike have credited the organization with agenda-setting many of the big ideas which have come to dominate the EU agenda. The most well known of these stories concerns its role in helping to achieve the shared goal of a European single-market project as a strategy for European wealth creation and business competitiveness. This story has been extensively used to provide evidence of how the relationship between the European Commission and outside interests can be used to explain the course of development of European integration (van Tulder and Junne 1988; Sandholtz and Zysman 1989; Green-Cowles 1995; Mattli 1999; Nollert and Fielder 2000; van Apeldoorn 2000, 2001).

In support of this account of the role of the ERT in the single-market project, the *FT* article cites Jacques Delors in recalling that 'the ERT was the right vehicle. Unice could not have done it. Discussions with the ERT were simple and straightforward' (ibid.:16). The clout of the ERT, with its involvement at chief executive level from household-name firms, undoubtedly made this 'the right vehicle' through which to build the support necessary among member states. Delors is quoted as remarking that 'these men are very powerful and dynamic ... when necessary they can ring up their own prime ministers and make their case' (van Tulder and Junne, in Mattli 1999:78). Certainly, the relationship between Delors, on the lookout for supportive allies, and the ERT, was a close one, with the two partners appearing together at press conferences. Mattli recounts how ERT members worked alongside, cajoled, and even threatened member state governments to achieve the necessary political support, first by citing an *FT* article in 1985 in which Wisse Dekker, head of Philips and later to become Chairman of ERT, said if there were no single market

> there were not so many reasons why ... Philips should stay in the Netherlands ... I am European enough to wait until the last possible moment ... (but) if Europe is neither able nor willing to develop its economic structure, then the consequences ... must be drawn. (Mattli 1999:80)

Mattli also reproduces the famous telex sent by the ERT to the June 1985 Milan European Summit meeting at which member state leaders were considering the single-market project:

> As leading industrialists based in the European Communities ...
> we urge you to exercise your full influence so that the forthcoming

top meeting ... will produce concrete results. STOP. Not only is the credibility of European political leaders at stake but European industry badly needs a clear signal that the major objectives of the Treaty of Rome will be realised within the next 5 years. STOP. Even a clear statement that this would not be the case, would – although not hoped for – be helpful as this would end the prolonged period of uncertainty with which industry has to cope under the present situation and which forms a significant obstacle on the way to expanding our activities and intensifying our efforts to build a strong a competitive European position. (Mattli 1999:80)

The reputed influence of the ERT has made it something of an iconic magnet for attention by anti-capitalism/globalization 'alternatives' activists throughout its history (Balanya et al. 2003). The *FT* article cites description of the ERT by one activist as 'a shadowy lobby group that has, for the past 15 years, exerted an iron grip on policy making in Brussels', and 'the political agenda of the EU has to a large extent been dominated by the ERT' (Betts 2001). The ERT's own website has in the past fed these prejudices by presenting its 'achievements' (ERT 2001; Richardson 2000). While ERT self-presentation is now notably more muted, stories told by friend and foe alike have fed a reputation about the influence of the ERT, supported by some accounts from commentators about its supposedly key role played in securing political agreement for the single European market (Green-Cowles 1995; van Apeldoorn 2001). These latter accounts need to be contextualized as seeking to present counter-evidence for the perceived dominance of 'state-centric' accounts of the process of European integration in the analytic literature, in which the Single European Act is seen as a grand bargaining trade-off between member states (Moravcsik 1993). Nevertheless, the role of the ERT is better seen more as a supporting agent, rather than a causal one, in the establishment of a single market, and which would have happened without their interventions.

On taking office, Commission President Delors searched for a project for his term of office which would find universal support among the member state leaders at the time, and the single market fitted the description. Several things combined to get things moving. Most member state governments had been elected on largely liberal market platforms by the early 1980s, replacing the more left-oriented governments of the 1970s. In October 1984, the European summit settled the UK budget rebate and Greek entry problems, which had stalled EU politics for so long, while the European economy was finally growing again after the oil crisis, unemployment was coming down and optimism was in the air. By January 1985, Commissioner Cockfield was working remarkably well with Delors, and had galvanized everyone with his White Paper on completion of the Single Market by the end of 1992. The 1985 Milan European Summit endorsed the White Paper and agreed that it could be implemented only if the Treaty were changed to allow QMV on Single Market issues. Even member-state leaders who were committed Euro-sceptics, such as Margaret Thatcher, were committed to see this goal through.

This scenario casts the ERT as supporting, rather than causal, agents for a process which would have happened anyway (Young and Wallace 2000). Undoubtedly, ERT sat alongside Delors at his press conferences and gave legitimacy to the single-market project. The popularity of accounts suggesting their influence was more causal is a flag of convenience for those who wish to portray it so. The ERT participates in the rarefied atmosphere of 'high politics', in which its voice is just one of a number seeking influence upon public policies, alongside forces such as national governments and the international environment. Undoubtedly, it contributes to the climate of debate, and to the influences upon some of these decision-making forces. But, as with all interest-group-based explanations of the policy process, the simple and uncritical connection should not be made between demands and public policy outcomes.

The reputed strength of the ERT derives from its membership profile and format. Its policy positions are built directly by its members, with one asked to take the lead on a particular issue through a working party. The member's company will then use its informal networks with others in order to build a position before returning to the formal structures of the ERT, followed by presentation in one of the twice-yearly plenary meetings. In addition to written communiqués and publications in which its positions are presented, members are used to take the message to the highest level, through face-to-face communication with Europe's leading politicians and policymakers (van Apeldoorn 2001). This rather flat and flexible membership-driven structure, together with its cohesiveness and ability to come to rich common positions, finds its supporters elsewhere in the business representation community. Its membership constituency is highly selective and relatively homogenous in both the size and structure of firms, and in drawing upon chief executives with broadly similar worldviews. It has no members to either represent or discipline, does not face 'governability problems' (van Apeldoorn 2000), and chief executives are in a unique position to lend the name of their company to ERT positions.

The ideas of seeking the involvement of CEOs, and a flat structure of decision-making, have been the sources of inspiration for change among other EU associations. A small number of other groups spawned in the ERT's image include the Association for the Monetary Union of Europe (AMUE), the European Retail Round Table (ERRT), the European IT Round Table, and the European Roundtable of Financial Services (ERFS). This means that it is now somewhat less unique, and to a certain extent its energy has been absorbed by its institutionalization into the EU political system (van Apeldoorn 2001). It is now somewhat different as an organization from the one created in the early 1980s, and is not therefore regarded as influential today as during the favourable climate of the Delors days. Membership turnover since rather questions the 'iron grip on policymaking' caricature.

The historic selectivity of ERT membership has drawn detailed analysis from a number of observers. Nollert and Fielder observed significant membership gaps in it, claiming that the centre of the ERT network had at one time been dominated by German, Belgian, and French businesses (Nollert and Fielder 2000). This broad assessment was shared by van Apeldoorn, who noted a tendency towards 'Rhinish' capitalism (van Apeldoorn 2000). Today, ERT's membership is more oriented across western, and northern, Europe, but it does have inevitable membership gaps, particularly in central and east European countries, reflecting the lack of large indigenous multinationals from that region.

Betts has also identified a predomination by big manufacturing groups (Betts 2001), while Sietses discerned domination by chemicals, oil, electronics, and 'agro-element' firms (Sietses 2000). This partiality has, in the past, led to it being unable to speak out on certain strategic issues because of the presence of certain members, and needing to give behind-the-scenes support to the more broadly constituted Business Europe to take up the mantle. ERT and Business Europe have come together in more visible ways, issuing regular joint communiqués since 2002. They are complementary organizations with mirror-image strengths and weaknesses, reflecting how interest groups emerge and survive by finding 'niches', and in which competition is limited because the organizations are not fishing in the same pool for members. The emergence of the ERT reflects general accounts of how a group comes forward through the work of 'entrepreneurs' (Davignon/Gyllenhammer) spotting and filling a niche gap in the representation population (Salisbury 1969; Browne 1990).

EUROCHAMBRES

EUROCHAMBRES has 46 national chambers of commerce (from Iceland to Israel) as member organizations, which in turn encompass regional and local chambers. In the EU 15, chambers of commerce are differentiated from national business and employer organizations as a distinct brand whose strength lies in regional and local organization, with a mass of SME members, and a strong service provision orientation to its members. In the EU-27 and beyond, national Chambers of Commerce have often played a role as the principal business organization. At the EU level, where political representation is the principal requirement of business associations because service functions are required less by national business member organizations, the identity of EUROCHAMBRES is squeezed. It lies somewhere between the predominance of Business Europe and the greater recognition of UEAPME as an SME representative organization. These realities mean that EUROCHAMBRES had to find its own distinct niche away from centre-stage. One has been to develop strong institutional ties with the Committee of the Regions. A second has been to be an EU learning forum for horizontal business interest organizations from central and eastern European countries, and an outlet for their political representation. A third distinct role has been an unusual one for EU business associations, a service-related role in acting as a point of contact for export advice, business partner searchers through its network, and advice in chamber development. A fourth role has been to act as a partner with the European Commission for the delivery of advice services to local level, playing to its organizational strengths in the member states. The deployment of its staff resources reflects these diverse niche roles. Some of its larger members see it more as a large network than an outlet for political representation. The network is one of its principal strengths, covering most of the landmass of Europe, and extending into the Middle East (Israel) and Asia (Azerbaijan), and the international department of EUROCHAMBRES accounts for one third of its staff members. These global links, its function as a network, and its service orientation are its principal strengths as an association.

The strong emphasis on service work relative to political representation partly reflects the diversity of its membership. A key cleavage is between national chambers which are recognized in public law, based on compulsory membership, and those established in private law and based on voluntary membership. Members range from organizations which are not central players in their national domain to the largest of all national 'business associations', the Wirtschaftskammer Österreich (WKÖ), a key component of governance (and to some observers indivisible from state machinery) in Austrian corporatism. Members from Central and Eastern European countries have tended to look to EUROCHAMBRES to provide them with credibility in their own countries, as they seek to establish their own identities and independence from state structures. Small members and those members from countries that are weakly represented elsewhere in EU business representational structures look to the organization for political representation, whereas those with alternatives do not. A number of national members, and large city chambers of commerce, have their own representations in Brussels, and which are not as well co-ordinated as can be found in the Business Europe, and UEAPME, structures.

UEAPME

A characteristic of SME associations in any territorial setting is the appearance, disappearance, and merger of organizations, more or less geared towards political representation, often with particular niches and territorial partiality. This process continues with EU-level organizations, although the clear leader representative organization to emerge is the European Association of Craft, Small and Medium-Sized Enterprises (UEAPME). Its full members are national SME associations, with some notable membership strengths from the Germanic world, reflected in the composition of its secretariat, following a period of Francophile orientation. The glaring membership gap is from the UK, where the principal representative organizations of SMEs in the UK, the Federation of Small Businesses, dominates the rival European Small Business Alliance (ESBA), while the second largest UK small business association, the Forum of

Private Business, resigned its UEAPME membership in recent years. In addition to these organizations, EUROCHAMBRES and Business Europe each have a substantial derivative SME constituency, with some membership overlap between UEAPME and Business Europe, either directly or by affiliations.

The internal cohesion of UEAPME arises from three sources. One is its Germanic (countries where the principal language is German) orientation and its powerhouse members, the German *Zentralverband des Deutschen Handwerks* and *Unternehmerverband Deutsches Handwerk* (ZdH und UDH), and the Austrian WKÖ. A second is the role it has fought to obtain in the highest level of EU social partnership (Chapter 2) alongside Business Europe, following a case it brought before the European Court of Justice (T-135/96). These result in inclusion in setting common positions on behalf of employers in the negotiation of the social dialogue in negotiation with the European Trade Union Confederation (ETUC). A third major coherence factor is the nature of its constituency. There are no large firms to by-pass it, and SMEs themselves do not have the resources to establish themselves in Brussels, leaving the UEAPME secretariat and its members relatively free to define the positions of the organization.

The organization has incorporated the resources of its membership to good effect. Its larger members operate from the corridor of the same building in which UEAPME is based, supplementing its resources considerably, creating a strong collective, almost family, identity, whereby members actively contribute to the work of UEAPME. The ZdH/UDH has contributed a relatively large number of staff, while some of the individuals from national offices are self-employed entrepreneurs selling their part-time services to UEAPME. UEAPME has proved adept at entrepreneurial activity, such as the creation of European Office for Crafts, Trades, and Small and Medium Sized Enterprises for Standardisation (NORMAPME) and the Academie Avignon. NORMAPME is the official representative of craft/trades and SMEs in the European standardization bodies, and has spawned a structure in itself, comprising a Technical Advisory Committee and a number of working groups. Egan is one observer who has been impressed at the results of its efforts to push SMEs towards compliance (Egan 2001).

There is a highly receptive environment for SME representation in the Commission, to the extent that some sector associations ensure that an SME entrepreneur is included within their delegation when going to meet with Commission officials. One major EU business association recently elected as President an SME entrepreneur as one means to tackle a perception in the Commission that the association was primarily an outlet for multinationals in the sector. In addition to dialogue with all avenues of SME representation, the Commission has advisory groups drawn directly from SME entrepreneurs, as a separate initiative to meetings held with SME representative organizations.

While it is usual for UEAPME to be able to reach common positions, it is also not unusual for it to reach a view that it is unable to reach a common position on an issue. It also often uses a system of majority and minority opinions, reasoning that where it is not possible for the organization to come to a common view, it is better for the organization to demonstrate the difficulties in doing so, and where the main points of difference lie. Because UEAPME is an SME association where there can be a problem of member participation and knowledge, its secretariat, rather than its members, write the initial draft of the position papers, thus enhancing its leadership capacity.

Sector associations and firms

A variety of caricatures of the capacities and significance of business associations, juxtaposed with those of firms, can be found in the literature. Many early accounts observed weaknesses in the decision-making capacities of such groups (Caporaso 1974; Kirchner and Schweiger 1981; Butt Philip 1985; Grant 1990; McLaughlin 1992). Bennett reports the views of a Director in (then) DG III (now Enterprise), that

> I think we understand that a European trade association is representing a very wide range of different interests and they do not invariably speak with one voice and have a single view. Some opinions that we have received have worked on the lowest common denominator principle, so that by the time they reach us they are of precious little use; they do not say anything. It would be much better to say 'well some of our members think this and some think that', because this builds up the picture and helps us to understand what is going on. (Bennett 1997b:10)

In this account, the main value of EU associations lies in pointing out where the main differences of opinion lie. He also drew attention to their lack of speed, recounting to a conference audience how 'we recently received the most beautifully set out, thoroughly argued assessment of a Commission proposal which had been adopted six months earlier' (White 1997:74).

These criticisms of the capacities of Euro groups are not without historic foundation, they are based on their relatively slim resource bases described earlier in this chapter, and somewhat broad-brushed. The reality is variation, ranging from a 'post box' 'association' through to some of the examples in Table 4.1. While a 1997 large sample survey of UK trade associations found that less than half of their sample of UK national associations saw their EU association as effective (Compass Partnership 1997), the equivalent exercise repeated in 2005 found that 88% did so (Trade Association Forum 2006). Bouwen (2006) found that EU associations had a higher degree of access to the European Commission and European Parliament than did other types of actors. Some EU associations have been identified in 'islands' of corporatist relationships with EU political institutions (Greenwood and Ronit 1994; Grant 1997). In a case study of information and communication technologies in standardization, Knill (2001) also found significant self-regulatory functions, and concluded that EU associations have assumed greater importance than they have been credited for. Clusters of cognate associations working on common agendas can be found working from the same premises in key sectors, such as chemicals (under the CEFIC umbrella) and engineering (under the ORGALIME (European Engineering Association) umbrella). In the latter case, something of a Brussels 'engineering house' has emerged in the Diamant building, in which national and European associations work together on industry-critical issues such as the development of the research framework programmes (Chapter 2).

Thus, there is a mixed picture among associations at EU level. Which factors predict the ability of an industrial segment to undertake collective action? My own research interviews among 50 EU business associations and 150 of their members examined the causal factors of variation in the ability of these associations to unify their members interests and to secure compliance with associational goals (Greenwood 2002a), known as 'governability'. One association General Secretary has calculated that around 50% of the time of associations is spent in reaching internal cohesion (Ager 2002). Beyond internal factors, the main causes of variation between associations in their governability are structural factors concerned with the extent to which there are shared interests between a relatively homogenous and clearly defined interest constituency. Thus, associations representing a limited number of firms of a similar size in commodity product industries (such as metals, oil, chlorine) are relatively undifferentiated in their interests, whereas associations representing interests across the product chain (such as wholesalers, distributors, and retailers) in diversely constituted industries are bound to find more difficulty in reaching common positions. Beyond the nature of the product sector, and structural properties of the industry, lie more contextual factors which are predictors of cohesion. Thus, industries facing problems of overcapacity seek policy instruments to help manage the problem, such as financial instruments to support industrial restructuring, rather than market solutions (such as a price war) which have uncontrolled regional consequences. Similarly, industry segments can find cohesion from their contestation by a 'common enemy'. Without the presence of such factors there is little basis for sustained collective action (Greenwood 2002a).

Most industry sectors with a large firm component now accommodate large firms through direct membership, or risk being undermined by the contacts such players inevitably make with EU institutions, particularly because the largest firms almost all have their own dedicated representative offices in Brussels. The European Banking Federation faces just this scenario because it is solely comprised of national associations of banks. Sectors which are almost wholly comprised of large firms have tended to develop associations which are solely direct membership organizations, and in which national associations have no direct membership. In turn, this brings its own issues where national associations are excluded from EU sector association membership because they can also find their own contacts with EU institutions; the automobile manufacturing sector is one example of this. The usual solution in such sectors is to admit both national associations and companies directly into membership, on the grounds that whatever the difficulties are in reaching common positions as a result of the wider membership base are overridden by the increasing sense of obligation which members will feel towards the collective policy positions of an association. An interesting alternative has been the development of a European-wide system of national associations in the plastics sector, with a European association hub and national association spokes. For a short time this looked like a futuristic model for EU trade associations, but the model has not been replicated, with some associations identifying reverse pressures for subsidiarity and decentralization. A sense of the importance of associations to companies is provided in a case study of Nokia, whose membership of one EU association with direct members was partly informed by that association's membership of another confederation (Kautto 2009).

Direct company membership associations and networks

As discussed in the commentary on business-wide associations above, direct firm membership structures, and federations of associations, each have different strengths and weaknesses. Some of these differences are expressed in findings about their contacts with EU institutions. Eising (2001b) found that associations of associations have more contacts with the Commission than associations organizing firms only – and even have more contacts than do associations that include both associations and firms in their membership. This was a broad finding supported by the work of Bennett, although he found that both types of structures which included associations as members had more contacts with the Commission than did associations of firms (Bennett 2000). This may reflect a point made earlier about the diffusion of control in federations, and the concentration of control within direct firm membership associations where the autonomy of the secretariat becomes highly restricted by companies whose main motivation is to prevent the association from doing any harm. Large firms have a variety of means and outlets for their different public affairs needs, and few, if any, are totally reliant upon their direct membership affiliations for all of them.

In addition to formal trade associations, a variety of informal networks have emerged in Brussels to link the public affairs staff of corporate offices. Some are occasional cross-industry lunch clubs, with a speaker followed by a discussion, organized by the offices of the rotating chair. Another model provides a forum for participants drawn from politics, international institutions, industry, and finance to think about world events (Nollert and Fielder 2000; Chabanet 2006). These satisfy a need among participants for discussion, interpretation, networking, and information, and to tune in to the latest thinking. While shared beliefs and mutual socialization are the basis for successful collective action, and all the usual benefits can be expected from routine networking activities, the importance of irregular gatherings should not be over-exaggerated.

Some informal structures are caucuses of firms seeking to provide a particular direction to the activities of a particular interest group. Typically, these are organized at the sectoral level, such as the 'Brussels Automobile Representatives' (BAR) structure linking all the public affairs managers of the Brussels offices of vehicle manufacturers, where all but one of the members of the Association of European Automobile Constructors (ACEA) are based. Some fora of large companies have also emerged in response to initiatives from the Commission. The most noted of these from the European side was the Transatlantic Business Dialogue (TABD), whose first conference in 1995 emerged into a company-led 'informal process where European and American companies develop joint policy recommendations to discuss with the EC and US administrations' (Coen and Grant 2001:39). In addition to this, the parties concluded agreements in their own domains with public governance impacts, such as Mutual Recognition Agreements which 'reduced the costs of testing and certification in seven key industrial sectors' (ibid.:41). The structure spawned a secretariat in Washington and Brussels, to assist the work of working groups, each co-ordinated by a joint EU/US company chair. The structure includes trade association executives working as issue managers in standards and regulatory policy (Coen and Grant 2001). More recent structures of significance have emerged from EU Research Framework Programmes, where 'platform' structures brought together players in a particular technology field who fed in to the design of public policy initiatives designed to develop strategic technologies. Some of these came downstream in more formalized structures once the initiatives emerged.

While some alliances develop into more formalized structures, others remain ad hoc or disappear as issues recede. Such alliances are a feature of all political systems (Wilson 1995), across the spectrum of civil society, and there is no shortage of examples at EU level which can be provided by a short Internet search. While some read 'corporate influence' from the presence alone of a website, such an interpretation can be a surprise to the rather loosely committed participants who see little more than meetings with intangible outcomes. Thus, one commentary cited an informal group of energy companies as a means to hurry on energy liberalization, although the ENERG-8 group of large consumers of electricity had little or no impact upon the dossier, such that they are hardly recalled at all by the main issue actors either inside or outside the Commission (Green-Cowles 1997; Greenwood 2002b). Informal structures continue to emerge, but are not always exclusive to firms. The European

Construction Forum (ECF) links trade associations and associations of the professions, across the contributing disciplines to the construction industry. Boleat gives the example of the European Partnership for Energy and the Environment (EPEE), formed to help develop effective European policies to reduce greenhouse gases from the use of refrigerants. This structure brought together companies, national associations and European associations active in the air conditioning, heat-pump, and refrigeration industry (Boleat 2002).

Large firms as EU public affairs actors

Unsurprisingly, commentators have found that company preferences for greater integration at the European level are determined by the magnitude of external threat to the industry, and the level of industry's transaction costs (Mattli 1999; Weber and Hallerberg 2001). Keith Richardson, a former General Secretary of the ERT, has claimed that multinational firms were kept out of the initial stages of European integration, and shunned in favour of trade associations, despite the fact that they were among the earliest to think in pan-European terms (Richardson 1997). Certainly, most of them did not become active until the early 1980s; Wessels found 314 corporate public affairs offices listed in EU directory sources in 1994 (Wessels 1997), and the 350 counted by Coen in 1997 (Coen 1999) do not appear to have been exceeded since. Not all of these are Brussels based, while the population of such offices in the Belgian capital shows some degree of turnover with exit (e.g. Boots, American Express) and entry.

Coen's analysis of the national origin of companies with EU public affairs offices in Brussels between 1997 and 2003 makes interesting reading in that the proportion of US firms has decreased from around a third to a quarter, with a relative growth in the presence of British firms (9% to 17%), and German firms (7% to 11%) (Coen 1999, 2009). Most corporate EU public affairs capacities are small, typically around two to three people. While some are staffed by senior personnel with support staff and a degree of autonomy, at the other extreme are those in a relatively junior position within their company, working alone in Brussels with part-time secretarial assistance. These latter personnel may have little scope for action without reference to sometimes disinterested line management in a public affairs headquarters in the member states.

Companies provide a complementary, and sometimes competitive, smaller segment to EU business interest representation than trade associations. There is a legacy of research investigating whether there are patterns evident in the use of particular channels by different actors, including companies (for a review of these, see Woll 2006). Among the earliest propositions is Sidjanski's suggestion that collective channels would be used for general purposes and to support proposals, while individual channels to combat details (Sidjanski 1967). More typical of recent research is work by Mahoney in focusing on the institutional and policy context in which players are seeking to act. She argues that 'advocacy is a process composed of numerous stages ... lobbying decisions at each of those stages are determined by a confluence of contextual factors including institutional, issue and interest group characteristics' (Mahoney 2004:iii). Her comparative research drawing upon samples of actors and issues in Brussels and Washington reveals plausible conclusions in suggesting that strategies to block or amend are related to the ease of achieving change in a given political system, and to the degree of democratic architecture in place, with a developed infrastructure leading to a greater use of appeal and alliance strategies. Knowledge of the EU political system is thus the strongest starting point for identifying political behaviour.

Levy and Prakash's analysis of the changing preferences of multinational corporations in international governance leads them to conclude that

> MNCs are neither omnipotent ogres nor gentle giants pursuing the common interest; rather, they bargain with states, NGOs, and other actors over the form and structure of international agreements and regimes ... the resultant indeterminacy of outcomes suggests that while MNCs are powerful actors, they do not always succeed in imposing their preferred regime type ... an endpoint when corporations rule the world is highly unlikely. NGOs and states are also building their capacities to coordinate their activities and act effectively in international arenas. (Levy and Prakash 2003:147–8)

These themes are taken up further in Chapters 6 and 8, but emerge from an analysis of the professions.

Professional interests

Of all types of civil society interests, issues surrounding interest representation by the professions are the least prominent in the literature. This may arise from their status as the most weakly organized category of civil society interest at the EU level. Most are based outside Brussels. The extreme national differences in the constitution and practising environments of professions, together with the defensive posture of many of the member state professions towards European integration, help explain this relative disorganization. There is a general pattern of small EU associations whose secretariats have positive outlooks towards European integration, but whose interests in developing it are frustrated by their much more sceptical and powerful national members. Where professions are correct in perceiving that European integration is on balance more of a threat, their nascent strength may ironically be their organizational weakness at the EU level, in that they deny to the EU institutions an alliance partner for policymaking or competency-seeking purposes.

The constitution of a 'profession' is a contested one and focuses on the processes of professionalization that has granted power and status to 'professions', acquired through the ability of representative organizations to attain controls over entry to the profession and the knowledge and training thresholds they can impose. The different historic abilities of the professions to control this process in different countries help explain the considerable degrees of variation between them in the power and constitution of professions, which in turn help explain their collective action problems at the EU level. There are different national traditions of organizing, with certain interests from the professions affiliated to wider units of organization, or operating independently. In turn, these differences are reproduced at the European level and create difficulties for some EU associations in defining the parameters of their own membership constituency. One branch of the profession from a particular country may well be represented by a different European association to its counterpart in another country. Thus, Italian civil engineers educate and license architects, who are organized separately elsewhere in Europe; dentistry in Italy is subsumed within general medicine; and there are no counterparts to British solicitors and barristers (Orzack 1991). French pharmacists have prescribing powers but their premises and establishment are licensed by government, whereas UK pharmacists have no prescribing rights but their premises and practice rights are controlled by their professional association. Architecture in France has primarily been regarded as one of the liberal arts, whereas in other countries it is treated as a technical practice.

After Brussels, the UK is the most important base for European-level associations of the professions, accounting for around one fifth of them (compared with one fifteenth of groups of all categories). The historic strength of the professions in the UK is a function of the much higher degree of powers vested in associations of the professions in the Anglo-American tradition, in comparison with that in Continental Europe, to organize and regulate their members. Many UK associations of the professions exercise monopoly powers through licensing and self-regulatory arrangements granted by state authority. In common with other types of EU associations, France, too, has historically been a disproportionately strong base for the establishment of EU associations of the professions, although fewer of them have migrated with others to Brussels, partly because of resource weaknesses. The French tradition of 'liberal professions' also fits alongside historic approaches to the development of EU regulation of them. To add to this picture of unevenness are contrasting degrees of developed competencies of the EU in different professional fields, and the selective impact of European authority upon different types of professions, described later in this chapter. A further factor involves the variety of concerns that comprise the livelihood of some of the professions, ranging from issues of public interest to those of private profit-making. By way of contrast to illustrate this point, the Standing Committee of European Doctors (CPME) is a member of the campaigning European Public Health Alliance (EPHA), while associations representing architects, and lawyers, are often exercised by single-market freedom issues about the rights of establishment to provide commercial services. For large practices of architects and engineers, the detail and operation of EU public procurement rules are also matters of considerable importance.

For Lovecy, the key variable to explain the variation to be found among the professions in their EU orientation is the degree of 'globalization' (Lovecy 1999). In this account, issues such as service trading, transnational mergers, and foreign direct investment have resulted in the professions of law and accountancy investing more in their EU associations than those subject to little globalization, such as healthcare. Even the former group, however, has invested relatively little in their EU associations in comparison to the substantial self-governing organizations to be found in some member states. Even in Lovecy's 'best case' scenario, the interests concerned have, on balance, tended to regard European integration as more of a threat to their established operations in the member states than an opportunity, and the corresponding associations are just a shadow of their national counterparts.

The construction of a free market has been a shock to the monop-olies which some of the member state professions have enjoyed on the supply of services. Nonetheless, it has been a limited change agent for many of them, and there are pockets to be found in some of the professions where the opportunities which European integration has provided have been recognized. Cross-border trade in archi-tectural services within the EU remains relatively modest, yet most medium-sized practices and above now collaborate in some way across borders, including outsourcing of detail design to low-cost countries. Architects in Germany, where there is no public regulatory regime of protection, saw in European integration an opportunity to seek restrictions on access to their profession. In France, architects also saw open markets as a threat because they are more vulnerable to foreign competition (Dankelman 1996). Dutch, and British, archi-tectural practices, sought open markets, with large practices such as Norman Foster Associates well above to benefit from open markets. As a group, European architects have looked to GATS to open up north American markets for them as a reciprocal measure. Engineers have established a voluntary, pan-European register of qualified engi-neers in order to facilitate cross-border practice. Lawyers have been able to preserve the integrity of sector-specific legislation against a recent tide of 'horizontal' legislation. Some law firms have sought to establish transnational multi-disciplinary practices embracing accountancy and public affairs. And the European Court of Justice continues to deliver interpretations and rulings on single-market freedoms with profound implications for commercial practices of the professions. Despite these realities, the national members of EU associations have had difficulty in getting the vast majority of their members sufficiently interested in transnational issues.

The focus in this chapter is upon both self-employed and sala-ried white-collar workers who are included within levels 1 and 2 of the International Standard Classification of Occupations (ISCO). These include fully qualified doctors, lawyers, architects, vets, dentists, pharmacists, civil and electrical engineers, teachers, nurses and midwives, librarians, writers, artists, ministers of religion, and middle-ranking and senior corporate and public-sector managers. Even this International Standard raises boundary problems, with level 2 classifications such as teachers, nurses, and midwives being organized in some member states by associations that are mid-way between trade unions and professional associations. These factors are reflected among the landscape of 'horizontal' organizations claiming a remit across the interests of the professions. As will be apparent, even this is problematic in that each of the 'peak' organizations has a selective view of the types of professional interests they are representing. In sum, many of the problems faced by the professions as organized interests at the EU level arise from the disputed and irresolvable definition of 'what is a profession?'

Peak associations claiming representation of professionals

At the peak level, there are three European-level pan-sectoral groups that claim representation of general professional interests.

1. CEPLIS, the European Council of the Liberal Professions, representing independent liberal professions.
2. EUROCADRES, the Council of European Professional and Managerial Staff, operates within ETUC, and represents salaried, unionized professional and managerial staff in both the private and public sector.
3. CEC, the European Confederation of Executive and Managerial Staff, representing independent organizations of salaried managerial staff, primarily in industry and commerce. CEC is not affiliated to ETUC.

There is a clear functional division between the three peak associations, with CEPLIS representing the independent liberal professions, CEC representing salaried private sector managers, and EUROCADRES representing unionized managers in both the public and private sectors. However, all three organizations represent similar concerns at the European level, all related to single labour market issues. Each has distinct membership constituencies with clear demarcation lines between them, and no membership turf battles.

CEPLIS

CEPLIS regards membership of the 'liberal professions' as excluding state employees. This results in a somewhat inconsistent application among its membership, with a fluid constituency which is variable across national contexts, as well as difficulties in locating common interest fields. It has no more than 10 inter-sectoral national members, while its European sectoral members are primarily engineering-related professions and organizations primarily grounded in a particular member state, rather than a spread of the main professions. Its foundation in 1974 reflects the account of interest group emergence arising from an 'entrepreneur' spotting a 'niche' gap in the representation market reviewed earlier in this chapter; until 1989 it was the only 'horizontal' organization in the domain. Nonetheless, the concept has never been sufficient for the organization to develop beyond four employees, and it has somewhat struggled over the years to make an impact.

The role of CEPLIS in sectoral matters is limited by its horizontal concept, and the differences between its members on various issues means that is has a limited ability to take up policy positions. Membership is thus partly informed by a wish among its members to prevent it being used as a vehicle for the positions of opponents. It has therefore been ill-equipped to engage the Commission's strategy since the 1980s of seeking to regulate the harmonization of the professions through a general, rather than sectorally specific, approach. CEPLIS was not consulted at all by the Commission during the draft and passage stages of the First and Second General Systems Directives, despite it being the only European-level cross-sectoral professional interest organization in existence in Brussels in this period. It was not among the organizations which responded to the consultation exercise for the proposals which led to a 2005 Directive consolidating previous legislation on professional recognition and creating a new operational system.

Another measure of the lack of influence of CEPLIS is that its best institutional contacts have historically been with the somewhat marginalized EESC, where it is a 'subgroup' of Group III. It is not recognized by the Commission as a social partner because a second successive evaluation of it (1999) instigated by the Commission concurred (Institut des Sciences du Travail 1999) with the first one in 1993 that 'its representativeness remains to be established' (Commission of the European Communities 1993:41). In response to this, CEPLIS negotiated an agreement with EUROCADRES in 2010 for the latter to represent CEPLIS positions at the table of the European Social Dialogue.

EUROCADRES

With roots in the trade union movement, EUROCADRES is a quite different type of organization to CEPLIS. Formed in 1993,

EUROCADRES seeks to group together (an estimated 5 million +) professional and managerial salaried staff in Europe who are organized in trade unions. Its direct members are national private and public sector unions across Europe (who in turn are required to be members of organizations which are affiliated to ETUC), and EU-level sectoral organizations (ETUC-affiliated) unionized professional and managerial staff. Its secretariat (of two executives and an administrative assistant) is located in the Brussels premises of ETUC, operating under the ETUC Secretariat and Executive Committee.

The main niche of EUROCADRES is thus its trade union constituency, which has afforded it excellent access to DG Employment and Social Affairs and to social partnership negotiations, and to DG Education and Culture. Its principal niche strength is the participation rights in social dialogue (Chapter 2) which it enjoys from its embeddedness within ETUC, and it is in its own right a partner in EU macroeconomic social dialogue, with membership also of the Standing Committee on Employment. However, it is active on core issues of concern to the professions, involving the mutual recognition of qualifications, obstacles to free circulation, including those presented by supplementary pension schemes, parental leave, and equal opportunities.

European Confederation of Executive and Managerial Staff(CEC)

Formed in 1989 from the International Confederation of Professions, the CEC is an independent organization (with French origins and orientation) representing salaried managers in industry, the public sector, trade and commerce through national cross-sectoral associations of managers, and European-level (though all with French addresses) sectoral associations. It has a dedicated office in Brussels, with four post holders from national member organizations sharing its workload. It comprises 18 national cross-sectoral associations of managers, and 10 European sectoral associations, ranging from bank to steel managers. All but one of these latter organizations have French addresses. The organization participates on the employee side of social dialogue, though it has good contacts with Business Europe, UEAPME, and EUROCOMMERCE. It is oriented towards European integration, assisting its members in finding practical measures to assist with European harmonization, and providing a network to promote cross-border mobility for its members.

EU sectoral professional interests

The majority of sectoral professional associations at the European level are not full members of CEPLIS, CEC, or EUROCADRES. While most have in common a federated structure (associations of national or European associations), the range of functional interests and type of organizations they span is vast, and reflects a high degree of specialization. Thus

- Professions with a single unified association in a member state may need to maintain affiliations to a number of organizations representing micro-specialisms. The British Medical Association, for instance, maintains affiliations to a range of EU medical associations covering specialisms such as senior hospital physicians, junior doctors, general practitioners, as well as the more generic Standing Committee of European Doctors and the European Union of Medical Specialists. In turn, some of these organizations themselves embrace other EU associations representing medical specialisms. While there is liaison between the principal organizations, there inevitably arise issues of co-ordination between them. Reflecting the definitional difficulties discussed earlier, some of the medical associations differ by representing salaried, and independent, practitioners. An examination of the membership lists of each of these organizations reveals that some have significant membership gaps, such as the European Association of Senior Hospital Physicians (AEMH), which has no member from the British Isles.

- Some professions have different associations for the same profession informed by different national traditions within the profession. In engineering, for instance, the principal association FEANI (Federation Européenne d'Associations Nationales d'Ingénieurs) has another association, ECCE (European Council of Civil Engineers), to contend with, which leans more towards the architecture profession to reflect the composition of the architecture profession in some countries. There are also a number of other specialized associations for engineering operating at EU level.

- Other professional domains have a selection of organizations at the EU level with different styles and emphases. Hence, in law there is the Council of the Bars and Law Societies of the European Union (CCBE), and the European Lawyers' Union

(ELU/UAE), as well as a plethora of specialist branch law organizations. In dentistry, there is the Brussels-based Council of European Dentists, the London-based European Union of Dentists, the Cologne-based Federation of the European Dental Industry, as well as associations covering specialisms such as orthodontics.

- Some professions, such as accountants, have separate associations to reflect the representation of business practice interests, and another to represent its broader interests as a profession. Some, such as pharmacists, are sub-divided between technical and research, and practitioner, associations. Some historic subdivisions reflect a legacy of intra-professional conflicts.

- At the other end of the spectrum are organizations representing very narrow specialisms a little adrift of the mainstream, often based in places far from the centre of EU decision-making, and sometimes attached to scientific institutes. Examples of these include the European Association of Handwriting Analysts and the European Association of Fish Pathologists. The European Showmens' Union and the European Association of Plastic Surgery are other examples of the vast range of highly specialized interests which have formed EU associations.

- The constituency of associations representing the professions includes more than its fair share of those which have been invented by an entrepreneur in search of a livelihood. Some of these are operated by a segment of Association Management companies, usually operating from a base in Brussels, or in the Netherlands where these arrangements are common. Some of these tend to be less oriented towards political representation than are most EU associations because their principal purpose is income generation for the creator, and professionals offer prospects as attractive high-income earners and good profile. At this quirky end of the spectrum are to be found the very few examples of associations with membership available to private individuals. There are also those which are driven by lone entrepreneurs with a website funded from advertising revenue. One example is the Federation of European Employers (FedEE), which re-invented itself from an organization (with start-up Commission funding) seeking to represent labour market interests of multinational companies to one positioning itself as a network of human resource professionals.

The professional groups most organized at the European level are engineers, lawyers, certain interests allied to medicine, architects, surveyors, and accountants. Many of the representative associations for these interests are long-established organizations. For instance, the European (general) engineers' federation, FEANI, was founded in 1951, and two of the principal organizations of doctors were founded in the 1950s. Many associations of the professions were established during the next two decades in response to a Commission agenda seeking to install a series of sectoral directives aimed at the mutual recognition of qualifications within their field (Laslett 1991), as described later. However, even the best-resourced EU associations are shadows compared with their national counterparts. For instance, the principal EU law association, CCBE, has seven executives, two trainees, and four support staff. Architects' Council of Europe (ACE) has four full-time employees. The Standing Committee of European Doctors has three Executives and three support staff, while the European Union of General Practitioners (UEMO) and the Permanent Working Group of European Junior Doctors (PWG) each rely on their members to provide the rotating secretariat. In most member states, associations representing doctors, lawyers, and architects are substantial organizations.

Some EU associations of the professions have made an attempt to add value through their unique EU status. Examples of these include FEANI's 'European Engineer' (EurIng) designation to aid cross-border mobility, and schemes to collate and disseminate best practice such as the voluntary one operated by the European Union of Medical Specialists for 'recognitions of quality', and CCBE's *Code of Conduct for Lawyers* engaged in cross-border practice. ACE has tried hard to find common ground with its American counterpart, with the two parties concluding a symbolic agreement on professionalism in architecture as the former tries to find ways to exploit its well-placed position (as a result of the Commission's function in world trade negotiations) to find a role in opening up north American markets through General Agreement on Tariffs and Trade (GATT). Attempts to locate a unique role are common for associations, and these latter types of activities are typical ones for EU associations of the professions. The nature of their agendas are constrained by the need to avoid the hallowed monopolies of some of their national members in controlling admission to, and continued registration in, their respective practices. In some of these fields, the role of EU associations is restricted to that of information disseminator. The balance of responsibilities in the implementation of EU legislation is vested more in national associations than in EU associations, for both sectoral and generalized directives affecting the professions (Evetts 2000).

Once implementation activities are undertaken by others, associations have to strive to find a role if they seek to become more than simply organizations based around the dissemination of information and the interpretation of EU legislation for their members. For most EU associations, this can be found through early detection and shaping of agendas, and in leading their members' analyses of what their interests are on transnational issues. Few of the EU associations of the professions are endowed with sufficient capacities to undertake these latter activities, and were one of the major reasons why the establishment of sectoral directives aimed at mutual recognition of qualifications either failed or took up to 25 years to complete. Even in the relatively better organized EU professional associations, such as the CCBE, contacts with the European Commission are insufficiently strong, and consequently the Commission still needs to turn to the national associations.

Given the differences in composition within the professions, the difficulties of their EU associations in achieving anything more than lowest common denominator positions between their members is inevitable, and it is little surprising that past authors have reached this conclusion (see, for instance, Arnison, in Neale 1994). In a survey of British professional groups, Neale found a marked preference for developing their own channels of interest representation to Europe, rather than using Euro groups (Neale 1994). National and sectoral differences remain so strong that collective interest representation is often dealt with on an issue-by-issue basis using different alliances of national associations. Thus, there was something of a 'free-for-all' among national, and sub-national, bar associations in making representations during the course of the 1998 Directive on the right of establishment for the legal profession. Such intra-country differences become magnified to extremes when attempts are made to reach collective views at the EU level.

A number of EU-level professional associations are joined in Brussels by outreach offices of their national members. Where these operate from the same premises, the relationship tends to be supportive, although the cost is a tendency towards domination by these members, and a loss of autonomy for the association. Some of these offices, and particularly those located apart from the

EU association, are there primarily because of perceived structural weaknesses of the EU association, and the activities they undertake contribute to these weaknesses through by-passing it. In the main, however, these offices tend to be very small affairs of typically one to two people in early to mid-career, reporting back to the international department of a national association from where most of their EU affairs are managed and co-ordinated.

The workload of the EU professional associations can sometimes be strengthened where their interests coincide with those of business associations (Neale 1994). Both CEFIC and EFPIA, for instance, have taken positions on core issues of interest to learned associations, such as wider European policy for science and technology funding (including the funding of higher education), while UEAPME has articulated concerns shared by professional interests in small enterprises. The Federation of Veterinarians of Europe has its premises in the same Brussels building as the representative business organization of animal health medicines, FEDESA. Some organizations with names resembling those of scientific and technical institutes have been established by business organizations, while others which are organizations of scientists may have become dependent upon business organizations.

Single-market freedoms

The professions were among the earliest targets of single-market-inspired attempts at European integration by the Commission. Most of the issues centre on the free movement of people and services and the related right of establishment to undertake business in the territory of another member state. As was described above, those areas of the professions where there are practices of a sufficient size to benefit from cross-border activities have demonstrated an interest in these opportunities, and the secretariats of EU-level associations have their own interests in taking these forward. Nonetheless, the professions in practice have on the whole been slow to recognize these opportunities, disinterested in them, or sometimes downright hostile for defensive, protectionist reasons.

As early as 1957, work commenced on developing systems for co-ordination and recognition of qualifications. In the professions, this proved a tortuous process, although a number of directives were eventually passed to eliminate national legislation and procedures that discriminated against qualified and licensed professionals in other member states from practising. Thus, measures were eventually passed to enable doctors, nurses, dental practitioners, veterinary surgeons, midwives, lawyers, architects, and pharmacists to practise in another member state, to offer temporary services in another country if requested to by a client, and to receive recognition of qualifications if migrating. In the most extreme cases, deliberations took almost a quarter of a century and ended up specifying on a country-by-country basis which qualifications issued by the various different authorities would be recognized. Inevitably, this attempt at detail gave rise to a series of loopholes, resulting in the Commission initiating legal proceedings against some national registering associations for engaging in discriminatory practices aimed at monopolizing service provision for their own members. Intra-sectoral and inter-sectoral competitions between professions have also hampered the passage of integrative measures (Orzack 1992; Lovecy 1993). In some sectors, attempts to agree upon directives were completely abandoned. These types of problems have required substantial Commission monitoring resources to enforce, and resulted in a change from the sectoral approach in favour of a generalized framework one.

This lack of progress on sectoral initiatives provided the basis for a sea change in approach in favour of outline generalized directives on the mutual recognition of qualifications. The first of these, the First General Systems Directive (FGSD), aimed at all professions not otherwise covered by sectoral directives, was agreed in 1988, and came into force in January 1991. The second, the Second General Systems Directive (SGSD), covering occupations requiring less than 3 years qualification (and therefore beyond the scope of this chapter), was passed in 1992. The third, on the recognition of professional qualifications, consolidating earlier legislation (and repealing most of the sectoral directives) was passed in 2005, against the wishes of many of the sectoral associations which had benefited from the sectoral regimes (the law profession has contributed to the retention of the sole survivor sector-specific directive). Lovecy (1999) claims that the CCBE played a role in gaining an exemption for law from the 1989 FGSD.

The most recent legislation is based upon mutual recognition of qualifications rather than harmonization of them and ensuring that barriers to recognition are removed. It is highly dependent for operationalization upon the work of national governments to co-ordinate and oversee the work of licensing authorities for each profession. In many cases, the competent authorities appointed by national administrations to oversee implementation are the national professional associations, which has in turn strengthened their role at the domestic level and vis-à-vis their European association counterparts.

Evetts has documented the work of transnational associations in producing their own mechanisms of harmonization. FEANI, for instance, created a register of higher and lower qualifications in 1970 and the award of an international professional title in 1987 (trade-marked as 'EurIng' in 1996) for those who meet certain standards of degree level and professional education (Evetts 1995; Jefferies and Evetts 2000). It is however not a licence to practise and carries no legal force, but an attempt to provide an internationally accepted benchmark. Nonetheless, the scheme has been widely reproduced, by organizations such as the European Communities Biologists Association (European Biologist), the European Communities Chemistry Council (European Chemist), the European Federation of Geologists (European Geologist), and the European Physical Society (European Physicist) (Jefferies and Evetts 2000). However, Evetts offers a more general assessment that

> European professions are moving at different speeds and sometimes, it seems, in different directions ... in the face of such differences between professions, the more ambitious internationalisation objectives (such as standardisation and harmonisation of licensing and regulatory practices) are being replaced by more realistic goals (such as bilateral agreements and mutual recognition of state education, training and licensing arrangements). (Evetts 2000:9)

In the main, national associations of the professions have tended towards protectionism and the maintenance of national regulation, while EU associations have interests which are much more aligned with the liberalization agenda. Where national professions are weak, and their interests coincide with the European agenda, the EU association can be a solution. In most cases, however, national associations would prefer for regulation to remain in their hands while their EU associations undertake a low-level monitoring and information service. Where the balance of power among EU association members is tipped towards national members with protectionist interests, this service-based role will remain. It is one built around providing national association members with assistance in interpreting EU legislation and a helping hand now and then to make it easier to implement it, or in establishing voluntary schemes to assist the small numbers of their members who wish to engage in cross-border practice. Beyond the sectoral level, the inter-sectoral associations have struggled to find any significant role, and some have statutes that prevent them from ever doing so. Where the sectoral ones can find a niche in supporting their national members and finding common mutual interests, such as the opening up of global markets through GATS liberalization, they have been able to make a contribution.

Conclusion

Business interests demonstrate a high tendency towards fragmentation, observed as the norm in collective associations, and within large multinational enterprises. The choice is between specialist collective organization, with low capacity to co-ordinate common interests across linked specialisms, or large umbrella organizations where co-ordination is possible but a high degree of collective action is difficult because of the problems of reaching common positions between divergent interests. Much membership of business associations is informed by the need to influence association positions (and particularly for damage limitation), rather than an expectation of a high capacity for collective action. Many trade association executives have limited autonomy to deviate from membership instructions, not least because the impact of losing a member is significant in associations where the number of members (national associations and multinational firms) is relatively low when compared to national counterparts, and because EU associations depend upon membership subscriptions because of their concentration upon political representation. Some multinationals also have little central co-ordinating capacity to reconcile the different positions of its product divisions. In general, business solidarity is less than that of environmental, or labour, interests because of the absence of a common outlook. Sectoral and product market characteristics mostly predict the governability of associations, such as the presence of a commodity product, and firms of a similar size. But the most common picture is that market power is a poor predictor of political power. The EU is primarily a regulatory regime, and regulation typically divides the interests of capital, producing competing forces, while business preferences can be difficult to construct because of the difficulty of calculating costs and benefits. The public affairs managers of companies spend a substantial amount of time trying to make common cause with environmental NGOs, in particular, because of the strength of environmental sentiment in Europe, and positioning themselves as part of the solution rather than part of the problem involves diluting their core interests. The professions demonstrate an even greater diversity than business, largely due to different outlooks about European integration, and because of the different composition of professions in member states. Together, these factors highly qualify the impact of producer interests upon public policies.

Chapter 5

Labour Interests

Labour interests have been heavily influenced by economic change, and the increasing internationalization of capital has posed considerable challenges to nationally based labour movements. In western Europe, labour markets have been transformed by neo-liberal tendencies, leading to a general decline in the influence of organized labour, and the establishment of a European labour market underpinned by qualified free market principles. The corresponding discourse in EU policymaking presents a difficult tide for labour interests to contend with, and EU powers in the labour market field have boundaries prescribed by the Treaties. EU social partnership with employer organizations have delivered limited results (Chapter 2). Recent landmark rulings of the European Court of Justice have placed qualifications on the rights to strike contained in the Charter of Fundamental Social Rights, and upon the scope of protection for domestic workers under conditions of free movement of labour.

Against this backdrop can be considered some contrasting perspectives. The core free market principle of free movement which underpins the European project creates substantial issues for the labour movement. Because this is a given, ETUC formally accepted the single market programme in 1988 (Dølvik and Visser 2001) and sought to do what it could to moderate the agenda by establishing some key benchmarks of protection for workers as well as seeking to use inherent contradictions and diversity of the European project to its advantage. Some member states have 'social model' traditions, and elements of a 'European Social Model' have emerged alongside core economic liberalization agendas to address cross-border issues. Some member states have shared interests with ETUC in preventing a flight of capital to low-cost production centres, and have sought to use EU legislation, with accompanying social rhetoric, to 'export' their own higher production cost conditions. These have resulted in basic standards of 'social protection' inside and outside the workplace, and some measures to accompany rhetoric aimed at the pursuit of social inclusion and equal opportunities. Some of the worst fears about the progression of the liberalization agenda in services have not been realized, with the 'Posted Workers Directive' (96/71/EC) providing some degree of protection against the use of cheap source labour to undercut national standards under conditions of free movement. Some of the judgements of the European Court of Justice have established significant principles of benefit to labour. Attempts to equip the EU with further democratic architecture open doors for organizations representing large numbers of members, and facilitates alliances with like-minded stakeholders. These also provide for good links with the European Parliament, via the socialist party. The internationalization of capital has stimulated transnational collective action. Social Dialogue continues to give labour interests high-level access, and some results. And the trade union movement has developed a significant structure at EU level, demonstrated a capacity for cross-border co-ordination, and demonstrated the ability for mass mobilization. These contrasting perspectives are articulated, evaluated, and weighed viz. each other below.

The recession which followed the oil shock of the 1970s contributed to the renewed ability of capital to assert itself against organized labour weakened by mass unemployment, and in consequence unions have enjoyed less of a central role in the operation of politics and markets than in the heyday of Keynesianism. Other contributory factors have been structural labour market changes from mass manufacturing and agricultural employment to more dispersed service sector employment with less secure working patterns and reduced scope for collective action. The emphasis has thus been on employment creation through deregulation, and enabling capital to exert more control over labour market costs, based on market principles. Against this context, membership of trade union organizations throughout western Europe has been in long-term decline, with the strongest decline in the private sector. Aggregate union membership fell by one sixth across the EU in the 10 year period from 1993 to 2003, with all but one of 20 countries for which information is available experiencing a decline in union density (total union membership as a proportion of the number of employees) over the same period (European Foundation 2005). The decline in density has been greatest in central and east European countries

(European Foundation 2009). The basis for trade union membership has shifted from collective action to individualized 'insurance
policies'.

The narrow scope of EU competencies in industrial relations is
limited to the working environment, health and safety, and equal
rights. Unanimity voting rules prevail (and are likely to do so for
the foreseeable future) for the sensitive areas classified as taxation,
employee rights, and social security, with QMV only for health and
safety and equal rights measures. Wage bargaining is excluded from
EU competencies, while legislation which would regulate the freedom
to associate and the right to strike is specifically excluded by the Treaty
(Erne 2008). The *Viking* Case (C-438/05) and *Laval* Case (C-341/05)
in the European Court of Justice qualify the principle enshrined in
the Charter of Fundamental Rights of freedom to strike by placing
the qualification upon it that it does not override the single-market
freedoms of establishment and to provide services. The *Rüffert* case
(C-346/06) also seems to elevate the right of freedom to provide services above those of collectively agreed wage rates.

Historic weaknesses among organized business and labour interests until the 1980s contributed to the lack of a social agenda to
develop, and until then this was the paradoxical strength of business. As long as organized labour was weak, business did not need
a highly developed employer organization. In any event, this might
result in the counter-organization of labour and the development
of demands for a social agenda. Only DG Employment and Social
Affairs of the European Commission, in some cases in partnership with the Germanic countries seeking to 'export' their high
production costs, were there to take the agenda forward. Among
the more hopeful historic moments for trade unions during this
period were the Collective Redundancies Directive of 1977, providing for workplace information and consultation, and the Transfer of
Undertakings Directive of 1979, which protected established working conditions when service contracts change and thus preventing
'social dumping' as a mechanism of cost cutting during competitive bidding for contracts. Around the same time the trade union
movement contributed to the drafting of the ambitious (and ultimately unsuccessful) Vredeling directive with its 'extra terrestrial'
provisions to empower workers in multinational companies with
information and consultation rights (Green-Cowles 1996). And the
notable Defrenne case (Chapter 2) from the 1970s was a landmark
in equality provision.

There has for some time been considerable scepticism of the value that the labour movement has extracted from corporatist, quasi-corporatist, or patron arrangements involving itself, business, and political institutions. In reviewing this literature, van Waarden noted how 'many authors doubt whether (union) concessions counterbalance the offer(s) (they) have made and whether the exchange is really symmetric' (van Waarden 1991:53). A similar, subsequent review by Erne, noted the persistence of these criticisms during the 1990s (Erne 2008). These doubts have been periodically restated in analysis of the principal trade union organization, ETUC, in EU-specific politics. These include both its involvement in social partnership arrangements (Chapter 2), where the deals it has extracted have either been symbolic or poor (Dølvik and Visser 2001), and its relationship with the European Commission. Martin and Ross (2001) conclude that it has been over-dependent upon its relationship with DG Employment and Social Affairs, and that this relationship has not delivered the goods for it. Consequently, Erne notes the subsequent development of a more independent strategy pursued by the labour movement, most starkly expressed by mass mobilizations. These include the organization of protest demonstrations mobilizing up to 100,000 individuals organized by ETUC and relating to EU generalized agendas from 2001 onwards (Erne 2008), but also more specific union mobilizations against sectoral issues, most notably the (ultimately withdrawn) European Port Services Directive.

The demonstrations built upon a successful cross-border mobilization in 1997 of 70,000 people at a demonstration against the closure of a profitable Renault factory at Vilvoorde, just north of Brussels. While the Vilvoorde closure went ahead, the notable case led to the strengthening of the position of European Works Councils, and accelerated the passage of a new Directive on Information and Consultation for workers (Erne 2008). It also provided encouragement to organize in subsequent disputes, but perhaps most importantly it reflected the paradigm that the multinationalization of capital also stimulates cross-border organization of labour (ibid.). This is one of a number of paradigms which has sustained the trade union movement. Erne argues that

> the unions are not passive victims of the EU integration process but agents that are also capable of politicising its contradictions ... unions can, at times, exploit these. (Erne 2008:199)

A key contradiction Erne highlights are Treaty provisions for 'a high level of employment and of social protection' on the one hand and 'an open market economy with free competition' on the other hand (ibid.). The extent of pursuit of social goals by the leadership of any political system always tends to be contextual upon overall economic performance, and the orientation of its leadership and the EU is no different in this respect; witness the difference in agendas between former trade unionist Delors, and neo-liberal Barroso, as Commission President. But as long as social goals remain, it will attract stakeholders who seek to hold political systems account-able for them (no 'cheap talk' – Lange 1992), and civil society actors will always be able to find common cause somewhere in each of the EU institutions. In the Commission there are various serv-ices, and parts of services, where trade union interests are seen as partners, most notably DG Employment, Social Affairs and Equal Opportunities, and within DG Education and Culture, although these have to contend with more market-oriented services. In the European Council and Council of Ministers, there is a constantly evolving turnover of political colours. And the European Parliament has a large party of socialists. The established links with the latter, together with the shift of strategy by ETUC from reliance upon institutionalization within the European Commission to mass mobi-lization, mean that the trade union movements' best institutional channels now lie with the EP, rather than within the European Commission. The dramatic outcome of the vote in the European Parliament on the Takeover Directive (Chapter 2) has been attrib-uted by one commentator partly to the lobbying work of ETUC in the European Parliament (Watson and Shackleton 2008).

The trade union movement has thus been able to combine mass mobilization strategies with those of institutionalized working. This is a niche which environmental organizations, such as Friends of the Earth and Greenpeace, have also been able to follow, linking social movements to institutionalized EU politics (Ruzza 2011). But the institutionalized role of the trade union movement includes a place at the Social Dialogue table.

Labour and the economic agenda

The reconstruction of rules of market exchange has led to high-standard member states seeking to 'export' their high-cost labour market regulation to ensure a level playing field in production.

The general tendency has been upwards in employment standards rather than to trigger a competitive 'race to the bottom' between member states. QMV is well established in fields such as Health and Safety at Work, working conditions, information and consultation of workers, gender equality at work, and the integration of persons excluded from the labour market. Where necessary, the Commission has resorted to 'playing the Treaty game' by classifying measures under sections of the Treaty to which QMV applies. The most renowned incident of this type concerned the 1993 Working Time Directive. In this case, the European Court of Justice rejected a challenge by the then Conservative UK government that this measure was not a Health and Safety at Work measure, and should be reclassified to enable it to be treated as one to which unanimity voting rules applied. The ruling enabled implementation of the measure by 1996, limiting the hours that workers could be required to undertake over an averaged out period. Despite some member states and employers using some loopholes in detailed implementation of the legislation, and the difficulties in securing member state agreement to redress these issues through extending the scope of the directive, the measure has made an impact in countries where there was previously little protection.

A key agenda for trade unions in responding to transnationalization agendas has been to avoid a 'race to the bottom' in wages and labour conditions, whereby competition leads to member states and companies undercutting each other to host production. This required cross-border collaboration, co-ordination, and a willingness for national union organizations to accept such intervention in their traditional territory of national bargaining. The final outcome of this was the establishment by the European trade union movement of a 'benchmark' for national negotiations whereby unions sought pay increases equal to increases of inflation plus productivity (Erne 2008). A stimulus to this was a 1996 Belgian law, setting a wage margin below the average of wage increases in Germany, France, and the Netherlands (Boucké et al. 2005). This resulted in a subsequent agreement ('Doorn', after the Dutch town where it was concluded) between unions from the Benelux countries and Germany in 1998 for the above benchmark, which was adopted months afterwards by the European Metalworkers Federation (EMF) and by ETUC in 2000 (Erne 2008). The EMF has led the development of cross-border co-ordinated wage bargaining in response to the potential for wage deflation posed by European Monetary Union, in which its lead German member, *IG Metall*, has played a lead role. These cross-border Interregional Trade Union Councils (IRTUCs) are therefore particularly established around German borders, but now benefit from co-ordination services hosted by ETUC.

The core single-market principles for freedom to provide services, and the free movement of workers within a cross-border labour market, have generated substantial challenges for labour interests. The original proposal in the 'Services Directive' (Directive 2006/123/EC) for a basis grounded in the 'country of origin' principle seemed to herald a 'race to the bottom' era of labour conditions, with the spectre of workers from the lowest cost/condition posted to jobs in higher condition countries to undercut established national provisions. However, employment law was excluded from the Services Directive, while the Posted Workers Directive stipulated that minimum wages, and safety conditions, to the job concerned are applicable in the country where services are provided. ETUC greeted the outcome as 'a success story for the European trade union movement, and an example of good cooperation with the European Parliament' (ETUC 2011a). This claim is corroborated by Crespy, who concludes that 'the role of the ETUC was absolutely crucial in securing a compromise which amended the Country of Origin principle' (Crespy 2009:16). ETUC had organized two mass mobilizations against the Services ('Bolkestein') Directive, including one attended by a claimed number of 75,000 participants in 2005. Subsequent rulings in the European Court of Justice, reviewed above, have tempered the mood of victory, with ETUC calling for a review of the directive and the installation of provisions in the Treaty to protect workers' rights. Nonetheless, the episode does illustrate the ability of the trade union movement to respond at EU level, with apparent effectiveness. The Posted Workers Directive is particularly important in the construction sector where the free movement of goods and services is the predominant issue, and the use of posted workforces, and efforts by construction firms to by-pass local collective bargaining agreements, has for sometime been commonplace. Erne (2008) recounts how the European Federation of Building and Wood Working (EFBWW) employed a dual strategy of lobbying at EU level for the Posted Workers Directive and working with its national members to restore national collective bargaining. The latter was particularly important in Germany, where high-standard conditions had resulted in the use of 60,000 posted workers in Berlin alone and a loss of local jobs of around half that number. The German member of EFBWW, IG Bau, worked to recruit migrant workers rather than create tensions with them, and sponsored the creation of the European Migrant Workers Union (Erne 2008).

Beyond direct economic agendas are those with 'spin-offs' for the labour movement. EU agendas geared at 'fighting exclusion' (from the labour market and mainstream society), equality, and anti-racism have evolved from the Treaties. The 1997 Amsterdam Treaty created a new title on Employment, with the objective of a 'high level of employment', and extended QMV to equal opportunities and treatment. The 1997 Luxembourg Jobs Summit created a European Employment Strategy (EES), in which the European Commission proposes new employment guidelines each year for member state consideration. Member states then draw up national action plans for employment. This was supplemented by the 'Cardiff' and 'Cologne' (summit venue) processes, which provide mechanisms to form, develop, co-ordinate, and review unemployment strategies. The 'Lisbon process' incorporated much of the EES, including the engagement by social partners in the national action plans through the Open Method of Coordination (OMC) of the Lisbon process, as well as 'anti-poverty'-related goals in which the European Anti-Poverty Network (EAPN) has been appointed to a monitoring role (Chapter 6). In turn, 'Europe 2020' has incorporated much of this agenda, with ETUC participation encouraged at the highest level in the Commission. The OMC has brought a variety of national union organizations into EU policy agendas, sometimes for the first time.

Equal opportunities are one of the four 'pillars' of the EES. In 1996, the concept of 'gender mainstreaming' was introduced, to ensure that the 'gender dimension' was considered in all aspects of EU policies, and formalized in the 1997 Amsterdam Treaty. An amendment to the 1976 equal treatment directive now introduces a number of measures on sexual harassment, one of the measures where agreement for legislation stalled within the social dialogue. 'Corporate social responsibility' is a further vehicle through which a variety of agendas are presented or re-presented from which labour interests have drawn benefit. An example is the sugar industry, where the social partners first signed agreement in 2003 on minimum standards for corporate social responsibility.

A pessimistic view of these initiatives highlights those which are rhetorical devices reminiscent of Edelman's concept of policymaking as theatre, with words that reassure and policies with dubious records of tangible achievement (Edelman 1971). In this view, they are symbolic actions that are long on analysis and short on real action, generating little but reams of statistics, propaganda, and reports. A more optimistic view of them is that they talk up prospects, create momentum, and enhance the scope for action. In this line of thinking, the value is the 'no cheap talk' dimension of action to which member states will become bound by interest constituencies. Those services of the Commission with interests in particular measures, together with the appropriate public interest groups (Chapter 6), have enforced support for them, taken the issues into the open debating arenas of the EU, and worked behind the scenes to implement measures designed to advance them. The embeddedness of the women's movement within Directorate General Employment and Social Affairs (Chapter 6) has been a major contributory factor to the advancement of this agenda. ETUC has latched on to these, working to create key alliances with a wide range of (broadly, left leaning) citizen interest groups to develop the European social agenda (Cullen 1999). To facilitate this, ETUC embraced wide-ranging social objectives within its own mission statement, including wide-ranging goals embracing the extension and consolidation of political liberties and democracy, environmentally sound economic and social development, the democratization of the economy, and a society free of exclusion and based on freedom, justice, and solidarity (ETUC 2007). These have featured less prominently in recent years in ETUC literature, which currently displays more of a 'back to basics' Union agenda. While regarded by some as something of a gatecrasher in the key umbrella alliance of European NGOs in search of a 'civil dialogue' to match the 'social dialogue', new alliances with citizen interest groups continue to emerge, such as the 2010 'Spring Alliance' 'to put people and the planet at the heart of EU policy making' (EEB 2010; Chapter 6). The citizen/democratic legitimacy agenda has been one avenue to engage the natural difficulties for a trade union organization operating within a core liberal discourse, and enabled it to form purposeful alliances. But the agenda and the alliances created do not, and could not, establish the wider labour movement at the centre of political decision-making in a system with a core liberal discourse.

Social Europe through a participative labour market model

Agendas on worker participation bring to the fore a basic intra-EU cleavage between different models of capitalism, between the quasi-corporatist, high-quality and cost labour market traditions of the Germanic (based language) countries with the contrasting low-cost traditions and ideas of the Anglo-American capitalist system, and the realities of low-cost countries to the south and east. Beyond the agendas of the 1970s, reviewed above, came the impetus provided in the 1980s by Commission President Jacques Delors, one time socialist minister in the French government, and trade unionist. Delors asserted during his Presidency that 'I want to make sure that the Trade Unions are written into Europe's social and economic decision-making' (Tongue 1989, cited in Compston 1992:28). He brought together EU employer and trade union organizations at the notorious 1985 Val Duchesse summit (named after the Chateau in the suburbs of Brussels where it was held), asking them if they would dialogue with each other, with the incentive for employers that participation would halt the flood of draft directives in the social field. Delors told the employers that 'if you want the single market to be completed, then you must obtain the support of the trade unions ... can you imagine me trying to create the single market against the wishes of the trade unions?' (Tyszkiewicz 1998:41).

Participation in the Social Dialogue provides ETUC with an elevated status in EU public policymaking, as well as for ETUC members in the national context, which helps these organizations recruit and retain members. Consequently, ETUC fought hard alongside Business Europe to maintain the mechanism and their respective roles in it in the Lisbon Treaty. Nonetheless, the actual achievements from social partnership are moderate (Chapter 2), and ETUC has needed to make significant concessions to individual agreements in an attempt to maintain the wider significance of the mechanism. The agreements on part-time work (Falkner 1998; Branch and Greenwood 2001) and telework (Pochet 2003) have been interpreted in these symbolic and sacrificial terms.

Beyond social partnership, participatory labour market agendas are developing at a variable rate. The European Works Council (EWC) Directive (94/45/EC) provides workers with a right to information and consultation companies via Works Councils, applicable in companies employing 1000 workers and which includes at least 150 in two member states. ETUC estimates that around 60% of the workforce could potentially be covered by such Councils (ETUC 2011b), but the European Foundation estimates that a much smaller proportion – around 14.5 million workers – actually are, with almost two thirds of multinationals covered by the scope of the directive yet to establish one. This is because the directive depends upon a management initiative or request from at least 100 workers across member states to establish one (European Foundation 2008). Where they have been established, identified problems include the ways in which the definition of 'information' and 'consultation' in the directive leads to variable interpretation in practice, and the requirement to meet once a year only. In some cases the result is little more than symbolic practice based on minimalist implementation, but there are more 'proactive cases' (European Foundation 2008:4) with more regular meetings and sub-committee structures with comprehensive information provision, though rarely extending into consultation over concepts. 'Proactive' cases are more likely to be found in companies where there are centralized structures. Until recently, the Volkswagen EWC was held up as a model of good practice, until Court cases in Germany in 2007/8 established how it had become used as a vehicle to bribe worker representatives into 'selling' reduced working time to its workforce (Timesonline 2011). Nonetheless, a failure to consult over significant company plans, such as a merger or redundancies, has led to temporary injunctions in some countries preventing the proposed action. Erne (2008) recounts the role of the European Works Council in the merger/ downsizing case of ABB-Alstom in co-ordinating actions in the face of competition for local production capacities among company subsidiaries, and in mobilizing at EU level which led to European Commission endorsement of a rescue package.

While the EWC Directive has not prevented the use of 'social dumping' mechanisms to move production to cheaper sites across borders, it has made it more difficult to do so without involving the workforce, in conjunction with other related measures. These include a 2002 Directive (2002/14/EC) establishing a general framework for informing and consulting employees (where a much lower threshold applies) with further information and consultation safeguards involving company strategic decision likely to affect their employment interests, and a 1998 Directive with minimal provisions for information and consultation on collective redundancies (98/59/EC). Such measures are hardly worker participation but they do provide for a basic level of legally enforceable rights to information and consultation.

Some of the large national confederations from high labour market conditions, and with strong relationships in domestic politics, have found difficulty in seeing significant gains through EU measures aimed at establishing minimal cross-border standards. Nonetheless, the EU does present an opportunity to seek to 'export' higher protection conditions to lower-standard member states in a strategy aimed at countering social dumping. The strong and well-resourced German trade unions have historically viewed the EU through this lens, as an additional arena which can be adequately dealt with through the national environment, and able to secure their needs adequately at the domestic level (Roethig 1994). In some other countries, particularly those in the south and east of Europe, the European level represents significant new opportunities to develop their interests. For some national confederations, membership of ETUC strengthens its role vis-à-vis its national members because it provides the main route for them to address the European level. A British trade union leader during the Thatcher era encouraged colleagues to see 'Brussels as the only card game in town' (Trade Union Congress 1988), although commentators have suggested that EU trade union organization is no substitute for domestic weakness (Roethig 1995).

There is no uniform trend of union embeddedness in political systems across the member states, or of changes over time, and the picture is complicated as governments change and the belief systems of parties, labour organizations, and governments evolve. However, the wider external forces to which member states have been subjected have made it difficult for unions ingrained in quasi-corporatist systems to maintain the full strength of the positions they once held in domestic politics. Where the labour movement has not been marginalized in domestic settings, it is difficult to see how its position could be significantly advanced by the context of EU politics in which they operate. Nonetheless, the stakes are too high for disengagement, and all have invested in EU-level organization. And trade union links with sympathetic national governments ensure that the movement has a spread of avenues of influence within EU policymaking to match those it enjoys within the EU institutions. Here, the trade union movement has institutionalized access to policymaking, particularly in Directorate General Employment and Social Affairs, with one member of the Delors cabinet once famously describing that Commission service as a 'union lobbying organisation, old style' (Ross 1994:507).

The natural links between trade unionists and the Party of European Socialists in the European Parliament provide it with important access, and the EP has been a strong supporter of a 'European

Social Model'. The Parliament's work includes a strong and effective trade union intergroup, with which ETUC meets monthly, and close connections between the majority Socialist party and European trade union leaders. ETUC has been able to table amendments in the Parliament through this route. Indeed, the relationship between these two actors has been so strong that the former UNICE Secretary General, Zygmunt Tyszkiewicz, once complained that 'ETUC has a privileged relationship with the European Parliament which shares its objectives and consistently passes resolutions by a large majority, advocating social policies that business finds unacceptable' (Stern 1994:141). A source of tension does however remain in the way in which the social dialogue procedure by-passes the EP.

Labour interests comprise one of the three categories of interest within the Economic and Social Committee, as Group II (workers). There are obvious limitations to the impact of this advisory body, but the effort invested by employers to ensure the organization is not reformed so as to embrace civil society interests and give labour interests a majoritarian alliance is testimony to its potential. Labour interests, too, devote some time to the work of the Economic and Social Committee, and in particular to making sure that business interests do not dominate the organization's positions.

A final factor working in favour of the wider labour movement concerns its generally greater ease of collective action than business. While business has a diverse range of issues to embrace across labour and product markets, and faces endemic fragmentation (Chapter 3), labour interests have a narrower focus and, while containing diversity, have greater homogeneity than business. Thus, the comprehensive organization of business interests cross-national project in the 1980s found an average of 16.4 business organizations to every single labour union (Streeck and Schmitter 1985; Traxler 1991; van Waarden 1991). There is also a greater homogeneity of belief systems among trade union actors, a greater tendency towards union solidarity, and a greater ability for trade union organizations to impact upon the attitude and behaviour of their members (Offe 1981). These general factors are useful background to consider during analyses of labour interests organized at the EU level.

The European organization of labour interests

Like other interests, labour concerns are represented in Europe through a number of channels. These include domestic channels of influence, where interests are incorporated into industrial and governmental decision-making, and actions by national unions approaching the European institutions direct. Transnational channels include cross-regional organization of labour, and dedicated structures based in Brussels, in interaction with the supranational institutions of the Economic and Social Committee, the European Parliament, and the Commission.

Dedicated labour structures in Brussels include a small number of national unions with their own Brussels office, well integrated with ETUC, some sectoral transnational unions, including 12 ETUC-affiliated 'European Industry Federations' (EIFs). Apart from ETUC there is the European Confederation of Independent Trade Unions (CESI), which organizes a relatively small constituency of workers in independent (i.e. non-ETUC affiliated) trade unions primarily in the public services. CESI has affiliates in around half of the member states, with notable strength of coverage in Italy and some central and east European countries, and three European organizations of workers. It has a small secretariat consisting of nine staff.

Labour sectoral actors in Brussels

Sectoral union organizations are mostly ETUC-affiliated European Industry Federations. These differ vastly in their membership size, structure, strategy, and potential. Most have developed from structures of international sectoral unions, and/or located within these premises. Most have engaged in social dialogue with their sectoral industry counterpart and are involved in formalized 'Sectoral Dialogue Committees' (Chapter 2). European Industry Federations have been particularly active in European Works Councils, where they are ideally placed to co-ordinate the role of their members across countries to serve on them. In most sectors, these have the right to make nominations for membership, and in some cases have the sole capacity to do so. Most EIFs have a low level of resources in comparison to national sectoral unions, although the European Federation of Metalworkers (EFM) and the European Public Services Union are notable exceptions, with 25 and 20 staff respectively. European Industry Federations are in general not designed to be self-sufficient labour representatives at the European level, but supplementary structures to ETUC for sectoral organizations and interests.

As the earlier reviewed example of IG Metall demonstrates, EIFs have played a significant role in the establishment and oversight of cross-national wage bargaining coordination mechanisms via IRTUCs. These are convened by ETUC, elect a Chair to represent them at ETUC Executive Committee meetings, and elect representatives on ETUC working groups. Although autonomous, European Industry Federations are also incorporated within the structure of ETUC. To be eligible for membership, each has to be open to affiliation to unions who subscribe to ETUC's national union confederations, and to subscribe to ETUC's aims. They have a seat, and voting rights, on all of ETUC's decision-making committees (except on financial matters because they neither contribute to ETUC nor take funds from it). This 'dual membership' structure of ETUC has occasionally caused conflict. Historic tensions have revolved around the dilution of power for the national confederations, where ETUC has wanted to take the lead on sectoral issues, and when members are represented by different positions within their national confederations, and the industry federations. Nonetheless, the successful incorporation of them has prevented them from developing into a parallel, and partly competitive, structure, and they now perform a complementary role in return for (a steadily increasing) influence in ETUC's internal structures. The success of the EMF, and that of other sectoral unions such as the European Federation of Building and Wood Workers in co-ordinating action and effectively responding to the 'posted workers' threat (Erne 2008), is to some extent mirrored by the story of change by ETUC, considered below.

The European Trade Union Confederation

The history of European trade unionism provides some clues to its historic difficulties in collective action. Prior to the formation of ETUC in 1973, and in its early years, the European organization was split between Socialist (International Confederation of Free Trade Unions – ICFTU), Christian Democratic (World Confederation of Labour), and Communist (World Federation of Trade Unions) confederations. These types of cleavages can be found in the national organization of labour interests, along with other dimensions such as religious denomination, and are reflected among ETUC affiliates. For instance, ETUC has six national confederations from Hungary, five from France (including the Communist Confédération Général du Travail (CGT)), and four from Spain and Turkey, while even small countries such as San Marino, Iceland, and Luxembourg each have two. These members can be broadly categorized between those used to working in Germanic, and Anglo-American, capitalist systems, French *etatisme*, the south of Europe, and those from Central and Eastern European countries. To add to this diversity are differences in organizational relationships between national confederations and their members, ranging from highly centralized organizations to those less able to co-ordinate the activities of its affiliates. Although these cleavages have to some extent become less important within ETUC over time, they are nevertheless ever present in the background. A further issue involves the tensions created by the 'mega mergers' of sectoral unions (Dølvik and Visser 2001), which has resulted in a net loss of industry federations. Diversity is perhaps the most important issue in comprehending European trade union organization. Like Business Europe, the encompassing nature of ETUC, with its confederate structure, is by design rather than by default.

In addition to the sectoral European Industry Federations, its principal membership pillar comprises 82 full national confederation members from 36 European countries, drawing members from a geographical area stretching from Iceland to Turkey. As with all confederations, both the parent and its affiliates therefore seek to build positions between a diverse range of constituents. The majority of ETUC's time is spent in seeking to overcome its internal diversity, and some commentators who have examined member positions and coalitions on key issues have viewed ETUC's collective action problems as insurmountable (Timmersfield, in Turner 1995). A further limitation it shares with Business Europe is that it lacks a wide-ranging collective bargaining mandate from its members.

The ETUC Secretariat (currently) comprises an elected General Secretary, a Deputy General Secretary (with provision for a second), and three Confederal Secretaries (with provision for a fourth), each with responsibilities for different functional areas. In total, it has 57 staff. ETUC's largest member and paymaster has historically been the German Deutscher Gewerkschaftsbund Bundesvorstand (DGB), although it has recently significantly reduced its funding level and has now been usurped by the British Trade Union Congress (TUC) as its single largest member. This reflects both differing views about what ETUC should be and the differential positions of these actors in domestic politics; on the one hand, an unwillingness among DGB affiliates, keen to maintain their relatively high domestic labour market condition standards, for ETUC to develop into a more powerful supranational actor, while for TUC the EU level has increasingly been a solution to their increasing isolation from the corridors of power in British politics. In the early years of its formation, ETUC was only just more than a co-ordination centre for national trade union confederations to engage the European level (Roethig 1994; Dølvik and Visser 2001). Early analysis emphasized overall weakness, with fragmentation and diversity, the unwieldy nature of its federal structure, the individualized activities of its members, a tendency to lowest common denominator positions, and an over-dependence upon the Commission to achieve its goals (Visser and Ebbinghaus 1992; Pedler 1994; Roethig 1994, 1995; Armingeon 1995; Ross 1994; Hoskyns 1996; Marks and McAdam 1996; Wallace and Young 1997).

These earlier analyses pre-date the full development of social dialogue at EU level, which brought to ETUC members a sense of the need for the organization to develop beyond a co-ordination centre, alongside a growing realization of the impact of monetary union. Looking back at the development of ETUC today, its greatest strengths have been its durability alongside the maintenance of its breadth, its ability to respond to the co-ordination challenges presented by monetary union, and to adapt from reliance on an 'insider' strategy to one which includes mass mobilization. This is significant because large-scale demonstrations are very unusual in EU politics because of the institutionalization of interest representation, the logistical difficulties of assembling cross-border protests, and the difficulties of engaging mass constituencies in EU-related issues. It has developed some way from the caricature of Martin and Ross of an organization which had become too institutionalized with little to show for it. Rather than being restrained by its members, it has to some extent turned the tables, with key constitutional reforms in 1991, 1995, 1999, 2006, and 2007 which have increased its autonomy from its members, most notably by removing the requirement for unanimity.

Rather than ETUC being dependent upon a Commission patron, the latter's funding is used to support ETUC specialist satellites (described below), and particular projects such as preparations for Works Councils (Dølvik and Visser 2001; Martin and Ross 2001), rather than ETUC's core operations. The Commission provides funds for the European Trade Union Institute (ETUI), founded in 1978 as a study and research centre for ETUC in the socio-economic field and for industrial relations, and now merged with other Commission-funded ETUC organizations, Trade Union

Technical Bureau (TUTB), and the European Trade Union College (ETUCO). The merged organization, the European Trade Union Institute for Research, Education and Health and Safety, was created in 2005. It has previously provided funding for other organizations hosted within ETUC, including EUROCADRES (Chapter 4), and the European Federation of Retired and Elderly Persons (EFREP/FERPA), although these organizations no longer receive such funding.

ETUC has a number of decision-making tiers, of which the most important are its Congress, the Executive Committee, and the Steering Committee. Congress, the supreme authority of the ETUC, is empowered to take decisions on the basis of a two-thirds majority. The Executive, also drawn from members in proportion to their membership, is also invested with a 'reluctant' two-thirds majority decision-making capacity. This is the key level that engages the Social Dialogue, sets the budget, and determines the positions of ETUC within the general framework laid down by Congress, and is assisted by an implementing/oversight Steering Committee.

Conclusions

Assessments of the role of the labour movement at EU level in the 1990s tended to focus on weaknesses, drawing attention to the negative cost–benefit balance sheet arising from the strategy of institutionalization in DG Employment and Social Affairs, but with the caution added by Dølvik and Visser in 2001 that

> without the strengthening of trade union cooperation and representation flowing from their role in developing European social dialogue and labour market re-regulation, they would have been in a worse position. (Dølvik and Visser 2001:39)

A single market in services and labour creates substantial issues for labour interests. Trade unions have accepted the concept as inevitable, mitigating its effects as well as progressing its interests through adaptation to make what it can of the changes it brings, and to focus upon the agendas presented by a 'European Social Model' and a 'Europe of the Citizens'. For 'free markets', read 're-regulation'. While this does not bring a European system of industrial relations, with limited outcomes from the Social Dialogue and Works Councils, the former has provided trade union organizations with an elevated status in

EU and national policymaking, acted as a recruiting sergeant for EU and national unions, as well as engaging national trade union leaders in EU policymaking at domestic and EU levels. And the labour movement has established a European benchmark, and significant cross-border co-operation structures, to respond to the potential for deflationary effects caused by monetary union.

Dølvik and Visser drew attention to the ways in which European trade union structures have been weakest at the sectoral level where national unions are strongest, and strongest at the peak level where national unions are weakest (Dølvik and Visser 2001; Martin and Ross 2001). While these assessments remain valid, union solidarity remains relatively strong in comparison with business. And there have also been considerable changes and mitigating factors. While sectoral union organization has developed little in breadth, it has developed substantially in depth, most notably with the extent of organization of the European Metalworkers Federation, and the European Public Services Union. These organizations, and others, have demonstrated the capacity to lead and co-ordinate in critical circumstances, developing new infrastructure to proactively engage threats and opportunities, to organize new segments of labour, and to combine lobbying at EU level with significant mass mobilization. ETUC has also notably pursued a dual strategy of institutionalized EU lobbying, and mass mobilization. This has contributed to the withdrawal of significant modification of legislative proposals such as port services, company takeovers, and general services, and the introduction of legislative safeguards, such as the Posted Workers Directive. ETUC has notably shifted strategy to add mass mobilization to its institutional lobbying, with a host of successful demonstrations to its name in an environment notoriously difficult to mobilize within. And its institutionalized lobbying has shifted away from reliance upon DG Employment and Social Affairs to relations with the Parliament where mass mobilization makes an impact. Attempts to create a 'Europe of the citizens' involves, at the least, measures of 'output legitimacy' for workers.

Chapter 6

Citizen Interests

A striking development is the 'coming of age' of citizen interest organization, mobilization, and representation at EU level. There is a dense landscape of NGOs organized and advocating at EU level for virtually every imaginable cause, from the unemployed to Muslim women to groups countering the long-held monopoly of producer groups in technical domains, such as financial services. There are over 50 women's transnational advocacy organizations active at EU level. A number of EU NGOs are also relatively well resourced. One segment alone, environmental NGOs, has over 150 EU-oriented staff, and self-declares an annual spend on lobbying the EU institutions of well over €4 million. The WWF European Policy Office and the European Consumers Organisation each have a staffing complement comparable to the group of best-resourced business organizations, bar one (Table 4.1). The Eurogroup for Animals, and Friends of the Countryside, each declare a spending on lobbying the EU institutions of more than €1 million each year on their respective entries on the European Transparency Register. EU NGOs have located a variety of new wealthy foundations from which to draw financial support. Individual NGOs are highly networked by formal organizations and informal structures within and across segments, sometimes working alongside one another in purpose-renovated buildings, often working on joint campaigns. Manifestos with a coherent outlook for 'people and the planet' (EEB 2010) are published together by coalition partners with a breadth of scope to match those of political parties standing for election. And, significantly, social movement structures which lie beyond the 'usual suspects' of institutionalized Brussels NGOs have been engaging the EU using various channels, linked to policymaking by 'bridge' organizations such as Friends of the Earth and Greenpeace (Hadden 2009).

As the European Community was driven by the single-market agenda in the period following the Single European Act a glance at any of the core contemporary debates since the Treaty on European Union (TEU) reveals that it has come to be gripped by discourse about its legitimacy. Much of the current debate about this focuses upon input legitimacy (participation and the means through which policies are made) rather than output legitimacy ('winning by results'). This model of 'participatory democracy', and the systematic empowerment of organized citizen groups as a means to achieve this (Chapters 1 and 8), explains why organizations articulating interests stated as those of the citizen have arrived at the centre of EU policymaking. Such organizations have successfully used the discourse of democratic legitimacy for this purpose, 'framing' their demands in these key terms. The linkage of policy agendas to popular discourse is captured by the concept of 'policy framing', where 'policy actors try to control the prevailing image of the policy problem through the use of rhetoric, symbols and policy analysis' (Baumgartner and Jones, in Mazey 2000:339). The all important ways in which issues are defined and 'framed' create policy priorities and their treatment in the policy process. These factors have helped to propel citizen issues to the fore of EU policy agendas.

A communication from the European Commission in 2000, 'The Commission and NGOs: Building a Stronger Partnership', issued in the names of its President and Vice President, lists six main reasons for co-operation with organized civil society:

- fostering participatory democracy
- as information relays
- representing the views of specific groups of citizens to the EU institutions
- contributing to policymaking
- contributing to project management and policy/programme implementation
- contributing to European integration (European Commission 2000b).

These roles are a mixture of 'input' and 'output' legitimacy and therefore help to explain the activism of EU political institutions in the formation and maintenance of interest groups. As well as responding to incentives provided by EU political institutions (Chapter 1), groups have also emerged to fill 'niches' which are identified and exploited by entrepreneurs. Citizen interest groups are the second largest category of EU interest groups, possibly now accounting for one third of the total, and have been the largest growth sector of all EU level groups in recent years (Chapter 1).

The landscape of citizen interest groups

The organizational landscape of EU NGOs bears evidence of its institutionalization, and in particular the emergence of 'family' NGOs. The most highly confederated citizen interest group is the EU Civil Society Contact Group, initially created as an umbrella group with which to engage the 2002/3 Convention on the Future of Europe, and which remained to develop a more permanent existence. It is a 'family of (8) families' of EU citizen interest groups, as shown in Table 6.1.

A variety of organizations fulfil horizontal niches within the citizen domain alongside the Civil Society Contact Group (CSCG), as shown in Table 6.2.

The Social Platform's emergence as leader organization for the sector has resulted in fewer horizontal organizations. The Platform was initially created as a joint initiative of DG EMP and the Chair of the Social Affairs Committee of the European Parliament in 1995 to pursue a 'Civil Dialogue' for input legitimacy with civil society, drawing a parallel with the 'social dialogue' for producer organizations. Its early work was geared at a widescale mobilization of citizen interests at EU level to this end, but progressively developed as an organization into an institutional interlocutor for EU political institutions (Geyer 2001; Smismans 2003; Cullen 2005). These have included bi-annual 'civil dialogue summits' with DG EMP, organizing NGO input into the Convention on the Future of Europe (Cullen 2005) and in meetings of the informal Council of Social Affairs and Employment (Alhadeff 2003). It has previously sought a system of accreditation for EU interest groups on the basis of 'representativeness' in the knowledge that such a system would leave it at the top of the tree (European Commission 2005b:5), arguing for the highest level of financial support to be reserved for it (Cullen 2005). Seeking to distinguish itself from other organizations, the Social Platform has developed criteria of representativeness which need to apply as criteria for other organizations to join it as a member:

> The network or federation must be composed of organisations (not individuals) in at least the absolute majority of the EU Member States. The network or federation must be established as

TABLE 6.1 *Members of the EU Civil Society Contact Group*

Social Platform	36 (full members) citizen interest groups in the wider social policy field. Initiated by EU institutions, now a leading organization in sector with elevated status in institutions. 10 staff. Hosts the secretariat of the Civil Society Contact Group.
CONCORD	European NGO Confederation for Relief and Development, comprising 18 international networks and 25 national associations across Europe. Lead partner of DG Development. 15 staff.
Human Rights and Democracy Network	Informal network organization of 38 outlets of international peace, and human rights, organizations, active at EU level, led by Amnesty International.
G10	'Family' network of 10 environmental NGOs active at EU level, which purposefully co-ordinates resources between participating organizations. 145 staff.
European Women's Lobby (EWL)	Confederation of 30 national organizations and 21 transnational organizations. Secretariat of 9 staff, plus interns.
Culture Action Europe	Formerly (until 2008) the European Forum for the Arts and Heritage. Family of 90 member organizations working on EU culture issues. 4 staff + intern/s.
European Public Health Alliance (EPHA)	85 national, regional, and European NGOs working in public health field. 11 staff + interns.
European Civil Society Platform on Lifelong Learning (EUCIS-LLL)	Umbrella of 20 networks active in education and training. 2 staff.

Data from: Organization websites.

TABLE 6.2 *Cross-sectoral EU citizen interest associations not in membership of the Contact Group of Civil Society*

Name (acronym)	Year established	Social Platform member?	Role
Association of Voluntary Service Organisations (AVSO)	1993	No	European platform of 22 national and international non-profit organizations active in the field of longer-term voluntary service. Presents itself as active in youth policy, legal status of volunteers, disability, inclusion, environment, EU citizenship and democracy, education and culture.
European Anti-Poverty Network (EAPN)	1990	Yes	Members are local, national, and European organization concerned with disadvantage. Has developed into a horizontal-type umbrella organization with a remit of social inclusion. Heavily institutionalized in DG EMP (Bauer 2002), and has assumed a formal monitoring role in the European Employment Strategy. 13 staff.
European Council for Non-Profit Organisations (CEDAG)	1989	Yes	French-dominated 'third sector' organization, with 32 members from 21 countries which are national and regional councils for voluntary organizations as members. One permanent employee, supplemented by member resources. Led the unsuccessful pursuit of a European Association

→

$\rightarrow$

Name (acronym)	Year established	Social Platform member?	Role
			Statute with DG XXIII of the European Commission in the 1990s (Kendall and Fraisse 2005).
European Citizen Action Service (ECAS)	1990	No	Direct membership organization, drawn diversely from over 100 EU, national (including one from Ghana and one from Cambodia) and regional NGOs, and those (including a small number of individuals) with interests in citizen issues/NGOs. Members drawn from fields of civil liberties, culture, development, health and social welfare, as well as general civil society development agencies. Active on civil society, free movement of citizens, and European governance. 13 staff.
European Social Action Network (ESAN)	1991	Yes	Horizontal mandate with specialisms in social, human rights, and development fields. Founded by UK and French national councils for voluntary organizations, members in 17 countries. Social Platform member.
Permanent Forum of European Civil Society	1995	No	Active on issues of citizenship and participatory democracy. Limited membership base.

Data from: Organization websites.

a not-for-profit and non-governmental organisation in one of the EU member states. The majority of the organisation's membership must themselves be legally established, not-for-profit and non-governmental. The network or federation must be active in the social sector, working to promote the general interest and contributing to social cohesion. The network or federation must demonstrate its representativity and that it is structured and managed in a democratic way, it is run by an elected body, whose decisions and membership must not be subject to approval by any extraneous body. (Social Platform 2010:8)

This criterion sets the organization apart from its competitors, clearly defining its niche as representativity. The Permanent Forum of Civil Society, for instance, is highly active on European citizenship and participatory democracy, yet it has only a handful of individuals as members. Similarly, ECAS is a leading organization in the domain based around its pursuit of citizenship, but whose voice does not depend upon its somewhat diversely constituted membership list. It was founded by an 'interest group entrepreneur' with substantial experience on the Brussels scene who saw a 'niche' gap in the advocacy market, much in the way in which specific business organizations have also emerged and differentiated themselves from one another (Chapter 4). There is space for them all because they all do something different, dependent upon each carving out its own distinctive niche. These differences are apparent in their approaches to particular causes. For instance, the European Citizens' Initiative has been a natural cause for ECAS to champion. And the leadership which ECAS (and the Permanent Forum) has given to a European 'compact' to govern, inter alia, standards of consultation with political institutions, draws upon the experiences of its widely drawn membership base, but it makes no pretence to 'representativeness'. For such organizations, their raison d'être is rather to advocate a 'cause' (i.e. they are 'what' rather than 'who' organizations), and the application of any instrument of representativity as access criteria by EU institutions would have a deleterious impact upon their work and status. This is discussed further in Chapter 8.

The European Citizens' Initiative is a new (from April 2012) route for one million citizens from at least a quarter of EU member states to petition the European Commission with a proposal for a legal act in a policy area which falls within the scope of the

Treaties. It requires an organizing committee of seven citizens from seven member states, whose proposal must first be checked by the Commission for admissibility. Once the green light is given there is a one month window to collect the threshold of one million signatures, which may be collected by designated electronic means or on paper, supported by accompanying measures to identify the signatory, and with safeguards for checks. Once the threshold is reached, the Commission then has three months to consider how to react. The extent to which EU institutions have already 'sold' the measure to the general public means that proposals will have to be given serious consideration, and outright refusals likely to be rare. The extent of organizational requirement to achieve the threshold of signatories, including responsibility for translation cost and for the privacy of data, as well as legal interpretations of Treaty powers, will depend upon professionalised organization to achieve it. European interest groups are therefore likely to have a significant role, although even for them the achievement of one million signatories accompanied by supporting identification information is a major challenge. Even before the measure came into place, with its detailed requirements for signature collection, most proposals failed to reach the required signature threshold. Even ETUC, with its extensive membership reach (Chapter 5), was unable to acquire this many signatories in a period shortly before the measure came into place (Bouza Garcia 2011). Organizations with experience of using such measures in the member states reckon on a general rule of the need to have five conversations in order to achieve one signature. However, the measure will increase the dialogue between EU interest organizations and their members, which until recently has been more focused upon advocacy with EU institutions (Sudbery 2003).

The European Citizens' Initiative arose from a campaign which fed into the fora drafting the failed 2005 Constitutional Treaty, which continued when the initiative was retained in the successor Lisbon Treaty. Of significance is that the campaign group was mainly composed of groups operating outside of the Civil Society Contact Group umbrella, such as the (Polish) Centre for Citizenship Education and 'Kid's Globe'. One author has pointed out that the initiative succeeded not because of large-scale civic mobilization but due to strategic lobbying of key policy members (De Clerck-Sachsse 2010). While this raises the key issue of the extent to which elite interest groups can be a source of democratic mechanisms, the paradox is of dependence upon such groups to operationalize democratic mechanisms.

The funding of NGOs

The Commission has been a significant source of funding for citizen interest groups organized at EU level. Their purpose in doing so has been to ensure the presence of checks and balances in the ways in which demands are brought to the political system, and to perform democratic functions (such as accountability pressures) because of the relative weaknesses of other mechanisms (low levels of public engagement, no EU-wide media or mass political parties, etc.). Funding is one of a number of mechanisms designed to empower NGOs. Virtually all such groups (Greenpeace and Amnesty International are notable exceptions) are beneficiaries of EU funding regimes, such that most NGOs at EU level get much of their funding from EU institutions.

It is difficult to establish a precise figure for the total extent of funding by EU institutions of NGO, with estimates from Commission sources varying from €1 to 2 billion. Thus, the Commission discussion paper of 2000 issued in the name of President Barroso and Vice President Kinnock recorded that

> [a]t present it is estimated that over 1000 million a year is allocated to NGO projects directly by the Commission, the major part in the field of external relations for development co-operation, human rights, democracy programmes, and in particular, humanitarian aid (on average €400 million). Other important allocations are in the social (approximately €70 million), educational (approximately €50 million) and environment sectors within the EU. Several hundred NGOs in Europe and world-wide are receiving funds from the EU. (European Commission 2000b)

On the other hand, the Commissioner announcing the European Transparency Initiative was keen to sell his new regulatory agenda in the estimate he identified when announcing the scheme:

> Annually the Commission channels over 2 billion euro to developing countries through NGO's. The word 'non' is quite fictitious. Some of the NGO's receiving funds from the Commission describe on their website one of their main tasks as: 'lobbying

the Commission'. Or to put it in the words of Sir Humphrey: 'the Commission is paying lobbies, in order to be lobbied'. The 'European Transparency Initiative' also seeks to increase transparency in these networks, for example, by improving the current registry of NGO's. It should also contain financial information. (Kallas 2005:6)

The more political overtones of this latter figure, coupled with the (as yet unsourced) 'external estimate' he cited for the number of actors active on the Brussels scene, would seem to lean more towards the first (€1 billion) estimate above. Most policy areas have budget lines for the support of NGOs, and some citizen groups organized at EU level receive most of their funding from EU political institutions. Two types of funding are possible: action grants (for specific projects, etc.) and operating grants (for core establishment funding). The European Transparency Initiative provides a means of identifying this funding. One part of the ETI is an online searchable database established by the European Commission of grant awards, and another part – the lobby regulation element – has some disclosure by organizations which states the proportion of income which comes from different sources, although there has been to date limited enforcement of this (Chapter 3) and it is possible to upload an entry without answering the question. The first data entry question seeks a total budget amount, whereas the second provides an estimate by the organization of the proportion of its funding which sources of finance, including a segment for EU grants, account for. Table 6.3 provides illustrative data for some organizations which appear in both information sources.

WWF has over 40 staff, and therefore approaching the staffing levels of the principal EU business association, Business Europe (Chapter 4). Additionally, such international NGO brands can draw upon the resources of branch offices based in other European countries, and upon those of some of its members for technical input. Outside of these global organizations, the organization with the highest number of staff is the European Youth Forum, with 27 staff.

The extent of EU funding raises questions about the independence of citizen interest groups. The view from leading organizations in the sector is that funding from EU political institutions is a source of independence (from needing to seek funds from business) rather than dependence, rather like state funding of political parties.

Table 6.3 EU funding of principal EU NGOs

Organization	Funding year	Financial Transparency Database (year if different to column 2)	Self-disclosure by organization on European Transparency Register of amount of EU funding/proportion of income
Culture Action Europe	2008	€104,000	€104,000/35%
European Anti-Poverty Network (EAPN)	2008	€1,281,661.92	€1,187,718.02/86%
European Citizen Action Service (ECAS)	2009	Not available	€701,124/76%
European Consumers Organisation (BEUC)	2010	€1,300,000 (2009)	€2,280,107/59%
European Council for Non-Profit Organisations (CEDAG)	2009	€111,060	€111,000/80%

→

European Environmental Bureau (EEB)	2008	n/a	€1,531,393/73%
European NGO Confederation for Relief and Development (CONCORD)	2009	€719,400	€772,221/54%
European Public Health Alliance (EPHA)	2008	n/a	€364,507.72/54%
European Social Action Network (ESAN)	2008	€33,900	€129,229/83%
European Women's Lobby (EWL)	2008	€825,600	€808,896/84%
European Youth Forum (EYF)	2008	€2,330,000 (2009)	€2,392,144/79%
Friends of the Earth Europe (FOEE)	2009	€813,721	€1,169,367/42%
Platform of European Social NGOs	2009	€680,000	€677,990/79%
World Wide Fund for Nature (WWF) European Policy Programme	2010	n/a	€677,244/13%
Average EU Funding			64%

Data from: European Financial Transparency Initiative 2010; European Transparency Register 2010.

The degree of critical engagement by such groups with EU political institutions, apparent throughout responses to proposed policy initiatives, suggests that such organizations may not feel specifically compromised; the Social Platform, receiving almost 80% of its funds from EU institutions, once famously pronounced in a press release that 'Mr Barroso, you killed the European Dream' (Fazi and Smith 2006:20). Nonetheless, there is a likely subliminal general effect that those whose livelihood depends upon such funding will tend to have a generally positive outlook to 'project Europe'. Some of the global NGOs, such as Greenpeace and Amnesty International, have taken the option not to seek EU funding. Some authors see the receipt of funding as bringing with it a set of perceptions about obligations, including a requirement to participate in (relatively inconclusive) open consultation exercises, which then helps to secure access to a second tier of more restricted participatory fora (Mahoney 2004; Quittkat 2011). The implications of this are considered further in Chapter 8.

There has also been a diversification of funding sources among the EU NGO community in recent years. These include the use of other established charities, such as Oxfam and Christian Aid, and foundations with funds historically derived from business wealth, such as the Joseph Rowntree Trust, the Sigrid Rausing Trust (whose website identifies a 2010 budget of £20 million, providing funding for three members of the G10 group of environmental NGOs), the OAK foundation, the Sir James Goldsmith Foundation, and the Isvara Foundation. The latter is unusual in that its funds derive from the Chairman (Ayman Jallad) of a Lebanese business importing and distributing 'Caterpillar' brand tractors, with funds distributed to beneficiaries through a Swiss bank account (Deighton 2011; Zadek 2011). A number of 'left to outside left' leaning organizations active at EU level have drawn upon a common pool of foundation sources, indicating the high degree of network overlap between them. These ties are strengthened by their presence in an NGO 'eco-house', purpose-renovated premises at Rue d'Edimbourg 26 in Brussels, the Mundo-b building, where building occupants share common social spaces including a canteen and a garden.

These realities mean that EU NGOs now have the ability to move 'beyond victimhood'. Self-positioning as victims can effectively play upon sensitivities that political institutions only listen to one side of the argument. But the EU NGO community now has the resources, the maturity of establishment, and the institutional means to move

Table 6.4 *EU NGOs in the Mundo-b building*

Central Eastern Europe Bankwatch Network

Climate Action Network

Corporate Europe Observatory

European Coalition for Corporate Justice

European Environmental Citizens Organisation for Standardisation

European Federation for Transport and the Environment

European Network on Debt and Development (EURODAD)

Food and Water Europe

Foodwatch

Forests and the European Union Resource Network

Friends of the Earth Europe

Jeunes et Nature

Nature Friends International

Seas at Risk

Terre des Hommes

Data from: Mundo-b website.

beyond access to participation. Chapter 2 provided an example of this through the participation of environmental and consumer organizations in technical standard-setting bodies, funded partly by EU institutions. Participatory mechanisms are also described in the sections which follow and in Chapter 8 where EU procedures designed to equip NGOs to participate as democratic agents (e.g. of accountability) are detailed.

Historic landmarks in the development of EU citizen interest representation

Consumer groups were the first citizen interest organizations at EU level, reflecting the focus of the European Economic Community, and quickly emerged in the years immediately following the Treaty of Rome. This wave was followed by groups representing world development and human rights concerns. Both sets of groups were heavily institutionalized in dialogues with the European Commission. A formal dialogue structure between consumer interests and the

Commission dates from 1961, and has continued (subject to a number of reforms), to the present day. Since the mid-1970s, a Liaison Committee with Development NGOs (later CONCORD) embraced an elaborate structure of organizations, acting as an institutionalized channel for dialogue with the European Commission. Amnesty International arrived on the scene in the mid-1980s, with other groups in the domain arriving following the establishment of EU competencies in the 1992 TEU. Animal rights groups were also an early citizen group on the EU scene. The European Environmental Bureau was established in 1974 as an umbrella body and institutional interlocutor for (and heavily financed by) the Commission, and remained the sole environmental public interest group in Brussels until the late 1980s. Those who came in the late 1980s, such as Greenpeace, Friends of the Earth, and the World Wide Fund for Nature, established outreach offices as co-ordinating devices for wider movements to address EU political decision-making.

A 1986 report in the European Parliament (Fontaine Report), leading to a subsequent EP resolution, put the 'third sector' of social and civic organizations on the EU policy agenda, recording that

> Europe needs inspiration to take a further step towards its destiny as a Community. Nonprofit organisations are an opportunity to be taken in this respect. Inertia must be overcome and this opportunity must be boldly seized. (Kendall and Fraisse 2005:283)

Most of the action followed during and beyond the TEU period, when a wave of organizations oriented towards poverty, disability, public health, voluntary sector provision, and justice/home affairs types of issues came to Brussels. The TEU included a landmark declaration, Declaration 23, stating 'the importance ... of cooperation between the European Community and charitable associations and foundations as institutions responsible for welfare establishments and services' (European Commission 2006a). Despite this, many such organizations operated at the fringes of Treaty competencies, clustering around the emerging social programmes and initiatives coming out of DG V, until the insertion of an article in the 1997 Amsterdam Treaty opened the gates for the development of social policy beyond labour market measures. Many of these groups also have their origins or spurts of significant development dating from major Commission White Papers of the early to mid-1990s, such as those on *Growth, Competitiveness and Employment* (1993) and *European Social Policy* (1994), or initiatives such as action programmes or mainstreaming (Chapter 5), which resulted in land-mark social action programmes for the remaining years of the 1990s. The Social Platform's organization of two large 'social forums' in search of 'civil dialogue' during this period were also landmarks, helping to develop the Social Platform's leadership role for EU civil society organizations. A new budget line for NGOs to pursue civil dialogue in 1997 supported these activities.

From the side of EU political institutions, DG EMP was a clear leader in these 'social policy' initiatives, whereas the leadership for another set of related, parallel initiatives running at the time in the social economy field was provided by a unit within a now defunct service of the European Commission, DG XXIII (now incorporated within DG Enterprise). This unit, together with CEDAG, proposed an ultimately unsuccessful mission for a European Association Statute, seeking a legal status for EU organizations in the wider frame of demo-cratic legitimacy (Kendall and Fraisse 2005). In 1997 the unit launched a Commission Communication on 'promoting the role of voluntary organizations and foundations in Europe' which argued that

> voluntary organisations and foundations foster a sense of soli-darity and citizenship, and provide the essential underpinnings of our democracy. In the light of the challenges now facing the European Community, these functions have never been more vital. (European Commission 1997:5)

This claim was followed up by the 2000 Commission Discussion Paper 'The Commission and NGOs', which argued that 'NGOs can make a contribution to fostering a more participatory democracy both within the EU and beyond' (European Commission 2000b:4). This thinking came downstream in the White Paper on Governance, aimed at structuring a system of participatory democracy as a wider solution to democratic legitimacy, and is the subject of extensive analysis in Chapter 8. In acting as a catalyst for the creation of a procedural framework for a systematic engagement with civil soci-ety, the White Paper followed up an agenda first set by the 1992 Sutherland Report (Sutherland 1992).

'Democratic legitimacy' was also a catalyst for the creation in the late 1990s of a structured dialogue by DG Trade with civil society in the formulation of external trade policy, and a direct response to the issues raised by the 'Battle of Seattle'. The dialogue embraces 600 organizations across the spectrum of civil society (spanning producer and citizen interests), structured through 14 organizations elected by civil society, and provides funding to allow the participation of organizations based outside Brussels.

The 'Lisbon agenda' has been another development agent for civil society organizations of all kinds, extending opportunities beyond those organized at EU level for EU engagement. Clause 38 of the original European Council 2000 declaration launching the Lisbon process states that 'the social partners and civil society will be involved using various forms of partnership'. Objective 4 of the distinctive OMC inclusion process is to 'mobilise all relevant actors'. Such relevant actors are explicitly envisaged as organized groups acting as representatives of, and proxies for, wider civil society. There have been mixed reports of success in engaging the diversity of organized civil society in the process (European Economic and Social Committee 2004; Kok 2004), but on the credit side the EAPN and the Social Platform have been closely engaged with the design and monitoring of the process. EAPN is highly institutionalized in DG EMP (Bauer 2002) and receives a significant strand of its EU funding for the purpose of promoting the participation and dialogue central to the OMC inclusion process (Armstrong 2003). Groups such as EAPN have been progressively drawn into the EES through its leading role on behalf of EU social policy NGOs in the Social Inclusion Strategy (Armstrong 2003; de la Porte and Nanz 2004). The EAPN's continued leadership is underlined by its position at the head of a coalition of over 40 European NGO networks aimed at ensuring their participation in the 2010 European Year for Collaborating Poverty and Social Exclusion. The network underlines the capacity of Brussels NGOs for collective action via coalition formation.

These historical landmarks help to explain the role of citizen groups in the EU policy process of today and their high degree of institutionalization. These are brought to life by the detail of segments of citizen interest representation, starting with the interests widely seen as having the greatest impact at EU level, environmental NGOs.

Environmental interests

As successive Earth Summits have revealed, the EU's environmental policies are the most advanced in the world. This reflects the reality that environmental issues are a central public interest concern throughout (particularly, northern) member states, and are highly politicized. Consumer behaviour displays significant environmental motives, and business has adopted significant aspects of the environmental agenda in response. Germanic Europe has concerns about acid rain, there are regionally acute issues about flooding and rising sea levels, and pollutants dispersed into the long, slow-flowing Rhine where dispersal takes time contribute to agendas of public concern. Eurobarometer surveys have repeatedly shown the popularity of the European level to tackle environmental problems based on the premise that 'pollution is no respecter of international boundaries'.

EU environmental action can be traced back to a 'landmark' summit held in Stockholm in 1972 which gave rise to the first of a series of 'environmental action programmes'. The sixth of these runs from 2002 to 2012. Beyond these are single-market-related issues, where high environmental protection countries in Germanic Europe have sought to 'export' their high-cost production conditions to lower protection countries, on the whole successfully. The Single European Market was the first formal recognition of environmental policy in European policymaking, extended by the TEU to the use of QMV and the addition of the precautionary principle. Co-decision powers now apply to most areas of environmental policy. The single market enabled countries to proceed with high standards of environmental protection than adopted at the EU level, provided they were compatible with the treaties. A landmark ruling in the Court of Justice in 1988, the Danish bottles case (C302/86 Commission v Denmark 1988, ECOR4607 OR 1989 1 CMLR 619), took environmental protection beyond single-market issues of a level playing field, enabling measures primarily designed for environmental protection even if they constituted a trade barrier. The number of environmental directives in the period from 1989 to 1991 exceeded those of the preceding 20 years (Young 1995). These were followed by the Environmental Fifth Action Programme (1993–2000), which gave a quantum leap to environmental policy with its motto 'towards sustainable development', a principle incorporated into the 1997 Amsterdam Treaty. Those years also saw the establishment of the European Environmental Agency (EEA) in Copenhagen, the fourth enlargement of the EU (adding high standard countries to EU policymaking), and environmental assessment policy mainstreaming throughout Commission policymaking and in external aid, trade, and international relations. In 1998, the EU signed the Århus Convention on citizens' rights in environmental matters, guaranteeing rights of access to information, public participation in decision-making, and access to justice in environmental matters (G8 2002). In 2001, the Gothenburg European Council agreed upon a Sustainable Development Strategy for Europe, adding the Environmental Pillar to Economic and Social Pillars as a core component of the Lisbon Strategy, and signalling the final arrival of environmental agendas as core to EU policymaking.

These factors raise the issue as to the extent to which environmental interest groups have been a driver of EU public policy in environmental protection, or largely operate within a set of favourable circumstances more shaped by other influences. This question can be addressed following an assessment of the population of groups and their action. The groups themselves tend to see their influences in terms of agenda-setting, of which a significant recent example concerns the REACH dossier (Regulation, Evaluation and Authorisation of Chemicals). While this is an item of EU legislation, it has a significant global impact in that anyone seeking to sell chemicals in Europe has to conform with it. The basic principle is that the responsibility lies with the producer to scientifically demonstrate to an independent regulatory agency that their products are safe, and in the case of reasonable scientific doubt the 'precautionary principle' (a presumption of danger) prevails. Tony Long, European Policy Director of the WWF European Policy Office since 1989, reflected that

> in REACH, without the persistent and very strong lobbying from the environmental NGOs, it would not have been possible for the Environment Commissioner to put forward such a proposal with such consequences for industry. (Long and Lörinczi 2009:176)

This extract emphasizes the agenda-setting role of environmental NGOs, which is further highlighted by a dilution of the final legislation when compared to the original version. Nonetheless, complaints by opposing sets of stakeholders that the regulation was too tough or too soft allows EU political institutions to claim that the balance, achieved after significant consensus seeking within and between the Commission, Parliament, and Council, is about right, and as such certainly reflects a typical outcome of EU public policymaking.

Beyond agenda-setting, environmental groups are also well equipped to undertake a 'watchdog' role (Long and Lörinczi 2009). The Water Framework Directive gives NGOs a specific monitoring and guidance role, and environmental NGOs are involved in 50 consultative groups of the European Commission (Fazi and Smith 2006). They are well capable of engaging policy-making at a scientific level, drawing upon EU policy offices which are among the best staffed of citizen interest groups, a highly committed network of volunteers, and in the cases of Greenpeace, WWF, and Friends of the Earth, the resources of global movements. As is described below, a core network of environmental organizations also co-ordinate their resources for EU-related purposes. Together, these enable the environment movement to match the resources which collective business organizations apportion to the environmental dimensions of their activities. For instance, Long, Salter and Singer. (2002) record how traditional energy source companies and some of the main business associations such as UNICE, ERT, and EURELECTRIC were 'not really on the ball' about a significant detail with potentially major ramifications affecting their interests, and failed to give it sufficient priority or engage in much active lobbying. These factors suggest that earlier eras in which business lobbying on environmental issues swamped the efforts of others (Butt Philip and Porter 1995) have now passed. Nonetheless, where necessary, business has significant resources to draw upon for the purposes of environmental policymaking. For instance, a staff member of the EU chemicals association CEFIC identifies the participation of 4000 industry experts on its network of expert committees (Thier 2009). The downstream oil industry has a specialist bureau, the Oil Companies European Organisation for Environmental and Health Protection (CONCAWE), attached to the Brussels offices of its trade association, Europia.

As well as conflict can be found degrees of collaboration between business and 'light green' interest groups, particularly where there is a coincidence of interests such as renewables, or where one segment of business is seeking to impose higher production costs onto another. At a more permanent, cross-sectoral level, the European Partners for the Environment (EPE), a Commission-initiated structure under the Environmental Vth Action Programme (Lenschow 1996, 1999), brings together some NGOs (such as WWF and the EEB) with business (such as Unilever and Procter and Gamble) and trade unions (including ETUC) and public (mainly local) authorities to

> build the ground for consensus on sustainability ... dialogue built through long-term relationships between partners and strengthened by trust leads to common practical action ... partners meet in an informal atmosphere to float ideas, seek common solutions and constructively engage in debate and projects of mutual interest. Each partner takes away this learning and feeds it into the work of his or her own organisation. (EPE 2010)

Some of this mutual learning can be found downstream in industry-organized voluntary environmental schemes to promote good practice, such as the issue of certificates of good environmental practice. The Marine Stewardship Council, for instance, was a joint initiative of Birds Eye processed fish foods (then a Unilever Brand) and WWF, involving the certification that fish had been drawn from sustainable stocks. Initiatives such as these are geared towards showing how good environmental practice can also be good business sense, through meeting consumer demand, providing competitive advantage and good positioning, and reducing overheads (Ruzza 2000). For business organizations, an alliance with an environmental NGO is highly prized because of the general need for alliance-making in a consensus-oriented decision-making environment and because of the strength of environmental protection sentiment in Europe. For these reasons, a European public affairs manager of one leading US multinational consumer brand reports spending more time talking to NGOs than to EU institutions. Nonetheless, achieving an issue-specific business-green alliance in detail is not easy, and often once achieved, is somewhat unstable. There are more examples of participation by 'light green' NGOs such as the EEB and WWF. The latter purposefully tries to lend its name to projects involving business organizations which have tangible benefits for the environment. EEB has entered into alliances with Orgalime, the EU engineering association, and with the IT and consumer electronics associations, about practical collection targets in the framework of the European Waste from Electronic Equipment (WEE) Directives. The risk of entering into such alliances is an apparent compromise to 'ideological purity'. The latter position may be more informed by the need to maintain membership levels and the funds they bring, and therefore a niche for some of the 'dark green' organizations is to undertake 'stunts' with high media visual appeal as a means of demonstrating to its members that the organization concerned is active about the things which concern them in a 'protest business' (Jordan and Maloney 1997). In practice, however, even 'dark green' organizations enter into issue-specific alliances with business interests on the Brussels scene.

As well as voluntary initiatives among producers, statutory framework initiatives to which the environmental movement has contributed have reinforced and contributed towards changes in consumer behaviour. And as well as specific interventions over policy measures, the key contribution of environmental public interest groups, at EU and other levels, are the influences they have contributed to the belief systems of policymakers and of business and consumers.

Not long after establishing an office in Brussels, the Director of the WWF European Policy Office (WWF-EPO) reflected that 'in general the environmental organizations are unable to exercise power' (Long 1995:678). Eight years later, he commented that 'all the talk in Brussels these days about the role of "civil society" and the need to consult more widely is not just words ... whatever the reason, civil society is becoming recognized as the missing element' (Davis 2003:66). By 2009, he was emphasizing the leadership given by environmental groups to the wider NGO community, including their ability to bring in much broader 'policy clusters' of coalition partners to key environmental campaigns (Long and Lörinczi 2009). Reflecting on the history of environmental NGOs at EU level from their early days, he records that

> [n]ow, after several decades of expansion, the (one time) new market entrant is seen by some as possibly part of a 'lobbying oligopoly'. (Long and Lörinczi 2009:183)

For these authors, environmental NGOs have been able to progress beyond their traditional strengths of agenda-setting, but a key question remains how capable they are of competing with business interests during other stages of the policy process. One of the dimensions of this concerns their ability to participate throughout detailed stages of the passage of legislation, of which their resource base is a key part.

Environmental citizen interest groups

Table 6.5 details the Brussels offices of the 'Group of Ten' (G10) environmental NGOs, a loose but co-ordinated network 'of the ten leading environmental NGOs active at EU level' (G10 2011) who 'coordinate joint responses and recommendations to EU decision makers' (G8 2002:3).

The G10 estimates that its collective membership is over 20 million people (G10 2010). The mass membership base of many of them, together with the skills acquired by European offices, enables them to combine institutional politics with traditional social movement activism. As is discussed later, groups such as Greenpeace and Friends of the Earth, act as a bridge between the respective worlds of institutionalized Brussels NGOs and radical social movement networks (Hadden 2009).

In addition to the G10 are environmental NGOs outside of the network but with a Brussels office. These include a number of occupants of the Mundo-b building (Table 6.4), as well as the EU Liaison Office of the Europe Regional Office of the International Union for Conservation of Nature (IUCN), and the European Cyclists' Federation (eight staff). There are also a number of regionally based environmental organizations. Commission funding supports the work of 28 environmental NGOs (Kirchner 2006). There are thus well over 150 staff working for environmental public interest groups based in Brussels alone, supplemented by the potential resources of other European offices of organizations, and countless supporters willing to contribute expertise and voluntary assistance. Greenpeace, for instance, claims to have access to over 1200 scientific environmental experts worldwide (Mazey and Richardson 2005:116), making for an interesting comparison with those of the collective chemical industry (4000), described above. Participation at a level of detail, it seems, is possible for environmental NGOs throughout the policy process, rather than simply relying upon the strength of environmental sentiment to agenda-set issues.

The preamble to the Common Position approving the last financial action programme for green NGOs indicates that environmental NGOs have made themselves indispensable to EU policymaking. It recorded that

> NGOs active in the field of environmental protection have already
> demonstrated that they can contribute to the environmental

policy of the Community ... by active involvement in concrete environmental protection measures and in activities to increase the general awareness of the need for the protection of the environment with a view to sustainable development ... NGOs are essential to coordinate and channel to the Commission information and views on the new and emerging perspectives, such as on nature protection and transboundary environmental problems ... NGOs have good understanding of public concerns on the environment and can thus promote these views and channel them back to the Commission ... they provide necessary balance ... in relation to the interests of other actors in the environment, including industry/business, trade union and consumer groups. (Official Journal C110 E/27 of 7.5.2002)

Apart from some tensions surrounding the position of the EEB, described below, and some frictions arising from significant differences in style, relationships between the G10 are generally collaborative and well co-ordinated. They meet together every month for purposes of information swapping and co-ordination, periodically with the Cabinet of the Environment Commissioner and with the Director General of DG Environment, and, on an annual basis, with the President of the Commission. The Environment Commissioner has been known to turn up, unannounced, at meetings of the G10 (Long and Lörinczi 2009). Most G10 members have excellent links throughout DG Environment, meet up in a variety of other fora, and get to share thinking. Co-ordination is particularly good between a core 'Gang of Four', comprising the EEB, FoE, WWF, and Greenpeace, who commenced the network as 'G4' in 1990 (Long and Lörinczi 2009). Most of the G10 have competencies in matters affecting the environment across the range of their interests, with an informal and unwritten division of labour to enable the organization with the natural specialism to take the lead on it. This division is not intended to be exclusive, in that most of the organizations undertake work on a core of related environmental issues. Long and Lörinczi have reflected that

NGOs might have an advantage over business groups in that NGOs find it easier to construct and maintain broad cross-national coalitions than do business interests who are essentially in competition with each other and who are differentially affected by EU regulation. (Long and Lörinczi 2009:177)

TABLE 6.5 The 'G10' environmental NGOs and their resources

Organization (acronym)	Total budget declared in ETR	% funded by EU institutions (ETR)	Number of Brussels office staff listed on website (or ETR)	Declared spend on lobbying EU institutions in ETR	Brussels office at Rd'E[1] 26, Brussels
European Environmental Bureau (EEB)	€2,097,502	73%	18	€700,000–750,000	No
World Wide Fund For Nature (WWF) European Policy Programme	€5,194,065	13%	41	€450,000–500,000	No
Friends of the Earth Europe (FoEE)	€2,802,560	42%	(24)	€600,000–650,000	Yes
Greenpeace European Unit	€1,339,000	0	14	€565,000	No
European Federation for Transport and Environment (T&E)	€1,020,000	26%	13	€400,000–450,000	Yes

$\rightarrow$

Birdlife International European Division	€1,499,655	26%	(9)	€360,000	No
Climate Action Network Europe (CAN Europe)	€794,363	33%	9	€650,000	Yes
Nature Friends International (NFI) (formerly Friends of Nature International – IFN) (Vienna HQ)	€782,682	39%	1+	'less than €50,000'	Yes
CEE Bankwatch Network (Prague HQ)	€1,382,103	53%	(7)	€200,000–250,000	Yes
Health and Environment Alliance (HEAL)	€525,037	68%	9	€150,000–250,000	No
Total	€17,436,967	37.3%	145	€4,195,000–€4,475,000	5

[1] Rue d'Edimbourg

Data from: European Transparency Register, October 2010; organizational websites.

The G10 claims that it

> successfully lobbied the European Convention to retain existing Treaty commitments to sustainable development, environmental protection and the integration of environmental concerns into each EU policy area. (G10 2010)

This claim once again raises the problematic issue of the extent to which environmental NGOs create policy outcomes or act as contributory voices to outcomes which would have happened anyway. There is some confidence among leading G10 participants on this point, with Long and Lörinczi claiming that

> [a] G10 letter to President Barroso in July 2005 was undoubtedly influential in saving the seven thematic strategies on the environment being proposed by Commissioner Dinas from disappearing off the Commission's agenda. (Long and Lörinczi 2009:175)

Once again, the power of EU environmental NGOs as agenda-setters is stressed by this reflection.

The organizational figurehead for the G10 is the EEB, as the first to be established in the field through the environmental services of the European Commission. As a confederation, it carries the usual advantages and disadvantages of breadth, much as the review of similarly structured business organizations (Chapter 4) demonstrated. This, along with the need for it to share its space alongside other environmental activists, has been the source of the organization's principal difficulties. Its diverse membership includes the conservative Campaign to Protect Rural England (CPRE), the (UK) National Trust, national branches of Friends of the Earth, Greenpeace, and WWF, to the European Union Foundation for Landscape Architecture (EFLA) and the European Foundation for City Farms. Nonetheless, the EEB is a good network organization for its members, and as an organization in its own right is well networked with other environmental NGOs on the global stage. As an organization geared to addressing the EU political institutions rather than a social movement, it has a wide-ranging set of institutional contacts. Consistent with its preference for EU level groups, the EEB has been used by the Commission as its main interlocutor across the range of environmental interests, and has institutionalized its presence across a range of advisory committee structures. It has an astonishingly symbiotic relationship with DG Environment, to the extent that Mazey and Richardson record that

> one Commission official suggested to us that the task force which preceded the formation of DG (Environment) was originally so weak that it sought the support of the NGOs and mobilised and supported them in order to defend itself. He believed that without NGO support DG (Environment) might have died in its early years. (Mazey and Richardson 2005:115)

Apart from meetings with the Presidents of the Commission and the Council, the EEB is a member of Commission delegations at Earth/Environmental Summits.

These strengths apart, the EEB has also had some problems of style. A past Chair of the EP Environment Committee once commented that 'instead of making it short and snappy they go in for awfully wearisome and hectoring briefings. Effective lobbying is about being selective with information' (*Financial Times* 1994). Inevitably, its influence has been diluted since other environmental NGOs established Brussels offices, and the EEB has not always welcomed the leadership the latter have sometimes given on particular environmental issues.

The WWF and the Birdlife International network are similar in outlook to EEB in working primarily through institutionalized channels at EU level. Their strong resource bases also enable them to engage policymaking at a highly technical scientific level. The WWF has something of an establishment image as the world's largest and best-established field-based nature conservation organization, and declares corporate sponsorship among the financial contributors to its European policy office. Alongside its 'cuddly panda' image and institutionalized links, its European office has self-consciously sought to position itself as a policy as well as advocacy-oriented NGO (Long et al. 2002). Besides using its established channels in the national delegation offices in Brussels, it has resorted to the European Court of Justice system where it is necessary to ensure that action is taken against member states for environmental violations of structural fund initiatives. It has also played an important whistle-blowing role, such as providing the European Investment Bank and the Court of Auditors with video evidence of environmental violations arising from the use of the structural funds in

Spain (Long 1995). In addition, it also makes use of its mass-membership base through letter-writing campaigns, co-ordinating with the Swiss-based Europe/Middle East regional office of WWF International (Graziano 1999). Birdlife International also has a mass membership base, with one million members in the UK alone (Graziano 1999), which it has used in EU politics. The popularity of its case is underlined by holding the record for the largest ever petition presented to the European Parliament with two million signatures, aimed at stopping the modification of the Birds Directive to extend hunting seasons, and claims this as a contributory factor in the withdrawal of its proposal by the European Commission. Like WWF, Birdlife also has the status, resources (with 100 staff based in the UK; Graziano 1999), and establishment reputation to work institutionally.

Like WWF and Birdlife, Friends of the Earth and Greenpeace are also equipped to engage EU policymaking at a technical level, through permanent resources and supporting scientists, and have the ability to turn science into politics through their mass mobilization base when required. Not for the first time, Greenpeace has also been able to triumph politics over science, when its mass letter-writing campaign over the drinking water directive helped achieve an EP amendment about pesticide limits which the Commission accepted despite the opinion of its own scientific advisor (Warleigh 2000). Graziano records that WWF 'is quietly critical of Greenpeace and its confrontational tactics, whereas the WWF embraces a philosophy whose central tenet is reliance on solid scientific evidence' (Graziano 1999:23).

Whereas WWF and Birdlife are 'light' green, FoE and Greenpeace are more 'medium to dark' green. Friends of the Earth Europe (FoEE) is a highly decentralized network of independent national environmental organizations across Europe. This degree of decentralization means that some FoEE national organizations have activities well beyond the environmental domain into general left of mainstream political goals, and some of these are highly networked in 'alternatives' circles. Its EU office has concentrated more on institutional contacts with the Commission and the Parliament, where it has a reputation as a valuable contributor of information, than on seeking to mobilize the movement's grassroots base. This illustrates the tendency for radical social movements to become tamed over time as they engage, become incorporated in, and be influenced by the routines of institutional political decision-making, despite one of its original motivations for coming to Brussels being the weakness and institutionalized nature of the EEB. At one point in the 1980s it sought to establish a rival cross-sectoral organization to the EEB, seeking to attract direct-action-oriented groups, which the EEB diverted by proposing greater co-ordination with and between the 'Gang of Four'. As a highly decentralized movement, the Brussels office of Friends of the Earth is more self-sufficient than is Greenpeace, whose work is more shared between its offices in the member states. Greenpeace is perhaps the most geared to direct-action campaigns and boycotts, although it has also learnt how to interact with the European institutions. Greenpeace actively supplements the resources of its Brussels office with those from elsewhere, in that responsibility for discrete EU policy areas often lies with national offices. Thus, Greenpeace Austria and Greenpeace Switzerland, for instance, have held responsibility for work on Trans European Networks, where these issues have high environmental impact and strong local mobilization, with specialists in the Brussels office only for chemicals, climate, electricity, and biotechnology. The Brussels office plays a co-ordinating role between these.

While the differences between the G10 organizations mean that they cannot always work together, the overall pattern tends to work well for environmental citizen interests. The G10 embrace ranges from the respectable and 'establishment-friendly' WWF and Birdlife to the more assertive, direct-action-oriented Greenpeace and Friends of the Earth. It encompasses the mass-membership power base of FoE and Greenpeace, and the institutionalized EEB, WWF, and Birdlife. Styles vary too, such as the interpersonal contact style of Birdlife, and the informal and loosely co-ordinated, but effective, Climate Action Network (Rucht 1993). The relationships between the G10 are more harmonious than are many business coalitions, and contain some close alliances, helped by the occupation by five G10 members of the Mundo-b building in Brussels. Because most are operational outreach Brussels offices operating with a high degree of autonomy, rather than membership offices, they do not have to be overly concerned with internal platform-building, enabling them to respond quickly to issues.

With the exception of Greenpeace, all of these organizations have been commissioned by the European institutions for investigative work. They all have the technical and political ability to turn science into politics by influencing the ways in which issues are perceived and defined, to become part of the knowledge communities which drive policymaking, and to engage public policy throughout the different stages of its formulation, implementation, and monitoring. And, crucially, they have helped shape not only the thinking of other policy actors such as the Commission and producer groups but also member state preferences towards environmental protection policies. WWF-EPO Director Tony Long is reported to have responded with delight to a Commission Green Paper on Common Fisheries Policy Reform with the words 'it could have been written by WWF' (Scotland Europa 2002:96).

Environmental NGOs have a natural ally in the shape of the EP, whose members are quick to take up concerns popular with their electorate. Surveys of 'lobbying effectiveness' among parliamentarians have in the past indicated that environmental groups were rated by MEPs as the most effective of all citizen interest groups (Burson Marsteller 2001). However, a repeat survey conducted in 2009 found that NGOs had been overtaken as 'effective lobbyists' in the estimation of MEPs by business interests, and particularly in the energy domain (Burson Marsteller 2009). This seems to reflect a changing need among MEPs for expertise as the Parliament has gradually acquired more legislative powers. The analysis by practitioners of an increasing ability on the part of NGOs over time to intervene in public policymaking beyond agenda-setting (Long and Lörinczi) is difficult to test empirically because of the difficulty of isolating the impact of environmental interest groups from other issues, not least of which is the general strength of the environment in public sentiment and its corresponding strength as an issue within the mechanisms of representative democracy.

Consumer interests

The Consumer Programme 2007–13 follows the principles of the landmark Consumer Policy Strategy 2002–6. A 2001 Commission report announcing this strategy reflected that

> in broad terms, the last few years have certainly been years of transition, with consumer policy moving to centre stage (European Commission 2001b:21) ... there has been a belated realisation, at both EC and national level, that consumer policy is not a luxury but rather an essential element of overall EU policy development. (ibid.:2–3)

This mini revolution in EU consumer affairs in recent years lies in stark contrast to Grant's assessment of a decade earlier that EU consumer policy was largely symbolic. At that time, Grant opined that European consumer groups were largely outsiders (Grant 1993). While that assessment was not shared by all other commentators at the time, it is fair to say that consumer groups have not been the catalyst for the sea change. The principal change catalyst has been the wider agendas of output legitimacy (a search for popular support for the EU through the impact of its policies), and the high, crisis, politics resulting from food safety problems, such as those over cattle and poultry. This resulted in the establishment of the EFSA in 2002, and the investment of responsibility in the Directorate General for Health and Consumer Protection (DG SANCO) for food safety along the entire food chain. Other safety crises, such as the discovery of phthalates in toys and infant equipment and their subsequent ban for use in this context, have also contributed to this development.

The search for output legitimacy issues include the high-profile targeting of particular consumer price issues, such as differential cross-border car prices, denied and late boarding of aircraft, and roaming charges for mobile phones used in a cross-border context. 'High politics' and a search for output legitimacy have done more to drive consumer policy to centre stage of the EU agenda than 40 years of continual effort by EU consumer organizations could. They have developed an agenda logic of their own, almost separate to that of wider consumer policy, following the discourse of 'consumer *protection*'. Elsewhere, consumer *policy* has largely been a story of incremental progression, and even potentially major catalysts such as mainstreaming and the Transatlantic Consumer Dialogue (TACD) have not lit the touch paper. This bears interesting comparison with more radical progression in the environmental domain because they share similar starting points of community action programmes (circa 1972), and some common development factors, including the embrace of the favourable 'citizen's first' discourse:

- *Mainstreaming.* Consumer policy was mainstreamed later (1997 Amsterdam Treaty; Article 153) than environmental policy (1992 TEU). Commission consumer policy papers continue to carry calls for more effective integration, contrasting sharply with the achievement of environmental policy (European Commission 2006b).

- *Institutional development and support.* In contrast with a history of significant and increasing funding for environmental policy, the annual EU consumer policy budget has declined relative to 1990. The environmental arena achieved DG status at a much earlier stage and has its own dedicated Directorate General, whereas consumer affairs only achieved DG status at a relatively late stage, and is incorporated within a Directorate General with a wider remit. There is around four times the level of support reserved for EU Environmental NGOs compared with consumer NGOs, and there has been no growth in funding for consumer NGOs in more than a decade. Consumer/Commission liaison fora have not progressed beyond dialogue and advisory status in over 40 years of operation. Consumer policy is somewhat submerged in a Council which also covers employment, social policy, and health, a re-organization decision taken without any prior consultation of consumer representatives (BEUC 2002a). Nonetheless, DG SANCO has witnessed substantial development of instruments with which to engage with civil society organizations in recent years, and in particular with the development of platforms in which companies have made public pledges which have the effect of advancing the consumer and health policy fields (Chapter 4). Nonetheless, the environment has had a 'social dialogue'-type mechanism for some time in the form of the European Partners for the Environment.
- *Different single-market dynamics.* Both areas acquired a firm legal basis for European-level actions as domains requiring action parallel to the single market and the use of QMV. While environmental policy took off around the time of the single-market programme and has enjoyed some radical development landmarks since, the single market was no radical launch paid for consumer policy, whose development has been more incremental and more dependent upon uneven crisis points. In environmental policy, progress has been made by 'leader countries' seeking to export their high-cost production conditions to 'laggard countries' via single-market measures. In consumer policy, the market advantage of high protection in consumer goods outweighed the competitive losses of higher production costs, giving leader countries the incentive to keep their market advantage to themselves (Young 1995).
- *Focus.* Consumer behaviour is more driven by the sharper focus of green considerations, whereas the constitution of a

'consumer' interest is more elusive. Consumer organizations have borrowed the discourse of environmental groups. Alliances between environmental and consumer groups have been driven more by environmental issues, such as the European Campaign for Clean Air, which brought together consumer, environmental, and public health organizations with a 'European Clean Air Campaign' to lobby for strict automobile standards (Webster 1998; see also Young and Wallace 2000).

- *Responsible agents.* While both agendas involve socializing the message 'it's good commercial sense for business', the construction of accompanying measures to enable and build consumer confidence in making cross-border transactions involves public authorities to build infrastructures rather than action that is within the gift of business to take. These infrastructures involve considerable transaction costs. While the adoption of standard currency measures (€, metrification, and labelling) has made cross-border transaction comparisons easier and some progress in reducing differentials has been made, variations are still considerable, and some sectors continue to confront consumers with trade barriers. Consumer and citizen organizations have helped the Commission to energetically confront these through 'whistle blowing'. The Commission has also supported from the consumer policy budget an EU-wide out-of-court complaints network for cross-border financial service issues, FIN-NET.

Differing degrees of centrality to business. Consumers engage the core operations of businesses in markets, and contesting business has been more difficult for consumer groups. Environmental agendas have been grafted on to business agendas by more mixed sources.

- *Collective action.* While the G10 has grown, the number of pure consumer policy-oriented organizations at EU level has shrunk to one (BEUC), and one concerned with input to technical standards bodies. BEUC is a confederation, whereas most of the environmental organizations are outreaches of wider movements, able to act quickly. There has been a considerable recent change in the landscape of EU consumer organizations in recent years. Three organizations have disappeared entirely, while another two have lost funding from the Commission. The Consumer Policy Programme continues to seek to increase the participation of consumer organizations in EU policymaking, despite nearly 50 years of institutionalized dialogue.

While BEUC is the sole European-level organization dedicated to the representation of consumer affairs in public policymaking, two further long-established organizations include consumer issues within their domain. One is a producer association of the co-operative movement (European Community of Consumer Cooperatives (EUROCOOP)) while another (Confederation of Family Organisations in the European Union (COFACE)) focuses more on family issues in its slimmed down format. A further organization at the technical level is the European Association for the Coordination of Consumer Representation in Standardisation (ANEC), established in 1995. ANEC was originally established within the structures of BEUC, and continues to operate from the same address, but is now an independent organization in its own right, and which includes other EU consumer organizations within its governance structure. It is substantially funded by the Commission, enabling it to employ nine staff, and involves 200 experts in the technical work of 60 European standards committees, deployed in a quite deliberate way to act as a counterweight to industry in them. These are concentrated in some of the most sensitive areas such as child and vehicle safety, as well as household appliances, and general services such as post, tourism, and road transport.

All of these organizations have supplemented their central resources by drawing upon those of its members, and BEUC has used this resource for particular needs. European Transparency Register data indicates that BEUC has an annual budget approaching €4 million, with 33 staff, as well as the ability to draw upon the substantial resources of its member organizations (the UK consumer organizations, for instance, employ around 400 staff). It has specialist organizational divisions responsible for legal affairs, food, health environment and safety, as well as departments for communications and training. These enable it to make a contribution to the detail of specific dossiers, enabling it to work across the range of issues in consumer affairs. Its relatively large legal department also equips it with the ability to handle conflictual relations where necessary (Wallace and Young 1997). There have been highly conflictual relations, with DG Agriculture (Young 1998), and with business interests, and in particular the pharmaceutical industry and automobile manufacturers. In the latter case, consumers have taken advantage of divisions among producer interests to form strategic alliances against the car companies with spare parts manufacturers and insurance companies (Young and Wallace 2000). Other automobile campaign activities have included press and publicity drives to publicize price differentials and trade barriers, whistle-blowing monitoring against individual manufacturers with DG Competition (Holmes and McGowan, cited in Young 1998), and in legal work, including supporting and working for referral of cases to the ECJ (Harlow and Rawlings 1992). BEUC has been a contributory factor to similar work within the Commission which has clearly had an impact on the car market.

BEUC has long been able to make a contribution to the detail of debate on particular issues. In a generalized sense, the consistency of its market orientation with those of core single-market objectives makes it easy to operate alongside its core partners in the Commission, although embracing members from high, and low, protection countries means that common platform building is not an easy task (Young 1998). BEUC meets each incoming Presidency, and enjoys regular meetings at the Director General level. BEUC went out of its way to welcome the Consumer policy strategy 2002–6, and has been involved in its delivery. A core of this strategy, and the Community action programme in consumer policy 2007–13, is capacity building for consumer organizations, and BEUC has delivered courses on Commission premises aimed at organizations from the new member states on subjects such as lobbying the EU institutions, paid by the EU institutions. The history of institutionalized dialogue on consumer affairs with the European Commission has not been altogether happy, with decisions slow in forthcoming, highly prone to compromise, and members reluctant to defend them. Infighting has characterized the history of institutionalized consumer consultative structures between the Commission and consumer organizations. The European Consumer Consultative Group (ECCG) comprises one member representing national consumer organizations from each member state, and one member from each European consumer organization (ANEC, BEUC). The Commission is free to ignore the decisions of, and rather little heed has been taken of them, or of those of its predecessors. Nonetheless, BEUC is represented in around 20 advisory committees across the Commission (Kirchner 2006).

Unsurprisingly, given its quest to represent civil society, the European Parliament has been a kindred force for consumer interests throughout its existence. Its high-status Internal Market and Consumer Protection Committee has taken on the mantle of its predecessor as a forceful promoter of consumer interests and a consistent critic of the Commission for its failings in the consumer policy field. Consumer organizations have been able to use this route as a means of inserting amendments into Parliamentary business, and BEUC's resources are heavily drawn upon by individual MEPs.

To a certain extent, the impact of the European institutions and consumer organizations upon each other has been mutually reinforcing. Consumer organizations have played a part in producing a general climate whereby consumer interests are taken into account at the European level, and European manufacturers have embraced consumer needs and desires through higher product standards. For influences in the other direction, the European institutions have played a part in improving consumer representation, at both national and European levels. Industry in Europe has become more oriented towards quality in the manufacture of products. The EU has been a contributory climate to this, with a General Product Safety Directive (1992; revised 2001), placing on manufacturers a duty to monitor marketed products for safety. Under the provisions of this directive, firms now have a duty to assess and investigate consumer complaints, to identify product batches and to sample-test marketed products, while legislators can remove any product from the market for up to a year. These factors indicate how far consumer issues have come on the EU agenda since their 'symbolic' days. Where there is unavoidable conflict with business interests, consumer organizations have been able to exploit the natural divisions between businesses. While the EU agenda has been driven more by individual crises incidents than by consumer organizations, the wider discourse of a 'citizen's Europe' has made it an easier climate for consumer organizations to operate in. This discourse has enabled consumer organizations to increasingly work together on an issue basis with environmental, citizen, and social organizations.

Social interests

The development of organized social interests at the EU level hinged upon the European Commission until the arrival of the European Social Platform in 1995. Many social NGOs originate from Commission initiatives aimed at creating a solid foundation for, and expansion of, European integration. The pattern of action in each case is very similar, with different outcomes. In the first instance, the Commission has taken the action of an initiative designed to create some momentum, such as a conference linked to a theme of the particular European Year of Action. Funds have been provided for a group by the Commission (sometimes historically on a doubtful legal basis), sometimes with little evaluation of the use to which funds have been put (Harvey 1995) other than the knowledge that a support structure would be in place to carry demands for integration to member states. These have tended to be in safe fields where member states would find the agendas difficult to openly resist calls for action despite them inevitably commencing a road leading to further European integration, such as equality for women, for people with disabilities, and actions in the anti-racism field. The establishment of Community action programmes provide a firm foundation of resources to create, and support to nurture, NGOs in the field capable of taking the cause direct to the doors of member states. Once this process is in place, the Commission then proposes the strategy of mainstreaming. This is followed by an attempt to insert the issue in the Treaty, enabling further action programmes. While the first 'best case' cause is being pursued, other, sometimes more difficult causes, are grouped together with the leading cause in a campaign for widely embracing action to be enabled under Treaty provisions. The 1997 Amsterdam Treaty provides a classic example of such a course of events. Following a sustained campaign by (then) DG V and social interest groups, told in further details below, Article 13 provided for 'appropriate action' to combat discrimination based on sex, racial or ethnic origin, religion or belief, disability, age, or sexual orientation.

Two further, linked, cases enable further exploration of the Commission/public interest axis in developing European integration, and provide classic examples of the role of DG Employment and Social Affairs in preparing the groundwork for, and building on, the Article 13 agreement in the Treaty of Amsterdam. They also demonstrate the limits to, and constraints of, Commission action in working with groups to develop European integration. To support the campaign for Article 13 in the Amsterdam Treaty, DG EMP (then DG V) proposed that 1997 be designated the European Year Against Racism. It added a €7 million funding package for projects in that year, including support for NGOs, the establishment of a European Monitoring Centre against Racism and Xenophobia, and a major network event in Brussels bringing together 130 anti-racism organizations to form the European Network Against Racism. The following year, 1998, with Article 13 safely in the Treaty, saw the Commission Action Plan against Racism, with 176 projects funded, and an attempt by DG V to introduce new legislation on mainstreaming (Guiraudon 2001).

The Commission's work on anti-racism dates from 1986. In support of this work, the Commission acted on an initiative of the Parliament to establish the (now defunct) European Union Migrants' Forum (EUMF) in 1991, actively intervening to shape the group's parameters and operations during its turbulent history (Geddes 2000; Guiraudon 2001). A later group was the Starting Line Group (SLG), a group of activist lawyers. SLG helped in the first instance by preparing a draft directive outlawing racial discrimination, modelled on the 1976 Equal Treatment Directive (Geddes 2000; Case and Givens 2010). While this was never implemented, post-Amsterdam SLG brought forward another proposal for a directive putting into effect the principle of equal treatment (Geddes 2000). Geddes comments:

> It is possible to detect the influence of the SLG's proposals on policy development within the Commission ... pro migrant lobbying at EU level has centred on the building of alliances between lobby groups and sympathetic EU institutions, particularly the Commission and the EP. (Geddes 2000:644–5)

Similarly, Case and Givens stress the impact of the SLG, but in particular, the support of the Parliament to do so, where there is a significant Intergroup on Anti-Racism and Diversity. The European Network Against Racism (ENAR), established in 1998 as an outcome from the 1997 European Year Against Racism, also claims some responsibility for the Commission launch of a new non-discrimination directive in 2008, covering aspects of discrimination beyond the workplace. ENAR is a core partner of a DG EMP-funded programme on 'promoting strategic litigation' that trains NGOs to identify test cases to bring forward which seem likely to push forward the frontiers of EU policy competencies in the field (Case and Givens 2010).

A similar pattern of Commission activism is evident from the case of homelessness, although the outcome has not resulted in an extension of EU competencies. In 1989 the Commission used a generous interpretation of a general clause in the Treaty of Rome (improving quality of life) to fund a conference on homelessness and housing provision. This was a subject in which there are very few EU competencies, and the conference was funded in the hope of kick-starting initiatives and finding a more permanent demand constituency that would be a supporting measure for European integration. It invested some effort into the creation of a group that emerged from the conference, the European Federation of National Organisations Working with the Homeless (FEANTSA). The Commission found useful things for FEANTSA to do, such as designating it with official 'observatory' status to supply it with information on the state of homelessness in Europe. The example is a highly typical one of each of the stages and the specific measures taken by the Commission to work with NGOs as agents of integration. Yet, almost two decades later, beyond the generation of reams of information, neither the Commission nor FEANTSA has much to show by way of changes to EU competencies in the housing field, other than generalized credit among a specialized community for taking forward a social measure.

The FEANTSA case lends support to an alternative interpretation, of the Commission–social NGO relationship as a 'frothy' one, generating much noise but little by way of hard achievement. While DG Employment and Social Affairs has rolled out programme after programme in social fields, with measures such as anti-racism and anti-poverty, the impact is little more than symbolic. The anti-poverty programmes, for instance, had a budget of €55 million over a 5-year period, supporting small-scale 'pilot projects', research, and networking needs of interests groups, in the context of an estimated 50 million plus EU citizens being trapped in poverty. DG V provided funding of €7 million in 1999 to fund anti-racist activities (Guiraudon 2001). In this view, actions such as 'theme years' of 'Solidarity Between Generations', 'Anti-Racism', 'Languages', and 'Sport' have been empty shells.

'Social Europe' has its origins as a series of measures adjunct to the single market. Until the Commission Green Paper on Social Policy in 1993, 'Social Europe' in 'Euro-speak' meant workers' rights. The soundest legal basis in the Treaties for 'social policy', until Article 13 of the 1997 Amsterdam Treaty became the gatekeeper for more traditional social policy, arose from measures to ensure a level playing field in production between the member states in the single market. Thus, the Treaty of Rome contained provisions for equal treatment of men and women, social security for migrant workers, and health and safety of workers, which came to be governed by QMV by later Treaty changes (Wendon 1997). In fields that could easily be related to employment, such as equal opportunities, training, exclusion from the labour market, disability, and protection and movement of workers, the Commission has had little trouble in developing and funding programmes and initiatives. Interest groups in the fields of women's rights, young people, disabilities, and refugees became well established and resourced, and well embedded into their patron's corners of the Commission. A caveat is that each of the fields spawned multiple organizations working within them, despite the presence of leader organizations. One of these examples concerns the representation of women, where a combination of circumstances makes it another 'most likely scenario' case to consider the impact of public interest groups on European integration.

The mixture of the EU labour market focus, an irresistible policy frame of equality, a committed patron, a strong network of grassroots organizations, and the ability to work in institutionalized politics combines to create a favourable set of circumstances for EU women's organizations. The Commission and the ECJ have become powerful institutional advocates of EU equal opportunities policies (Mazey 2000), and the women's movement has long been embedded within DG Employment and Social Affairs (Mazey and Richardson 1999). The European Women's Committee was among the first advocacy organizations to emerge, in 1984, created by a group of women working in the European Commission, seeking to build upon dramatic successes achieved in the European Court of Justice arising from the 1976 *Defrenne* case. Once again, the Commission was the first and main activist on the EU scene, and funded conferences the first vehicle for action. These factors gave rise to a series of densely organized European women's advocacy and network organizations covering a variety of niches, with, by 2010, around 55 women's organizations currently active at EU level. The lead organization, EWL, was itself formed in 1990 from a coalition of traditional and radical feminist groups. Its member organizations, comprising organizations in 30 countries and 21 European-wide networks, themselves embrace 2500 member organizations. It uses this network to undertake EU public education campaigns in the member states, undertaking 'roadshows' to explain the potential impact of new Treaties, and satellites its board meetings around different national venues. These efforts make it notable among the wider constituencies of EU interest groups by seeking to engage with citizenry direct and popular within the EU institutions, particularly within DG Employment where it is heavily institutionalized (Mazey 2000). A past secretary general of the EWL who went on to work in the Commission has reflected that its 'survival and effectiveness depend on friendly individuals inside the European Parliament and Commission' (Helfferich and Kolb 2000:148). The expected close relationship between the EWL and the Women's Committee of the European Parliament has been confirmed by Cullen (1999).

At a very early stage, the Commission established a Women's Employment and Equality Office inside the Employment and Social Affairs Directorate responsible for policy promotion and co-ordination (Harlow and Rawlings 1992), and which later became the Equal Opportunities unit (Pollack 1997). Gender equality at work came under QMV rules at the TEU, while the Treaty of Amsterdam introduced a number of significant new gender equality initiatives, including provisions applying beyond the labour market, gender mainstreaming, and a new provision for equal pay for work of equal value (Helfferich and Kolb 2000). A number of other gender equality provisions were also reinforced, such as those enabling member states to take 'positive actions' in the labour market and anti-discrimination provisions. Helfferich and Kolb remark that Treaty amendments passed to extend gender equality at the Amsterdam Treaty were

> at least partly the result of a co-ordinated lobbying campaign of the European women's movement spearheaded by the EWL. (Helfferich and Kolb 2000:143)

and that the EWL was

> one of the few European public interest groups in the social policy field that was successful in having its demands taken by the governmental representatives negotiating the new Treaty ... the active campaigning of the EWL was crucial for the extent of the changes. (ibid.:144, 147)

According to these authors, EWL's Spanish member convinced the Spanish government to adopt EWL positions as their own, and from there got the position into Treaty negotiations. The authors do specify that 'the final outcome would fall well short of the Lobby's expectation, but it was nevertheless greeted as a success by the organisation' (ibid.). A further, stronger dose of caution should be added to the interpretation reached by the authors, in that the story is told by a former secretary general of the EWL at the time of the 'campaign', who claims that the EWL went 'one step further than the other groups working on the treaty revisions' (p. 156). Just as the ERT was not the prime agent responsible for the single market, neither was EWL single-handedly responsible for the Article 13 measure in the Treaty. The authors do acknowledge that the 'campaign' came at the right time, when there was considerable concern within elite circles that there might be a repeat of the TEU scenario and a rejection of the Amsterdam Treaty. Other authors, too, have lent a similar interpretation. Mazey has argued that women's organizations have been important agents in the adoption of mainstreaming strategies in EU and member states. Using similar arguments to those presented by Helfferich and Kolb, Mazey has highlighted the importance of mobilizing networks and 'political opportunity structures', and draws upon her earlier work to outline the importance of a sympathetic 'policy frame' in the relevant DG in determining the degree to which mainstreaming has had an impact (Mazey 2000).

The European Commission has successively launched 5-year strategy programmes for equality between men and women. The CSCG claims that the adoption of the 2006–10 programme arose from lobbying by the European Women's Lobby, noting that

> it covers approximately the same areas as the EWL Roadmap and contains some of the same vision and strategies for gender equality, although the official measures foreseen are not as strong, far reaching, and precise as the ones suggested by the EWL text. (CSCG 2006:17)

Similarly, in 2010 the EWL issued a press release in which it 'welcomed the launch of the EU's much anticipated new 5-year strategy for equality between men and women', noting in particular how 'women's rights groups are positive towards the envisaged annual top-level Gender Equality Dialogue amongst key stakeholders and stress the importance of the presence of key women's organizations at such fora' (EWL 2010). The latter is a further reference to the continued institutionalization of EWL, with the dialogue involving, inter alia, the Parliament, Commission, Member States, Council Presidencies, and the EWL.

Social movements

The increasing engagement of the European Union by 'social movements' has been viewed in a more or less hopeful way by a number of commentators (Tarrow 2006; della Porta 2007; Erne 2009). Della Porta claims that

> it is possible to already delineate some elements of an emerging European movement, in which a set of organizations and discourses are interwoven in extremely flexible organizational structures, with identities that are tolerant of difference. Common denominators of such mobilizations that seem anything but a passing fad include demands for social rights and a democratization of European institutions, not least through the creation of a supranational, critical public sphere. (della Porta 2007:205)

Such movements appear to be drawn more from globally oriented activism rather than national origins (Tarrow 2006), ironically mainly to the theme of 'anti-globalization'. A common feature of 'new social movements' is their 'alternative' perspectives'. Leigh cites the way in which Anheir, Kaldor, and Glasis characterize this as

> an experiment in and demonstration of new ways of living and new types of social relations – non-hierarchical and consensus-based. (Leigh 2009:5)

A key issue concerns the point at which – and whether – a distinction can be drawn between organizations which are 'social movements' and those which are part of the 'usual circuit' of Brussels-based institutionalized NGOs. A usual caricature is that between advocacy 'insiders' to activist 'outsiders' (Tarrow 2006), ranging from institutionalized charities headed by royal patrons through to the ATTAC (Association for the Taxation of Transactions for the Aid of the Citizen) network and beyond to 'loosely affiliated anarchists' at the other extreme (Hadden 2009:13). There are normative overtones conveyed by labels such as 'new' social movements, or idealized juxtapositions between 'professionalized and bureaucratized associational civil servants' on the one hand, and 'radical' organizations populated by 'grassroots activists' (Saurugger 2009) pursuing 'the politics of the street' (ref.). This is to some extent also evident in Saurugger's definition of a social movement as

> collective challenges to existing arrangements of power and distribution by people with common purposes and solidarity in sustained interaction with elites, opponents and authorities. (ibid:8)

A key point is the extent to which the activities of such actors contribute to, or detract from, EU legitimacy. Is, for instance, the occupation of business association offices (there were such incidents at CEFIC, and ERT) by activists to be interpreted as a positive sign of engagement and populating the public space with debate? Erne claims that 'most political scientists concur that social actors contribute to Euro-democratization if they contribute to the rise of a European public sphere' (Erne 2009:2). He argues that

> social actors contribute to Euro-democratization if they contribute to the making of a European public sphere, act collectively on a European level, and politicize the EU integration process in the transnational European public sphere. (Erne 2009:4)

Hadden takes a critical view of the message that 'any engagement is a positive contribution to legitimacy by creating a public space' on the basis of an assessment of the activities and perspectives of 37 organizations and a variety of activists. She casts the perspectives of 'radical' organizations based around anti-globalization lenses as potentially de-legitimizing for an EU seen by such activists as broadly pro-liberal. Her analysis confirmed the presence of two distinctive segments of actors at EU level, split between 'conventional' actors and those that use 'contentious actions', with organizations such as Greenpeace acting in a brokering role as a bridge between these two worlds (Hadden 2009). Nonetheless, some organizations are forced to play the institutionalized game by the need for policy advocacy and funding (Leigh 2009; see also Sikkink 2002). There are also 'hybrid' cases where 'protest and institutionalized contention go hand in hand, with some actors among civil society pursuing dual strategies' (Crespy 2009:16). The European Social Forum has been a venue for these various types of players to meet, with participants balanced more towards 'outsider' than 'insider' organizations (della Porta 2007). The Forum has met on a more or less bi-annual basis since shortly after the 'battle of Seattle', but there are preparatory meetings four times yearly with up to 400 activists present at events (Doerr 2009).

Ruzza shows how social movements have found a niche which fulfils a variety of functions they need to meet (Ruzza 2011). They become 'norm entrepreneurs' at EU level, bringing ideas into the EU environment and contributing to otherwise limited understanding of issues, as well as providing a voice for otherwise marginalized parts of civil society, and a check and balance upon producer-oriented lobbies. Sometimes they put forward an often utopian vision of desirable policy change that other more moderate organizations can utilize as a negotiating standard. Characterizing a type of organization which lie somewhere between traditional social movements, and institutionalized actors in the political system, he moves beyond traditional caricatures of once independently minded organizations whose destiny is to become progressively institutionalized and removed from their grassroots origins. He identifies a set of intermediate organizational forms that retain some of the features of social movements but have also acquired some of those distinctive of NGOs, including a degree of professionalization, service delivery roles, and better legal skills. Direct representation arises through organizations which are part of the social movement 'family', such as Greenpeace and Friends of the Earth, but who can also play the 'institutional politics' game, apparently without too much compromise or tension (Ruzza 2011). These 'broker' organizations are highly skilled in alliance-building; they were key agents in the formation of the ALTER-EU alliance in the creation of the European Transparency Register (Chapter 3), and where required they build alliances with producer organizations for common cause campaigns, such as genetically modified organisms (GMOs) (Parks 2009a). The ability to create alliances with producer constituencies is also a noted skill of WWF, considered earlier in this chapter.

Protest and direct action have always been the traditional tools of 'outsider' movements, now facilitated, empowered, and extended by the use of 'cyberactivism' (Thomas 2004). The key point is that the internet allows activists to find and communicate with each other, allows activists to engage in attacks on the IT domains of opponents ('hacktivism'), and provides an unprecedented platform for mobilization and broader public communication. The latter has been used in a way which is oriented towards public accountability of either political institutions or opponents, influencing public

policy through public message, and by confronting opposing interests. Websites are carefully constructed in a way to attract the casual
browser, using satire as a weapon (Balme and Chabanet 2008),
aimed at striking chords with populist outlooks about the influence
of finance in politics.

At EU level, these activities have been used in a way to de-legitimize
the EU polity (Balme and Chabanet 2008), with opposition to the
European services directive proposed by Commissioner Bolkestein
a particular rallying point, and a means of connecting with institutionalized NGO actors in the EU system. Crespy notes how

> [t]he Bolkestein Directive therefore constitutes a hybrid case where
> protest and institutionalised contention go hand in hand, with
> some actors among civil society pursuing dual strategies. (Crespy
> 2009:16)

Of significance is that mobilization on the Services Directive was
particularly aimed at the European Parliament (Fazi and Smith
2006), making the direct connection between citizens and their
representative organization. This aspect also drew in traditionally
'outsider' organizations to institutionalized EU public policymaking
(Crespy 2009; Parks 2009a). This included groups such as ATTAC,
who also became drawn in during the early days of dialogue with
DG Trade and during the Convention period drafting the constitutional treaty, and through the ALTER-EU alliance (Chabanet 2006)
(Chapter 3).

Conclusion

The breadth and depth of citizen interest mobilization at EU level
is substantial. New organizations are constantly emerging to fill
advocacy causes and niches, now extending to embrace social movements. 'Family' organizations and networks of cognate NGOs have
emerged with purposeful co-ordination and a division of labour
between them. A range of issue alliances across segments demonstrate the presence of a 'citizen interest community'.

Of the three segments of citizen interests reviewed in this chapter,
environmental interests appear to be the most organized, related
not only to the resources upon which they can draw but also to the
breadth and range of advocacy organizations and the niches they
fill, the structures which link them together, and the power of the

environmental discourse in Europe. Their impact can be demonstrated not only in fields of agenda-setting but some way beyond. Niche organizations in the social/citizen field are by now also highly established, as well as institutionalized. Whether organizations which receive more than three quarters of their funding from the EU political institutions are well placed to help political systems develop input legitimacy will always remain an open question. However, a new development since the last edition of this book has been the diversification of funding sources for NGOs. Consumer affairs present a slightly different story, although the main NGO in the field is very well resourced. Here, significant policy landmarks have arisen not from agenda-setting by consumer groups but from crisis events involving food or consumer product safety, and from the quest by EU institutions for output legitimacy through the pursuit of populist measures, such as regulating cross-border mobile phone roaming charges.

Together, a whole range of issues arise from this chapter for the democratic legitimacy of the EU, and particularly the extent to which the activities of interest organizations as well as engagement of the EU by social movements can be a route to the democratic legitimacy of the EU. These are considered in Chapter 8.

Chapter 7

Territorial Interests

The focus of this chapter concerns sub-national, regional, and local interest representations at the European level, which are dominated by the perspectives of territorial public authorities. Much of the 'hype' of one to two decades ago about regions becoming a 'third level' of EU multi-level governance (to member states and supranational institutions) has long since evaporated. Much of this hype seemed aspirational, and it is notable that the subject field attracted contributions from writers originating from or based in countries where there have been significant issues of regional conflicts or at least a history of centre–regional issues, such as Belgium, Scotland, Italy, Germany, and Spain. It seems somewhat doubtful that arrangements for some countries to be represented by regional entities in specific discussions in the Council of Ministers, and for regions to be partners in policy instruments, 'have transformed the European Union from a primarily state centric system of authority into a system of multi level governance' (Hooghe 2002:370–1). The slogan of a 'Europe of the Regions' gradually gave way to 'Europe with the Regions' (Hooghe 1995) to one of, at best, 'Europe with … some of … the regions'. Yet, incremental developments in territorial interest representation continue to yield a succession of issues surrounding the presence of the 'Brussels offices of the regions'. These are reviewed in turn.

Since its establishment, the Committee of the Regions (CoR) has disappointed the principal movers behind its formation by failing to progress beyond advisory status or to find a significant niche for itself. A promising window in the 2001 White Paper on Governance, which briefly offered 'radical decentralisation' as a forthcoming EU agenda, melted into timidity (Metcalfe 2001). There has not been the development of a significant 'by-pass' route for the 'regional lobby' around member states (Sutcliffe and Kovacev 2005), and notable is that, in general, the greatest recipients of structural funds have been the least represented among the 'Brussels offices of the regions'. As is reviewed later, some of these offices have limited roles which are constrained by national and regional restrictions. Brussels has become another venue for the respective players to act out domestic centre/regional relations struggles, rather than radically reforming centre–local relations struggles (John 2000b; Schultze 2003; Fleurke and Willemse 2006). In some circumstances the 'regional lobby' has been a means for the Commission to pursue its ends with member states (John 2000a), and the history of regional interest lobbying is littered with examples of local government organizations misunderstanding the basic ways in which the EU takes decisions in fields which influence them (see, for instance, Greenwood et al. 1995; John and McAteer 1998). As is reviewed below, some regions established offices in Brussels without any clear purpose in mind at all, although some of those which have been left to find useful things to do have developed significant agendas.

But despite the absence of dramatic new developments, incremental changes have strengthened the hand of regional governance players. An EU-oriented network organization of regions with legislative authority emerged from the 2000 Intergovernmental Conference, REGLEG, which claims to have influenced recognition of the concept of a region with legislative powers in a European Council Declaration of that year. There has been the progressive extension of decentralization in some member states, and where decentralization has arisen it has increased the capacity of regions to make the centre accountable in the implementation of EU regional policy. Devolution has not, however, increased the number of staff working on EU activities by local authorities (Sutcliffe and Kovacev 2005). As is described later in this chapter, while some of the 'peak' associations of regional and local government have not progressed their role and influence, some of the sectoral regional associations have done so. Thus, those representing cities, peripheral maritime regions, and areas dependent on traditional industries have grown in resources and capacity and in the ability to influence some of the smaller structural fund programmes. Most regional and local authorities of any size are involved in the implementation of cohesion policies.

The number of regions directly represented in Brussels has continued to grow, with an extract from a listing provided by the Committee of the Regions yielding a total of 216 (Committee of the Regions 2009). As is described later, some of the offices from the Federal Länder, and the autonomous communities of Spain, are now impressively large affairs. A highly dense collection of thematic networks of regions has emerged from the EU structural fund programmes, and particularly the Community initiatives. These have added to the ability of the Commission to monitor whether structural funds are getting past the hands of central government to their intended targets and whether the rules are being adhered to. Environmental organizations have also assisted in this role (Chapter 6).

In practice, distinctions between territorial public authorities and territorially based interests are difficult to make because territorial public authorities work to attract, promote, and protect key private interests within their domain. For this reason, public authorities have been specifically exempted from the need to make an entry on the European Transparency Register; yet in a significant change to the operation of the scheme, some representative offices of territorial authorities to the EU are expected to register in the new scheme, reflecting the embrace of such offices as a channel of diverse types of interest representation (Chapter 3). Indeed, the levels of complexity involved in territorial interest representation are perhaps greatest of all because a territorial level can be a channel of influence for private interests, and a set of interests within itself, and because what constitutes a region means different things in different member states. The Committee of the Regions (CoR) is both a decision-making structure for regions and a source of interest representation in its own right. Collective action issues applicable to other actors do not arise in the same way for territorial public authorities because they are a distinct level of governance, sometimes intertwined with national interests, sometimes separate, and with a whole range of competencies and interests. Indeed, the territories of the regions comprise the entire EU itself and there is economic competition between them, and, to an extent, for regional funding initiatives. However, there are also a number of reasons to collaborate and territorial authorities do work both individually and collectively to pursue their interests in the EU, spanning both formal and informal varieties. The ambiguity over whether their activities are considered as 'interest representation' in the EU system is reflected in the rule for the current scheme that public authorities of any kind are not expected to register, and in the draft rules for the amended forthcoming scheme that certain kinds of EU representative offices from the territories are expected to register.

Regional governance in western Europe

Various typologies of member state decentralization exist, most of which pre-date the accession of Central and East European (CEE) countries (Leonardi and Nanetti 1990; Leonardi 1993; Bullmann 1997; Schneider 2003; Mamadouh 2001; Keating and Hooghe 2006; Hooghe et al. 2010). These have developed progressively more complex elements to them and include EU 'NUTS' (Nomenclature of territorial units for statistics) data. They also incorporate criteria which reflect the position in central and eastern European countries (Swianiewicz 2002) but in essence break down into a variant of a 'high, medium, low' axis embracing political and administrative decentralization (Table 7.1).

Most countries in the 'low' category have been major recipients of EU structural funds, including those from central and eastern European countries, as well as traditionally centralized countries such as Greece, Portugal, and Ireland. The latter created 'administrative' 'paper' regions for the purpose of conforming to structural fund rules (Hooghe and Marks 1996).

This differential degree of regional autonomy conditions the response of territorial interests to the European level. Where there is high regional autonomy, the EU has strengthened it. For instance, Article 203 of the Treaty on European Union enabled regional governments to represent and vote for their country in the Council, an instrument used to varying degrees by the countries with the most significant regional powers. At the other extreme, the position of member states as the gatekeeper of structural fund applications and the disburser of funds enhances its control in centre–local relations, and 'regions' in the most centralized states, where they exist, are little more than paper entities.

Table 7.1   *Degrees of devolved authority in the EU member states*

Predominate classification category	Country
High	Austria, Belgium, Germany, Spain
Medium	Denmark, Finland, Italy, Netherlands, Sweden, UK
Medium to low	France, Poland
Low to medium	Hungary, Czech Republic
Low	Other EU member states

Data from: Leonardi 1993; Loughlin, in Mamadouh 2001; Mamadouh 2001; Keating and Hooghe 2006.

Beyond these factors lie other complexities. In some federal, quasi-federal, and mixed devolution countries, there is also considerable control by central government over EU regional policy issues (John 2000a). However, in countries where regions have gained powers viz. the centre, there has been a weakening of the centre's absolute ability to dominate aspects of the interface with EU regional policy initiatives. For instance, regions had the power to agenda-set 'additionality' disputes (issues surrounding the requirement for matching funds for EU grants in member states) to significant levels (John 1996; McAleavy 1994; Greenwood et al. 1995; Bache 1999). In Wales, this led to a chain of events contributing to the resignation of the first Minister and to the release of further funds for Wales, while a central government junior Minister also resigned as a way of raising the issue for his home region.

Concerns with uneven regional development were referred to in the preamble to the Treaty of Rome and were always a concern of the Coal and Steel Community. At the conclusion of the EU steel regime, a sectoral regional organization representing steel-dependent regions, CASTer, claims the credit for successfully obtaining the residue of this for spending on their constituencies (van der Storm 2002). The EIB, providing low-cost loans for major projects in and across the European regions, was formed in 1958. Measures to support regions with particular difficulties were thus present from this period, although not in the context of an overall regional policy because of the anticipation that the common market would automatically reduce regional disparities (McAleavy 1994). In the absence of such a scenario, regional policy initiatives developed slowly, though controversially, in the 1960s. These included a major conference on regional disparities in 1961, the addition of the ESF in 1961 and the Agriculture Guidance and Guarantee Fund (EAGGF) in 1964. Further measures taken during this start-up decade include the Commission's first regional policy memorandum to the Council in 1965, and the formation in 1968 of a Directorate General for Regional Development (Deeken 1993).

Regional policy took a quantum leap forward with the accession of the UK, which, as part of the accession negotiations, sought a 'pay-back' for its budget contributions in the shape of the availability of European-level regional funding programmes for its declining regions dependent upon traditional manufacturing activities. Italy, with its own marked regional disparities, had for some time also sought an active European-level regional policy. The result was the creation of the European Regional Development Fund in 1975, the major pillar of the structural funds, and a constituency of inter-ests seeking receipts from this fund formed by membership acces-sions in the 1970s and 1980s. These accessions of Ireland, Greece, Spain, and Portugal placed regional unevenness across the EEC in sharp relief. After a succession of reforms, particularly in 1988–9 and 1992–3, when these funds were doubled in absolute terms on both occasions, structural expenditure came to command approxi-mately a third of the entire budget of the European Union, a level at which it has reached a plateau. Further landmarks worthy of note in European regional policy include the establishment in 1988 of the Consultative Council of Regional and Local Authorities (CCRLA), annexed to (then) DG XVI of the European Commission, compris-ing representatives of regional and local authorities. In 1993, this was replaced by the Committee of the Regions.

The growth of the structural funds is largely related to the single-market project. Although there is no agreement on the regional economic impact of the single-market project, one interpretation was that it would concentrate economic development. Metaphors to capture this have included a 'golden triangle' between London, Paris, and Milan; a 'blue banana' (stretching through Frankfurt); and a 'brown doughnut' of peripheral regions largely excluded from the benefits of the single market (Armstrong 1995; Benington 1994). The concept is a somewhat contentious one, given the pres-ence of prosperous city regions on the so-called periphery, such as Aberdeen, Barcelona, Bordeaux, Copenhagen, Helsinki, and Stockholm. Nonetheless, the concept of the single market as a cata-lyst to geographically concentrate wealth is a plausible one, with a common interpretation being of the structural (regional) funds as a 'side-payment' to the poorer member states from wealthier countries in return for agreement for the single-market project (Moravcsik 1998, 2002). There is some evidence for aspects of the side-payment argument. Keating (1995) attributes Ireland's large positive vote for the Maastricht Treaty to the ability of that country to gain from the structural funds. A new Objective 6 for Arctic regions was created almost certainly with the intention of influencing the accession vote in the Nordic countries, only to later disappear in future rounds. However, the 'side-payment' explanation is weakened because the regional impact of the single market remains disputed; indeed, it is possible that peripheral regions will attract inward investment in Europe from firms shopping around for the lowest production costs. Marks (1992) therefore argues that the growth of the structural funds arose more because of the vulnerability of potential losers in the event that the single market does concentrate wealth in the core of Europe at the expense of the periphery.

EU competencies, rather than structural funds or a national 'by-pass', seem to explain the engagement of local authorities with the EU (Sutcliffe and Kovacev 2005). The liberal ethos of the single market seems to provide much of the explanation for the extent of growth in the European-level regional dimension. Apart from the uneven development caused by market forces, the single-market project involved a whole host of new or revitalized initiatives and competencies deeply impacting upon territorial authorities. Competition policy has outlawed protectionism. Public-procurement legislation has disrupted favoured local–supplier relationships between producers and territorial authorities. As employers, landowners, and monitoring, enforcing, and licensing bodies, local authorities are deeply affected by the range of competencies and activities of the EU. Martin (1993), for instance, estimated by 1993 that some 85% of trading standards legislation came from the EU, while some regional authorities estimate that 80% of the environmental legislation they work with originates in Brussels (Bavarian State Ministry 2006). To this list could be added issues concerned with transportation, local economic development, encouragement to local interests to participate in Europe by way of information and advice, technology transfer and research framework programmes, the supply of public utilities, transfer of undertakings, and anti-poverty initiatives. All these competencies have attracted some territorial interests to set up camp in Brussels and to network extensively, albeit, as is evident below, in a rather uneven pattern from across the EU.

Some regional alliances pre-date European competencies, whereas others have been stimulated as much by the encouragement of the European institutions themselves as by the presence of Euro competencies. The Commission and the Parliament, in particular, have encouraged alliances with regional interests, partly as a means of by-passing member states and reinforcing the authority of the central institutions. The 1988 reform of the structural funds established the notion of 'partnership' between territorial authorities and local interests, creating, enhancing, and/or institutionalizing local interest communities in the implementation of structural fund assistance. As is discussed later in this chapter, the Commission has enabled a dense series of trans-regional networks to form and develop through funding under its successive INTERREG and URBAN programmes, designed to support cross-border regional development and co-operation.

A major window of opportunity for regions came with the start of the White Paper on Governance process. The lack of progress with a 'Europe of the regions' agenda was one of the major issues identified in the original (October 2000) draft for the programme, offering the spectre of 'radical decentralization'. Of the six work areas chosen to embrace the governance concept, territorial interests were central to two, including the decentralization of European executive responsibilities to territorial tiers of governance, and the 'open method of co-ordination' with tiers of national and regional governance. One working group focused on decentralization involving regional and local actors, and another on networking regional and local levels. Upgrading the role of the Committee of the Regions was one of the themes, alongside a greater reliance upon regional and local authorities in policy provision and enforcement. The report from the team to the College noted that the strongest reaction to this initial agenda was from local and regional players, talking up their 'underrated involvement' and 'dynamism' (European Commission 2001c:4). All the major associations identified in the sections below made an input, taking the opportunity to try to 'beef up the regional agenda'.

The final White Paper proved a disappointment for regional actors (Metcalfe 2001). The process was long on analysis (such as the need for better interaction with regional and local government, and more involvement of them in the EU policy process) and short on solutions. The recommendations themselves were insubstantial, such as using regional authorities as a channel of communication, and reminders of previous decisions such as a more decentralized approach to regional policy. The regional agenda became subsumed under the wider heading of 'coherence', with generalized principles, such as establishing a more systematic dialogue at an early stage with regional and local actors, and flexibility to take account of local conditions. The Committee of the Regions was urged to do better by being more proactive and organize best practice, and to review and report back. Member states were told that the principal responsibility for involving regions and local authorities in EU policymaking lay with them, blamed for not adequately involving them in preparing their positions, and told to listen to regional and local experiences. They were told that they should promote the use of contractual arrangements with their regions and localities. Promises included little more than examining how transnational coopera- tion of regional or local actors could be better supported. However, while the paper disappointed and the agenda melted into the Future of Europe debate, the wider climate of raising the issues is likely to come downstream in some future agenda initiatives for regional and local actors. For the moment, however, the process has disappointed many, and did not re-launch the enthusiasm of a 'third level' of EU policymaking from a decade ago.

The organization of territorial public interests at the European level

Sub-national territorial public authorities engage the European level directly in a number of ways. There are multiple access points. The first 'channel' to consider is institutional sources. Some regions play a role in national representation through the Council of Ministers, though the arrangements depend upon the delegation of author- ity by the member state concerned. While this mainly involves federal-type states, it has occasionally involved member states where a region has an intense interest in a particular issue (Scotland has represented the UK in fisheries discussions in the Council of Ministers). Another forum for ministerial contact, albeit outside the framework of the EU, is through the Council of Europe, which has a secretariat and forum for the regions, the Congress of Local and Regional Authorities of Europe (CLRAE), first established in 1957. This forum discusses matters concerned with local and regional authorities throughout Europe and submits advice and opinions to the Council's Committee of Ministers and Parliamentary Assembly; organizes public hearings on local and regional matters of interest; is active in town twinning; maintains close relations with conferences of European Ministers responsible for questions of local adminis- tration; and maintains direct contact with the EU within the frame- work of the relations established between the Council of Europe and the EU. In 1986 it opened a joint office with the International Union of Local Authorities (IULA), as a means of engaging the EC (Keating 1995).

In the Commission, the foremost regional structure is the Directorate General for Regional Policy, which has developed strong links with regional and local authority interests. As major employ- ers, a number of territorial interests have also developed good links with DG Employment and Social Affairs, while the peak public sector employers' organization, the CEEP, is a 'first-level', or 'macroeconomic' social partner (Chapter 2). The Parliament also contains a natural constituency of interests in regional affairs, and it was this institution which proposed the establishment of the CCLRA, the predecessor to the CoR. The Parliament has a dedicated Committee on Regional Development. Whilst individual members of the CoR have to hold a regional or local authority mandate (since the Treaty of Nice), the selection of members rests in the authority of member state governments. This means that territorial authorities have no formal role in EU representative democracy, despite their roles as elected entities in their own territories, but take their place among other types of interests in the EU's participatory democracy stream (Piattoni 2011).

Some regions have sought to create an overt sense of identity for communities of officials working in, and interfacing with, the European institutions, such as directory books of citizens from a particular region working in Brussels, or have sought to capitalize upon the regional identity of commissioners. Most, if not all, regional and local authorities of any size have appointed European officers to manage the EU interface. Most territorial public authorities of any size have set up their own Brussels offices, and/or participated in formal and informal trans-regional networks in Europe. The latter two strategies are considered in detail below.

The Brussels offices of the regions

The Brussels offices of the regions embrace considerable diversity, from ministries of federal regions staffed by civil servants through to economic development agencies through to membership associations of territorial civil society organizations. Table 7.2 identifies the number of 'regional offices' by country.

The diverse population of (a shade over 200) offices from the regions in Brussels range: from representations tied to a regional government; collaborative arrangements of territorial authorities for Brussels representation; and membership services offices which are public private partnerships, and sometimes open to subscription for entities from a region. There have also been a very small number of cross-border trans-regional offices, although these have waned since first arriving on the scene in the early 1990s. The traditional 'diet' of activities which the Brussels offices of the regions perform

Table 7.2 *Territorial representation offices in Brussels*

	Sub-national territorial general entities
Germany	21
Austria	7
Belgium	9
Bulgaria	2
Cyprus	0
Denmark	5
Spain	22
Estonia	1
Finland	8
France	20
Greece	0
Hungary	5
Ireland	1
Italy	23
Lithuania	0
Latvia	1
Netherlands	14
Poland	18
Portugal	0
Romania	0
UK	29
Slovakia	8
Sweden	9
Czech Republic	12
Croatia	0
Iceland	0
Macedonia	1
Total	216

Data extracted from: Committee of the Regions (2009).

includes: acting as a two way conduit for information between their territories and EU institutions; policy input and lobbying for territorial authorities and the specific interests they have, or for interests within a territory; and (facilitating, and in some cases conducting) project work linking regions supported by EU funding.

The emergence and development of the Brussels territorial offices

Offices from the regions started to appear in Brussels in the mid-1980s, rising to 170 in 2001 (Mamadouh 2001). In the Marks et al. survey of 2002, offices from Germany, Austria, Belgium, and Spain spent an average of €447,000 each year, with single regional offices from these countries occupying up to 1000 m^2 space (Marks et al. 2002). The Brussels offices of the German Länder together employ more staff than are employed in the German permanent representation (Moore 2006); the office of Bavaria, operating from its notable 'chateau', is the largest, with over 30 staff. The lowest quartile of all offices in the Marks et al. survey were, unsurprisingly, from countries without powerful territorial authorities, operating with budgets of less than €150,000 and floor space of less than 80 m^2, sometimes where a small group of localities in the same region share the resource of part of the time of one person. Because regions from 2004 and 2007 accession countries have a tradition in which regional devolved authority is typically low, so this is reflected in a relatively small population of Brussels offices. However the most established case is that of Poland, where the 18 administrative regions from Poland are the most represented, with staff capacities of up to three. The most recent arrivals on the scene are from the candidate member states.

In part, the Brussels territorial representations have followed predictable EU milestones in the development of regional policy, including the Committee of the Regions, Treaty agreements on subsidiarity, the possibility of representation of member states by regional government in the Council of Ministers, and a variety of funding instruments. But underlying such general stimuli was a lack of specific focus as to how regions could specifically engage with these. The establishment of a Brussels office reflected more general concerns about being where the action was (Huysseune and Jans 2008), having a status symbol, 'flying the regional flag', or an 'arms race' with competitor regions. These generalized stimuli offered little guidance as to what to do once an office had been established, so it could be a case of 'finding things to do', hoping to attract support constituencies along the way which would help keep offices going. Where this was not forthcoming, offices disappeared from the Brussels scene, creating an ever-changing population.

The desire to be better positioned to access EU funding, or as a means to support political claims for credit when funds were dispersed, appeared to be a motivation behind the establishment of some of the early offices. For many countries, however, the reality is that member states are the principal gatekeepers of EU regional fund applications, deciding which regions to submit for various schemes ahead (Greenwood et al. 1995). An initial orientation towards the structural funds became supplemented by more focused agendas, whether in stimulating new cross-national networks, addressing poor information flows from federal ministries (Knodt 2002), or a policy orientation (Marks et al. 2002). Tatham argues that

> all the Brussels offices are not playing the same game. While most 'second league' regions are usually hunting for European projects, funds and subsidies, 'first league' regions seek to influence European public policy itself.   (Tatham 2008:508)

Among the 'first league' regions, Brussels had become a venue in ongoing power struggles in member state politics between the centre and the regions. This came to a head in constitutional court cases during the 1990s surrounding the establishment of offices from the German Länder, the Spanish Communidad Autonomas, and Italian regions with special domestic status. In these countries, the presence of regional offices in Brussels raised substantial national sensitivities about who had the right of external representation, In each of these countries there were cases referred to the national constitutional court seeking to establish whether a regional 'representation' in Brussels was compatible with national law. Offices from the German Länder consequently chose low-key names in the early days, such as 'liaison bureau'. When a formal legislative instrument providing the right to liaise directly with EU institutions (for 'inner-state' tasks, not as a 'diplomatic mission') was made in 1993, so the names did also, with most (though not all) choosing the name 'Representation' (Moore 2006), emphasized by the use of titles such as the 'Free State of'. Similarly, from Spain (Case STC/1654/94) and Italy (Law 52 of 1996; Case 428 of 1997), territorial offices in Brussels initially had to operate under a 'camouflage' (e.g. a chamber of commerce or specialized agency) (Badiello 1998). Today, the Communidad Autonomas (or their proxies) have substantial representations in Brussels, including names such as the 'Autonomous Government of …'. Regional authorities from Germany and Spain have established arrangements between them for the co-ordination of input to the Council of Ministers.

The extent of tension in issues of centre–regional relations which these cases reveal from member states with highly devolved territorial models also informed the deployment of staff. This involves the secondment of regional government employees to Brussels outlet offices, working to highly prescribed agendas including monitoring central government, with limited autonomy to develop other activities. For the German Länder it has been a common arrangement to send civil servants to their Brussels office for a period of 2–3 years (Moore 2006), and have an authority staff member working in Germany to 'shadow' the work of a counterpart in the Brussels office working on the same dossier (Badiello 1998), measures which would help prevent Brussels staff from 'going native'. The regional offices from Italy employ a mixed model of office staffing based on a core of 'civil servants' sent by, and tied to, the regional authority, but sometimes supplemented by a number of more independent 'consultants' recruited from the pool of EU specialists in the Brussels job market where specific projects are involved.

Another model again is where a diverse set of stakeholders equips Brussels territorial representative offices to be able to take up and pursue a wide range of initiatives. Scotland Europa, for instance, includes within its membership the Scottish Trades Union Congress, the Scottish Environmental Protection Agency, Scottish Natural Heritage, the General Medical Council Scotland, and has recently included the Scottish Council for Voluntary Organisations. The Dutch 'G4' (large cities) office also offers a model whereby the influence of any one stakeholder is diluted. Where the territorial offices have been less tied to specific constituencies, they have tended to recruit staff from the Brussels pool of 'EU experts'. For instance, the Committee of the Regions (COR) repertoire lists 17 individuals leading the Brussels offices of UK regions (from 69 listed – i.e. around one quarter) who bear non-British names, and who have been recruited from the 'Brussels circuit' rather than from the ranks of the regional/local authorities themselves. Such staff have a

European orientation, are highly networked, and tend to have interests in working on issues which are related to building European integration, rather than tied to a remit of a 'principal' which is a sending authority. In this model, those who lead the offices have a greater freedom to manoeuvre, and the space to develop self-generated agendas which they can 'sell' to their own 'principals'. It is from this cadre that actions related to the development of EU democratic legitimacy have arisen, and in particular the development of a dense set of networks linking Brussels territorial offices which are concerned with 'citizen'-related issues, most notably on public health and social exclusion (Greenwood 2011). And a 2008 survey with the Directors of 40 Brussels offices by Olsson found that these saw their role as communicating 'the regional goals achieved in Brussels to the constituents at home' and 'bringing Europe closer to the elites at home' (Olsson 2009:26). Another survey involving the participation of 123 of the Brussels regional offices found that each office hosts an average of 635 visitors each year (Huysseune and Jans 2008).

From these considerations arise a plausible hypothesis that Brussels territorial offices from 'medium' devolution countries (such as the Nordic countries, the Netherlands, and the UK) are most likely to be involved with activities which are oriented towards EU democratic legitimacy goals. Offices from highly devolved member states are too oriented towards issues of centre–regional conflicts, while offices from centralized member states – if they exist at all – are too weakly resourced to do much beyond a focus towards regional economic development.

Territorially based EU collective action organizations

As has been evident from other chapters, formal collective structures with wide constituencies suffer from coherence and lowest common denominator problems, and those representing territorial interests are no different. At the European level, the structure, funding, competencies, and democratic legitimacy of the territorial authorities across western Europe differ significantly. Both of the 'peak' organizations have a much wider basis than the EU, with roots in the Council of Europe. These are the Assembly of European Regions (AER) and the CEMR. The AER started life as the Council of European Regions in 1985, changing its name in 1987. Comprising 270 member regions from 33 European countries and 16 interregional organizations, its membership profile and Strasbourg base (with a current secretariat of 21) belie Council of Europe roots, although there is also a Brussels outreach office with five further staff, and a small outreach in Romania. Because representatives come mainly from elected regional assemblies, there are significant membership gaps in the centralized states of Greece, Ireland, and Portugal, contributing to a somewhat quirky membership profile in which regions from Romania comprises a disproportionate component of all regional members. Its objectives include the promotion of co-operation between the regions of Europe, and to promote regionalism and federalism in Europe. It performed a semi-institutionalized role with the European Commission prior to the formation of the Committee of the Regions, doing much of the preparation work (Hooghe 1995). While Hooghe claims that both it and CEMR framed the debate about the CoR (Hooghe 2002), at least one author doubts the impact which AER has (Jeffery 2000).

The CEMR has much earlier roots, dating from the European section of the Hague-based IULA, formed in 1913. This section has its roots from 1951 as the Council of Municipalities, which became the CEMR in 1984, and later merged with the IULA. It has twice had a Brussels office. The first of these closed in 1976 due to lack of use and finance (Keating and Waters 1985), while the second has been open since 1990. It has a total staff complement of 22 (slimmed from 30 in 2002), split approximately evenly between a Paris and Brussels office. It is a federation of national representative associations of the various local authority categories among Council of Europe countries, and houses a variety of working groups on functional issues, as well as hosting substantial twinning arrangements. John (2000b) notes competition between the CEMR and the CLRAE, and also notes that the CEMR has not been effective in its EU engagement.

While the AER is more geared towards regional interests, the CEMR primarily represents local and municipal interests. Both have members drawn from across western and eastern Europe. Like the Committee of the Regions and its predecessor, CCRLA, they have been beset by conflict, both within and, mainly, between these organizations, which are largely divided along the lines of the regions (AER) and the municipalities and local authorities (CEMR). A more distinct form of such conflict arises between urban and regional needs. Both organizations perform similar roles; typically, this leads to a limited degree of collaboration as well as competition, not least because the actors have had to work together on a range of issues, including shared institutional involvement (including the nomination of members) in the CCRLA. They are nonetheless the most representative outlets of territorial authority for the Commission to engage with.

Beyond these organizations lie European 'sectoral' organizations of regions with particular themes, such as cities ('Eurocities'), maritime regions (Conference of Peripheral Maritime Regions), and border regions (Association of European Border Regions). These are significant organizations, described in further detail in Table 7.3, along with a variety of networks linking territorial interests. A range of political, social, and economic networks of regions, or regions clustered around European programmes dedicated to bringing regions together for particular purposes, emerged from the 'Europe of the regions' agendas of the 1990s and 2000. Some originated from the Community initiatives, which had the explicit purpose of transregional network formation, or in the regeneration schemes aimed at particular problems, and/or in the management of structural fund programmes (Balme 1991; Marks 1993; Hooghe 2002). INTERREG (currently in its fourth phase) and URBAN (two phases up to 2006 for 'sustainable urban development in the troubled urban districts') programmes have been particularly significant. Most of these operate as networks, although some have developed into more formal organizations with a secretariat attached to them. Chalmers has compiled a list of around 80 network organizations spanning a substantial breadth of shared interest fields (Chalmers 2010), from the general (such as regions with legislative assemblies), to the geographical (such as metropolitan regions, or 'Northern Sparsely Populated Areas') to thematic ones (such as the European Chemical Regions Network). While many of these are oriented towards general territorial authorities, some are organizations of territorial authorities with functional responsibilities, such as regional and local authorities focused on public health. Examples of regional networks are listed in Table 7.3.

Beyond these organizations, networks from diverse clusters of territorial interests have periodically emerged, embracing regions dependent on motor car manufacturing, wine-growing regions, ceramics, seaside towns, defence, and conference towns, with varying degrees of durability. In many cases the Commission has been the principal instigator of these networks, using limited period funding instruments in the expectation that the networks will be able to develop longer-term independent funding models.

The list of networks in Table 7.3 illustrates the diverse interest and activity fields of the Brussels territorial EU offices, and further examples are apparent from the websites of these organizations. As argued above, networks with citizen orientations are most likely to involve offices from 'medium' devolution scenarios. Thus, the west Sweden EU office is active in a variety of agendas surrounding health, social policy, youth, and education, and participates in the European Network of Social Authorities (ENSA), based around territorial authorities. ENSA has ongoing projects involving disability and inclusion, care of the elderly, and youth inclusion, as well as past projects focusing on immigrants' integration, foster carers, and child protection. ERRIN, the European Regions Research Innovation Network, has a health-specific network which includes in its mission the assistance of NGOs with international co-operation and development projects. The 'European Regional and Local Health Authorities' (EUREGHA) network includes among its objectives 'to improve the collaboration among Brussels Regional Offices' as well as 'to cooperate with relevant stakeholders such as NGOs and universities' (EUREGHA 2011). A variety of Brussels territorial offices have also engaged in the European Local Inclusion and Social Action Network (ELISAN), which declares itself 'towards a social Europe that fulfils the citizens needs' (ELISAN 2011), and the Social Inclusion Regional Group. The presence of such networks reflects the public remit of regional and territorial authorities, and these are widely linked through specialized networks organized in citizen domains, embracing fields such as the environmental, social action, health care, and consumer protection. These organizations are by nature networked with independent NGOs working in the related fields.

Among the associations there are claims of influence for both Treaty insertions and policy-related issues. The Islands Commission of CPMR also claims to have successfully lobbied to insert references and enabling policy instruments into the Amsterdam Treaty. The AEBR and the Atlantic Arc Commission of the CPMR claim to have influenced the design of the INTERREG programmes. AEBR has been extensively involved in the implementation of the INTERREG programmes, and has an officially designated (by the Commission) information 'Observatory' status. Schultze has linked EUROCITIES as a leader of a lobbying campaign which resulted in prolonging the URBAN structural fund initiative, and mainstreaming of the urban dimension in the structural funds, as well as acting

TABLE 7.3 *Principal sectoral EU trans-regional associations and networks*

Name and acronym	Role (if network, 'Network')
	Associations
Association of European Border Regions (AEBR)	Founded 1971, focused on issues facing border and cross-border regions. Based in offices of EUREGIO (a Dutch/German geographical cross-border development, enterprise and cultural partnership, established in 1958). Membership composition (currently 95 members) is oriented towards northern/central European border regions.
Conference of Peripheral Maritime Regions (CPMR)	Founded 1973. Focus is centre–periphery disparities. 160 regions from 28 countries working in thematic working groups, and in six Geographical Commissions, including:
	Atlantic Arc, drawing in members from south of Spain to Scotland. Established 1989. Focus on Atlantic Area of INTERREG programme and specialist sectoral networks. Claims to have undertaken studies which have guided strand B of INTERREG 3 programme.
	Balkan and Black Sea, with members from Bulgaria, Greece, and Romania, as well as Croatia, Turkey, and Ukraine.
	Baltic, drawing in members from Baltic sea country regions. Active throughout regional policy and sectoral project domains.
	Islands. Regional island authorities. Claims to have influenced content of both the Amsterdam Treaty and 2004 Treaty establishing a Constitution for Europe on territorial related issues. Sub-networks such as ISLENET, the European islands network on energy and the environment.

	Intermediterranean. 50 regions from 10 countries, including associated members such as Morocco and Tunisia.
	North Sea. 161 members from 28 countries, with particularly active Norwegian and UK profile. Oriented towards EU political lobbying for North Sea Basin on a variety of sectoral and regional issues.
European Association of Regional Development Agencies (EURADA)	150 regional development agencies from most member states. Brussels based.
EUROCITIES	140 city members in over 30 countries. Brussels based. 36 staff. Covers virtually all EU issues, 'horizontal' and regional. Extensive networks attached to it.
Networks	
GMO-Free	Network of regions (168), provinces, and local governments declaring GMO-free policies; over 60% of region members from Greece, France, Poland, and Albania. Linked to NGO network 'GENET-NGO'.
IRE (Innovating Regions in Europe Network)	235 participating regions, positioning for economic development purposes as 'innovating' regions.
METREX (the network of European Metropolitan Regions and Areas)	Network of 50 metropolitan regions. Glasgow (UK) based. 'Provides a platform for the exchange of knowledge, expertise and experience on metropolitan affairs, and joint action on issues of common interest' (website).
Conference of Regions with Legislative Powers (REGLEG)	Network, with 73 members from eight member states where regions with legislative authority, which 'campaigns to extend and improve the rights of legislative regions in respect of subsidiarity' (website).

as a co-author with the Commission on a key policy paper on urban regional initiatives (Schultze 2003). Historically, the RECHAR funding initiative for the adaptation of coalmining regions was proposed by the Coalfield Communities Campaign, a grouping linking coalfield communities in the UK, Germany, Belgium, France, and Spain. Similarly, the steel region network CASTer claims to have influenced the extension of the RESIDER funding initiative to 1999 (van der Storm 2002).

Conclusions

The logic of the single market led to the development of a number of compensatory initiatives in regional policy, of which some stimulated local and regional actors throughout and beyond member states, and these have formed demand structures for the development of regional policy initiatives. The Commission has not been an impartial actor in this process, deliberately cultivating bridges directly between the territorial and supranational levels where it is able to, assisted by the Parliament. Sub-regional mobilization cannot therefore be accounted for by the growth of EU competencies alone, although the single market has undoubtedly altered the structure of political opportunities, and the nature of regional policies, in Europe. Rather, institutionalist explanations focusing on the actions of the supranational institutions, together with issues concerning regional identity, and the relationship between sub-national actors and member states, are also important factors in explaining sub-national mobilization in Europe.

In some member states, territorial interests have sought a presence in Brussels because they seek to stiffen the resolve of central government actors in the interests of regional players. The European level has contributed to the development of regional bureaucracies in countries with weak traditions of decentralisation, and to the mobilization of interest coalitions around them. In federal states, the European level has involved a partial strengthening of regional interests vis-à-vis member states. But the overall analysis is nothing like as simple as this. Responsibility for regional policy has not been removed from member states. Member states remain the decision-makers in key areas of European integration, and in matters concerning regions and localities, such as structural fund global financing and applications, and the development of the CoR. Yet some member states have clearly been caught out by rules which they themselves signed up to, such as additionality. There is no clear-cut 'national bypass', and nor is there a clear pattern of the European level strengthening, or weakening, of the position of member states vis-à-vis the regions and localities. The sub-national level is neither superseded nor made subordinate, and nor is there a nascent 'Europe of the Regions' emerging, as a result of the European level. Nor are regional interests straightforwardly enhanced by the EU. Notable trans-regional networks have arisen and developed, and a significant quantity and quality of partnerships of regional, local, national, and European-level interests have been created. As John (1996) remarks, there is a complex interplay of interests involving a triad of local authorities, national governments, and EU institutions; sometimes all of these can be winners, and sometimes different actors can be. To this complexity might be added the cleavages between regional and local interests. Collective action is also complicated by patterns of inter-regional competition and collaboration.

It is these complexities which have led a clutch of authors to search beyond state-centric accounts of European integration (Chapter 8) to adequately conceive of a 'Europe with the Regions' (Hooghe 1994; Hooghe and Marks 1996). The question is not so much what the territorial level does to the position of member states in the EU but what dynamics arise from the sub-national level itself, and throughout interactions with the European level. Marks (1993), and Hooghe (1994, 1995), in particular, therefore propose the label of 'multi-level governance' as

> a system of continuous negotiation among nested governments at several territorial tiers – supranational, national, regional, and local – as the result of a broad process of institutional creation and decisional reallocation that has pulled some previously centralised functions of the state up to the supranational level and some down to the local/regional level. (Marks 1993:392)

Two decades on, these ideas have not come to fruition in any substantial way. John and McAteer note how 'an emerging body of evidence available on European lobbying by local authorities does not indicate a high degree of influence' (p.108), and that 'lobby success reflected rather than affected bureaucratic faction fighting within the Commission' (ibid.). In their analysis, the main value of the 'regional lobby' has been as pawns to the Commission in their battles with member states, and as agents of implementation (John and McAteer 1998). This outlook does not however reflect the incremental growth and embeddedness of some core EU sectoral regional associations, their involvement in both the design and the implementation of Community initiatives, and to the historic density of grassroots EU-oriented networks. There has been a wider process of decentralization, and the devolution of power has weakened the centrality of states in EU regional policymaking. Nonetheless, there are now welcome doses of realism in contrast to the over-exuberance around the time of the creation of the Committee of the Regions. It is not the case that permissibility for regions to represent member states in the Council of Ministers and partnership in cohesion policy for sub-national authorities 'have transformed the European Union from a primarily state centric system of authority into a system of multi level governance' (Hooghe 2002:370–1). Perhaps of greater significance is the way in which regional tiers of governance, as representatives of general public interests within their domain, have the potential to be contributory agents to the democratic legitimacy of the EU. This chapter has suggested that some of the Brussels offices of the regions are contributory agents to this endeavour. In particular, offices from member states with 'medium' degrees of devolved powers are now displaying a substantial workload on citizen-oriented issues, although those from 'high' devolution countries continue to be dominated by domestic centre–region relational issues, and those from 'low' countries are hardly present.

Chapter 8

Organized Civil Society and European Integration

Early 'neo-functionalist' accounts of European integration (Haas 1958) stressed the transfer of civil society loyalties from the national to the European level. This raises definitional issues as to what is meant by 'civil society', as well as the criteria by which a transfer of loyalties can be assessed. There is an established debate on the parameters of civil society, and particularly over the question of whether business interests can be included. The European Commission's all-embracing definition (European Commission 2001a) settles the matter empirically. A transfer of popular loyalties means more than the establishment of an interest group constituted at EU level as a means of addressing regulatory competencies, and a preference for a transnational regime to solve a cross-border issue does not imply a transfer of loyalties. Everyday activities of producer associations cannot therefore be taken to imply a transfer of loyalties. The few who participate in the work of associations in Brussels can 'go native', but the numbers are very limited. While producer associations do provide a gateway for more individuals to participate in EU-oriented policymaking at a level of detail, in activities such as standard setting or technical committees, such levels of elite participation are hardly likely to create mass 'we-feeling' (Hrbek 1995) of identify formation. And because most citizen interest groups organized at EU level are primarily associations of other associations, they have never been placed to become agents of loyalty transfer.

What therefore remains in debates on European integration involving organized civil society are whether interest organizations are, or could be, agents for the EU to acquire democratic legitimacy, and competencies. The contemporary literature is more focused on democratic legitimacy than the acquisition/extension of competencies. This partly reflects a public preoccupation with the first of these agendas, but also because the literature on the role of interest groups in EU competencies had become comprehensively established first. Political institutions use organized civil society as a means of pursuing their ends, be it for legislative or Treaty-related outcomes; thus, Woll (2009) illustrates in detail how EU institutions use a variety of interest groups to influence member states so as to achieve their ends in trade policy. Likewise, the 'success' or otherwise of organized civil society in pursuing their goals depends upon the extent to which these goals fit with those of political institutions. And the extent to which a joint coalition of political institutions and organized civil society will achieve shared goals depends upon the balance of interests and forces at play in the matter concerned. In between these apparently simple truisms lie sophisticated nuances. Thus, Bouza Garcia (2010) finds that NGOs work out first what is acceptable to political institutions and create their agendas within those parameters. Woll and Eising have shown how business associations can do a complete about-turn where they find they are 'frozen out' because their outlook differs so fundamentally from those of the Commission, changing their positions on core issues from protectionism to being in favour of liberalization (Chapters 4 and 6; Eising 2009; Woll 2009). These perspectives rather put EU political institutions as a driver of the EU system of interest representation rather than the puppets of lobbying favoured by cartoon caricatures.

Organized civil society and the democratic legitimacy of the EU

Mainstream economics views interest groups as 'rent-seeking' agents in their interactions with government, distorting wealth creation and imposing public costs by extracting special privileges (Olson 1971). And there is a long-standing tradition of scepticism – and even hostility – to the idea that interest groups could be agents of democratic legitimacy. In popular culture, particularly in the south and east of Europe, the word 'lobbying' carries pejorative overtones. A letter published in the UK *Independent* newspaper also summarizes a number of dimensions:

> Pressure groups are inimical to democracy because they are unaccountable to those whose lives would be affected by their policy prescriptions. They represent sectional interests but dress them in the language of social concern. In doing so they evade the responsibility of those who form public policy to consider how

best to reconcile conflicting values or competing claims to scarce resources in a peaceful and consensual manner, and how the costs of alternative policies may be equitably distributed. (Kamm 1995)

The core problems are thus identified as those of factionalism, accountability, mediation, and public cost. There are counter-perspectives to each of these accusations, although the difficulties of finding mechanisms to satisfactorily mediate between competing claims is the most difficult to address; clearly, there is nothing like the mechanism of 'the vote' in representative democracy to resolve competing claims. Beyond addressing these issues, there are also perspectives which make the case for the positive contribution which organized interests can bring to democracy, particularly in the process of 'authorization', that is, bringing substantive issues to the table of policymaking and legitimacy for them to be addressed (Kohler-Koch 2010a). And everyday goods, such as expertise and information, can deflate the public costs of policymaking.

The first complaint, of factionalism, is the counter-perspective to the traditional pluralist view that public benefits can arise from sectional interests acting as checks and balances upon each other. The EU system is essentially built upon the latter premise, with significant funding channelled to NGOs to ensure the presence of a substantial constituency of interest groups at EU level which is capable of acting as a counterweight to other types of interests with the resources to establish themselves, and to ensure that a variety of citizen-oriented perspectives are heard in the policy process. A variety of procedures empower groups to perform these and other roles, such as freedom of information measures for ease of 'Access to Documents', and to keep EU political institutions accountable given the relative weakness of popular participation and mechanisms which would otherwise create a 'public space', such as an EU-wide media. In effect, organized interests are used as surrogate democratic agents, as agents of 'unofficial opposition' in a system which otherwise has few adversarial mechanisms. Even the new European Citizens Initiative, ostensibly a direct democracy measure, in effect relies upon the professional organization of interest groups to operationalize it (De Clerck-Sachsse 2010).

The second complaint, of a lack of accountability, depends upon the starting point. Kohler-Koch makes a key distinction between 'liberal democracy' (in essence, systemic participatory rules underpinned by principles of formal equality of access and checks and balances between a wide variety of participants, and setting out expectations of participants), and 'deliberative democracy' (contributions to the public sphere, underpinned by public reasoning) (Kohler-Koch 2007, 2010b). If the aim is that of public deliberation, the 'problem' does not really exist at all because the emphasis is to encourage as many contributions to public reasoning as possible:

> To make this happen at the EU level, civil society organizations need a friendly institutional environment that provides opportunities for building a public space. Consequently it makes little sense to ask whether individual civil society organizations are representative or accountable. What matters is their communicative capacity, the diversity of views offered in the public arena, the quality of the deliberative discourse and the publicity it receives. (Kohler-Koch 2010b:107–8)

If, however, the starting point is that of 'liberal democracy', then 'accountability' does arise as a substantive issue for organizations which have crossed the boundary between 'voice' to enter the realm of participation in public policy, which is the reality of the highly institutionalized world of 'Brussels'. For some kinds of civil society organizations, notably 'who' rather than 'what' organizations, representativeness is also an issue because their legitimacy derives from their encompassingness. The extent of mechanisms connecting 'organized civil society' with 'civil society' differs for both of these types of organizations, though for organizations claiming legitimacy from the extent of constituency they cover, it obviously matters more.

A general critique of organized civil society is that they are 'professionalized organizations' removed from (an ill-defined) 'grass roots' civil society by virtue of the expert knowledge of their staff about the way in which political systems work, and the circles of dialogue with political institutions in which they move. Such 'professionalized representatives' are caricatured as 'hired hands' on the (here) 'Brussels circuit', evidenced by CVs demonstrating advanced training in how the EU works, rather than a background of activism or experience in the interest segments they advocate for. In this caricature, business associations are staffed by 'industrial civil servants' lacking company experience, while Saurugger casts a sceptical eye towards the movement towards professionalization of Brussels-based NGOs, in particular citing postgraduate qualifications obtained at the College of Europe (Saurugger 2006, 2009). These are more caricatures than rigorously tested propositions but they reinforce the spectre of a narrow circle of elite dialogue in which 'Brussels talks to Brussels', with limited potential for EU 'democratization' because of the lack of mass participation. An alternative frame is to see the vigour of democracy as always to some extent dependent upon elites (such as journalists), and that high degrees of educational attainment and specialized knowledge can result in enlightened figures capable of perceiving, the common interest (Gouldner 1979), and using their autonomy to represent it. Pitkin (1967) noted the inevitable disjuncture between 'represented' and 'representative', and the ways in which professional 'trustees' can use their autonomy and expertise to the benefit of the interest represented. With the autonomy to define and develop their work in whatever way they see best, together with their expert knowledge of EU institutions and of the Brussels circuit of organizations, such professionals can develop networks and activities which have the effect of deepening the EU's democratic connections. This was apparent in Chapter 7, in particular, where professionalized representatives from the Brussels circuit with the knowledge and autonomy to develop their work, develop deep networks with NGOs, and inject citizen-related issues into the EU arena. In Chapter 6, 'bridge' organizations such as Greenpeace and Friends of the Earth, largely staffed by 'professionalized representatives', connect to 'activist' organizations on the fringes, and draw them into the EU arena. A significant development in recent years has been the presence of well-funded anti-globalization 'alternatives' organizations on the Brussels scene in purpose-developed buildings in Brussels.

In order to harness their role as positive contributory agents to both types of legitimacy and to avoid negative externalities, political systems need to structure their engagement with civil society interests, whether in strands of representative or participatory democracy. Like the United States and Canada, the European Union has developed, and continues to evolve, such systems for engagement with civil society, and in particular for engagement with organized civil society. This regulatory framework is particularly important for the EU's democratic legitimacy because it has long pursued a developed strand of participatory democracy as a means to compensate for structural weaknesses in its system of representative democracy. This is now 'constitutionalized' through Article 11 of the Lisbon Treaty (Chapter 1) on Participatory Democracy, where the emphasis is upon institutions which *shall* involve organized civil society, as a supplementary mechanism to representative democracy.

The weakness of EU representative democracy is grounded in its lack of 'public space'. The multi-level, multi-component, decision-making architecture of the EU is oriented towards consensus seeking and leaves little room for adversarial contestation. Each of the three main decision-making institutions is itself founded upon multiple elements, with any majorities issue-specific and liable to shift. There are no mechanisms of adversarial party politics to make and bring controversies to the people, such as can be found in majoritarian systems. The parties of the Parliament are organizational devices within that institution and lack popular recognition, and thus do not become conveyer belts to bring 'politics to the people'. There is no EU-wide media to air debate or to provide for systemic accountability. The space vacated is populated by supplementary democratic mechanisms.

This structural (if secondary) role for participatory democracy, together with the needs for political and policy support by EU institutions (Chapter 1), makes the EU's systemic dependence upon organized civil society interests unusually high relative to that of other political systems. Because of this, coupled with the reality that organized civil society contains particular constituencies of interests seeking to capture advantage specific to those constituencies which may be quite different from the diffuse general interest, there is a strong need for the EU to have a highly developed set of rules for engagement with organized civil society if it is to aspire to democratic legitimacy.

The 2001 White Paper on Governance (WPG) has been a landmark in structuring the engagement of organized civil society in participatory EU democratic channels. The initial thinking devoted to democratic legitimacy which went into the WPG raised the prospect of advancing democratic legitimacy through both output and input means. In terms of output legitimacy (developing policies which are popular with citizens), concentrated effort was identified by the WPG in areas such as environmental policy and consumer protection, with Eurobarometer polls consistently recording high public support for EU action over a long period of time. Further developing environmental policy was always going to be difficult in a political system with the strongest regime of environmental protection in the globe, but limited consumer protection achievements left scope for further action. Consequently, measures such as consumer redress for denied and late boarding of aircraft and tackling high cross-border roaming charges for mobile phone use have been energetically pursued by EU political institutions. Such measures have the advantage of bringing quick results. In the former, the number of claims against airlines for redress tripled in the UK in the year following its introduction in 2005 (BBC 2006), while in the latter a number of high-profile mobile networks halved roaming charges in 2006 as an interim measure.

The current debate about the respective roles of output and input (participatory based) legitimacy in the EU political system has its origins in landmark contributions by Majone and Moravcsik. Because regulatory policies have more limited requirements for legitimacy than do re-distributive policies due to the technical functions they undertake, a focus upon legitimacy based primarily upon outputs may suffice (Majone 1996; Moravcsik 1998). Further, because interest groups seek specific benefits from such policies which can distort the general interest, the task for Majone is to some extent to insulate regulatory policymaking from such pressures, through the establishment of regulatory agencies. A popular retort to these authors is that output legitimacy is a necessary, but insufficient, condition for democratic legitimacy in a modern era characterized by the decline of political deference and the diversification of forms of political participation. Wincott argues that 'while many scholars still regard the EU as effectively legitimized by efficiency-oriented functional "outputs", this "once upon a time" story now has a "fairy-tale" quality' (Wincott 2004:231–2).

The policy mechanisms to which the White Paper on Governance subsequently gave rise contain an assumption that output legitimacy alone is insufficient for the EU to acquire democratic legitimacy. These include measures concerned with 'better law-making' and 'better regulation'. The 'better law-making' action plan is introduced on *Europa* with the reflection that

> people nowadays take an interest both in the effectiveness of the rules handed down 'from Brussels' and the way they are drawn up. The advent of a democratic conscience is strengthening the

need for accountability ... in the way the powers vested in the European institutions are exercised. This need is expressed more particularly in transparency, clarity and the willingness to stand up to scrutiny. (European Commission 2006c)

The 'better law-making' umbrella embraces the advance announcement of legislative intent through publication of an annual work programme, consultation plans, consultation procedures, and consultation reports, impact assessments, and the collection and use of expertise. Other significant procedural initiatives aimed at enhancing procedural democracy include those concerned with transparency, and a 2001 Regulation on Access to Documents. Taken together with arrangements for funding (Chapter 6) and institutionalization (Chapter 1) of interest groups, they constitute a system of empowered pluralism in which an activist bureaucracy has sought to create a level playing field between business and other types of interests, and to create mechanisms of accountability for the EU political system, through empowering civil society interest groups. The degree of institutionalization of interest groups in the EU political system is what makes it unique. Groups are used as agents of support for policy-making, integration, and input legitimacy purposes. As well as maintaining groups through funding, etc., the Commission has been highly active as an agent in citizen group formation in pursuit of its goals, and is deeply responsible for the landscape of such groups (Chapter 6).

A transparent dialogue with civil society

A Declaration annexed to the 1992 Treaty on European Union stated that 'transparency of the decision-making process strengthens the democratic nature of the institutions and the public's confidence in the administration' (European Commission 2006a). The European Commission responded to this declaration with a statement that

> the Commission views this declaration as an important element of the Community's policy on transparency. Improved access to information will be a means of bringing the public closer to the institutions and of stimulating a more informed and involved debate on policy matters. It will also be a means of increasing the public's confidence in the Community. (Harlow 2002:37)

A case in the European Court of Justice brought interpretation from the Advocate General:

> The fact that citizens are aware of what the administration is doing is a guarantee that it will operate properly. Supervision by those who confer legitimacy on the public authorities encourages them to be effective in adhering to their initial will and can thereby inspire their confidence, which is a guarantee of public content as well as the proper functioning of the democratic system. At the highest level of that system, providing the public with information is also the surest method of involving them in the management of public affairs. (Harlow 2002:41)

Transparency is therefore seen as a pre-condition for the operation of democratic mechanisms. A key means to equip such groups with the ability to act as democratic agents in the EU political system has been to enhance their ability to access information through a Regulation on Access to Documents. The Treaty establishing the European Community recognized a right of access for citizens to documents of the European Commission, Parliament, and Council. Regulation 1049/2001 on Access to Documents provides a legislative basis to this, supported by a public directory of documents on *Europa*. For the requestor, this makes accessing documents a simple process requiring the submission of a one-page internet form. Documents are normally to be supplied within a 15 working days deadline, with the requester able to specify a preference for the media of delivery, which includes email (and through that the ability to elect for anonymity). While there are safeguards involving matters of security or personal and commercial confidentiality which can result in a denial of a request for access, all categories of documents are covered by the right of access, including those originating with third parties. Any denial of access can be appealed to the European Ombudsman. For its part, the European Commission has implemented the Regulation with zeal, interpreting it retroactively, that is, to include any document originating from previous to the entry into force of the Regulation. Documents originating with third parties are also included, and while such sources are consulted to see if they have an objection to the release of documents, the final decision as to whether to do so rests with the Commission. Thus, authors of documents prior to the measure would not have known that their work would be placed in the public domain. The operation of the scheme is clearly oriented towards public domain release, with around 85% of documents released on first application, and most refusals arising from the need to protect audit investigations and the like, or where companies were using the mechanism to seek information about their competitors (European Commission 2010b). In the relatively few cases where the Commission has refused release, the European Ombudsman service and the Court of First Instance have delivered a series of judgements which lean on the side of release. The Court has contested the use by the Commission of general grounds (such as dis-incentivizing the participation of experts), and the use of privacy grounds by insisting on proportionate judgements viz. the wider public interest in disclosure.

While these instruments are easily accessible for anyone sufficiently interested to want to use them, it is well recognized that their use will be dominated by civil society organizations. Many documents are freely available on *Europa*, whereas documents of committees, and internal and preparatory documents, are more likely to be of use and interest to those with specialist knowledge. These instruments have been quite deliberately designed to empower civil society organizations as part of a pluralist system, to acquire information so as to be able to act as checks and balances upon each other, and as accountability agents upon EU institutions. Use of them by journalists and academic researchers is also reflected in the usage figures, the work from whom can be expected to come downstream into the public domain. In 2009 there were 44,538 visitors to the Openness and Access to Documents portal on *Europa*, and slightly over 5000 applications for access to documents (European Commission 2010a). A similar conclusion arises from usage statistics of the European Ombudsman service. Over one third of the 121 complaints of maladministration against the EU institutions in 2009 involved issues of transparency (European Ombudsman 2010a), many originating from NGOs. Occupants of the Mundo-b building have been particularly active recently in using the Ombudsman complaints service as a means of furthering their causes (car omissions (European Ombudsman 2010b)) and Expert Advisory Groups are recent examples). The Ombudsman has acquired a reputation as a transparency activist, using NGO relations as a key means of asserting the office, extending actions to recruit the Parliament as a means of controlling the Commission. Once again, the issue is the extent to which the agendas of institutions, and outside interests, coincide.

Consultation

Two strands of the better law-making action plan have involved 'promoting a culture of dialogue and participation' and 'systematizing impact assessment'. The first of these reflected that

> [t]he aim here is to establish who is really consulted as part of the Community legislative process. Are the smallest voices really and always heard? What are the subjects of consultation? To what extent are people's opinions actually taken into account? ... The purpose is to enable the legislator to be sure of the quality, and particularly the equity, of consultations leading up to major political proposals. These standards are motivated by three concerns: to systematise and rationalise the wide range of consultation practices and procedures and guarantee feasibility and effectiveness; to ensure the transparency of consultation from the points of view of the bodies or persons consulted and of the European legislator; and to demonstrate accountability vis-a-vis the bodies or players consulted, by making public, as far as possible, the results of the consultation and the lessons that have been learned. (European Commission 2006c)

Protocol 7 annexed to the EU Treaty of Amsterdam (1997) stipulated that 'the (European) Commission should consult widely before proposing legislation, and, wherever appropriate, publish consultation documents' (European Commission 2006d). These requirements are now translated into Article 11 of the Lisbon Treaty. The key point is that the procedures are used in such a way so as to ensure that access to political decision-making is possible for the widest possible range of stakeholders, that the Commission listens to all sides of the argument, and that no one type of interest routinely dominates.

All policy initiatives which are foreseen are first announced in advance in the European Commission's forward programme of work, a statement which is produced annually and posted on *Europa*. Thus, all interests have an opportunity to know what is upcoming. Proposals for legislation are preceded by Green and White papers. Green Papers set out a range of ideas presented for public discussion and debate and White Papers contain an official set of proposals in specific policy areas and are used as vehicles for their development. And the publication of legislative proposals is accompanied by 'impact assessments', in which the potential impact upon the various stakeholders is publicly outlined. Accompanying an impact assessment must be a 'consultation roadmap', in which the European Commission identifies how it intends to conduct consultations pursuant to the requirements set out in Article 11 of the Lisbon Treaty. Responses to consultations are supposed to be public domain territory, and once the consultations have been completed the Commission is supposed to respond to them by summarizing what the responses said, and stating how it responds to them in summary form.

Each impact assessment produces a consultation 'roadmap' with statements about the proposed conduct and duration of consultation, including the objectives of the consultation; elements upon which consultation is being sought; policy options and a comparison of them; target groups for consultation; and consultation times and documents. The three categories of consultations are expert consultations; stakeholder consultations; and public consultations, with most of these containing a number of sub-categories (Quittkat and Kotzian 2011). Quittkat and Kotzian make a key distinction between the degrees of openness of a consultation, with a greater dilution of potential for influence where the consultation is fully open. However, expert consultations rarely provide a lobbying platform because of their composition, which is mainly geared around experts from academia and national administrations (Quittkat and Kotzian 2011). An analysis of seven 'High Level Groups' within DG Enterprise and Industry by Friends of the Earth Europe in the Barroso 1 Commission found the presence of a range of civil society interests, and notes a preponderance of business interest representation (Friends of the Earth Europe 2008), but it is unsurprising that this should be so in expert groups advising the Commissioner overseeing DG Enterprise and Industry. A more comprehensive review of participation in all the 1237 expert groups in operation at the beginning of 2007 found that around half of the groups comprised national administration officials only. Industry/enterprise groups were present on 28.5% of groups, and NGOs and consumers were present on 24.5% of groups (Gornitzka and Sverdrup 2010). Despite the apparent balance, the Commission is introducing further procedural measures to ensure that further partity is achieved in the advice it receives from Expert Groups (European Commission 2010a).

A set of consultation standards in force since 2003, and modified in 2010, govern the conduct of the consultation exercises themselves (and were also subject to a comprehensive public consultation process). During this process, some citizen groups asked for the standards to be given a legal basis. While the standards are mandatory across the Commission services, it stopped short of giving them legal effect, responding that

> [a] situation must be avoided in which a Commission proposal could be challenged in the Court on the grounds of alleged lack of consultation of interested parties. Such an over-legalistic approach would be incompatible with the need for timely delivery of policy, and with the expectation of the citizens that the European Institutions should deliver on substance rather than concentrating on procedures. (European Commission 2002:10)

In the final Communication, the Commission committed itself to a transparent consultation process, in which the process of consultation is clear throughout, including the impact the consultation had upon decisions in the formulation of policy. Thus, the European Commission voluntarily commits itself to transparent public accountability in explaining how different input to the consultation process had guided the course of action taken and rejected.

The Consultation Standards set minimum standards for application across the Commission services, and as such meet a longstanding criticism of variation in practice. They provide an integrated framework of historic and emerging practice into a common application (Tanasescu 2009). To support even application across the institutions, the EU institutions produced a public internal service guide (European Parliament, Council and Commission 2003), and an interactive intranet site to give guidance. The minimum standards repeat key points from the Commission standards, but expand upon them in a number of ways of emphasis. This makes explicit that those affected by the policy in the widest sense should have an opportunity to express their opinions, including the need to involve non-organized interests and the need to strike a balance between a wide range of interests. Nonetheless, there is also reference to the need to take special account of interests organized at EU level, as well as the track record of participants in previous consultations. The latter remark does raise various questions. It may be an understandable bureaucratic wish to incentivize civil behaviour and screen out aggressive outsiders who refuse to play by the rules of the game, but in doing so it may skew participation towards the 'usual suspects' who learn the best way to please the Commission by supplying it with the policymaking inputs it is looking for.

The two main categories of consultations which involve avenues of civil society interest representation involve stakeholder, and public, consultations. Among stakeholder consultations, Quittkat and Kotzian line up the sub-categories of these as consultative and advisory groups, policy forums, and platforms. Of the first sub-category, consultative groups have the most direct involvement of organized civil society. These can range significantly in breadth. Membership of consultative committees is prized as a means of raising issues with the Commission, hearing the thinking of political institutions and of other stakeholders, and preventing opposing stakeholders from obtaining any kind of advantage. Places on them for civil society interests are handed out first through EU associations. These factors help explain, why, for instance, the European fishing association, Europêche, continues to survive, despite apparently irreconcilable differences between their members. But consultative committees are, as their name suggests, not decision-making bodies, and their importance should not be exaggerated. The Consumer Consultative Committee and its predecessors, reviewed in Chapter 6, provide an example of this.

The European Commission has also stimulated the development of a number of 'Forums', including 'Stakeholder Forums' in a variety of policy domains, which can develop beyond policy consultation into policy implementation. Some forums are open to the public, with one category in the form of events, and another category online in the form of 'European Business Test Panels', involving 6–8 online consultations per year of around 15 minutes in duration each, designed to assess the potential impact of legislative proposals. Around 3500 companies have registered for these. Other forums are more focused upon a particular audience, with the emphasis upon balanced representation throughout civil society (Quittkat and Kotzian 2011). A variety of 'Multi-Stakeholder Forums' have arisen in recent years, in which the main actors are brought together by the Commission services to develop a 'Vision Document' to help develop the technologies concerned over a 10–20 year time frame period. The European Health Forum is an open forum event in public which typically attracts 300 attendees, meets in plenary in the morning, and has parallel sessions in the afternoon in which the agenda is created, and organized, by NGOs. The wider structure also embraces the

European Health Forum Permanent group (EUPHF), a group of 10 organizations comprising NGOs, hospital providers, doctors, and pharmacists, and the umbrella organization of social insurance funds. One commentary sees this more restricted tier of 10 organizations as evidence of a two-tier consultation structure with elite bias, highlighting the receipt of industry funding by three participants (pharmacists, patients, and the European Heart Network) (Greer et al. 2008). Even putting aside the degree of influence which such funding really might create, the network also includes the European Public Health Alliance, the European Consumers Organisation, and Euro-Health Net (national agencies for health promotion/public health), alongside the European Hospital and Healthcare Federation, the European Health Management Association, and Standing Committee of European Doctors. A restricted membership based around those with specialist knowledge to contribute to debate does not therefore in itself provide evidence of elite bias in the Commission's consultation regimes. The EU institutions are very sensitive to the accusation that they might only be listening to one side of the argument, and have sought to ensure that its participatory structures have a balanced composition. Thus, the European Commission has established a Forum of Financial Services Users ('FIN-USE'), as well as the Financial Services Consumer Group (FSCG) as a sub-group of the European Consumer Consultative Group, bringing together consumer representatives from each of the member states to discuss financial services policies of relevance to consumers (Stichele-Somo 2008). MEPs in the European Parliament have established a 'European Parliamentary Financial Services Forum' (EPFSF) with the aim of becoming a 'Greenpeace of Finance' (McCann 2010:12), explicitly intended as a counter-lobby to international banks. At the time of writing, the Commission is 'examining possible ways of facilitating the capacity building of civil society organisations to represent their interests in financial services policies at EU level' (Hall 2010).

'Platforms' are similar to forums in progressing beyond policy consultation into policy implementation. Quittkat and Kotzian (2011:4) described these as 'highly formalised consultation instruments marked by a clear-cut agenda, an imposed self-commitment of those who participate, and by the presence of formal or informal monitoring-procedures'. DG SANCO, where the Director General had a record of innovation in consultative mechanisms, has a number of these, including the Platform on Diet, Physical Activity, and Health. Jarman records how companies make public commitments on platforms to tangible outcomes, such as the reduction of salt or sugar in foods (Jarman 2011) (Chapter 2).

Public consultations involve open events as well as online consultations. Open public consultations on specific policy initiatives are announced at the single access point for consultations, the 'Your Voice in Europe' web portal. In 2006, there were 129 online consultations, accounting for almost 60% of all consultations undertaken (European Commission 2007). In 2010, the Commission extended the standard time period for responses to online consultations, from 8 weeks to 12 weeks. The open format of such consultations means that they are likely to be pluralistic in nature, with lots of input from widely differing perspectives which have the effect of cancelling each other out. This diversity gives the Commission increased room for manoeuvre, and is reflected in the European Commission guideline document for consultation, which advises that consultations are unlikely to provide a representative picture of opinions, and cautions would-be consulters not to be unduly influenced by the views of one particular group, no matter how professionally presented (European Commission 2005a). There is always a possibility in any bureaucracy that consultation becomes a 'tick-box' exercise, and that 'consultation can replace the thinking' (Tanasescu 2009).

The highest number of contributions recorded to online consultations has been for animal welfare-related issues, with the highest at 73,153. However, this is exceptional, in that the average response to online consultations is 1029 (Bozzini 2008). There is a general tendency towards the under-representation of interests from southern Europe, and from central and eastern European countries. Public authorities are notably high participants (Hüller and Quittkat 2009).

Quittkat and Kotzian have undertaken a comprehensive analysis of participation in the range of consultation instruments, and the Commission's response to them, taking 89 exercises conducted by DG SANCO and DG Employment between 2000 and 2007 involving 2528 participants. They found that business interests comprised around a third of contributors and NGOs over a quarter (Quittkat and Kotzian 2011). There is little scope for any one type of interest to routinely dominate consultation fora. While consultations which are not open to the public may carry the potential to be over-focused upon one set of interests, the design of them is carefully undertaken such that they involve a variety of key contributors and participants.

Hüller and Quittkat found from their analysis of the consultation exercises from DG EMP and SANCO that only around half of the responses to consultations were made publicly available, and that reports were only available for only one third of the consultation exercises conducted. Beyond this, they found very limited public reporting from the Commission as to how the consultation exercises had informed the choices it had made in proposing legislation (Hüller and Quittkat 2009). On the basis of detailed case study insights, however, Tanasescu concludes that 'when consultations are conducted in a timely and correct manner, stakeholder input does make a difference and is reflected in the final version of the impact assessment report' (Tanasescu 2009:223).

Drawing on the work of Hüller and Quittkat as well as her own empirical investigations, Kohler-Koch sees a formal regime of open consultations in which participation is seen as a pre-condition for access to a more prized secondary system of elite involvement. In this view, participants expect little by way of outcomes to their contributions to open consultations, other than to demonstrate a willingness to play the rules of the game. In this perspective, recipients of funding contribute responses to open consultations as a result of perceptions about a set of obligations which funding brings (Kohler-Koch and Quittkat 2011). Citing Mahoney (2004) and Brodscheid and Coen (2003, 2007), Greer et al. argue that

> [t]he Commission uses funding and closed forums to select a subset of groups with which it will regularly communicate, using the promise of enhanced access to induce lobbyists to communicate useful information rather than their preferred and obviously tendentious arguments. (Greer et al. 2008:409)

Coen sees 'elite pluralism' from a two-tier system of procedural regimes, comprised of one tier of apparently open access, but supplemented by a second tier of elite access (Coen 2009). Richardson and Coen see 'chameleon pluralism' from this system, with levels of access changing over time, from a relatively open initial stage, through to a more elite stage later on in the policy cycle where the technical details are hammered out. A key point is the extent to which participation in this 'second tier' produces routine dominance of certain kinds of interests, and if so, which types of interests. The composition of restricted access policy 'forums' and 'platforms' does not suggest there is a systematic disproportionate imbalance between 'producer interests' and 'NGOs'. Both of these types of actors are highly present in the population of EU NGOs, and sufficiently resourced to participate (Chapter 6). The main cleavage is thus more between the highly institutionalized organizations of civil society on the Brussels circuit, and more occasional passers-by (Greer et al. 2008). These latter authors argue that

> it is not a simple story of exclusion by the Commission. What distinguishes the insiders ... is not that they belong to particular insider forums but that they engage with many different forums ... insiders are simply the groups that expend the time and energy necessary to participate in multiple forums. (Greer et al. 2008:427–8)

Use of expertise

The Consultation Standards were issued on the same day as a Commission Communication Paper providing guidelines and principles on the collection and use of expertise (Commission 2002). Again applicable from the start of 2003, this was aimed at assisting with the evidence basis upon which policies are developed, and that the process of collecting and using expertise should be credible. The guiding principles are of independence of experts, pluralism of viewpoints, and transparency in the ways issues are framed, experts selected, and the results used. To help put this into effect, public web registers of experts, consultative and comitology committees have been available since 2005, and are currently under re-construction to provide further public information. Experts are called upon to justify their advice when required, by explaining the evidence and reasoning upon which it is based and making this accessible to the public. Any persistent uncertainties, and diverging views, are made public. Any proposal submitted by departments for Commission decision should be accompanied by a description of the expert advice considered and how the proposal takes this into account.

The development of procedural initiatives

Curtin is one commentator who expects EU 'process democracy' to address the potential for asymmetries of power between producer and citizen interests (Curtin 2003). The various procedures described above and in Chapters 3 and 6 are likely to be further developed in pursuit of a general strengthening of participatory democracy surrounding the exchanges between EU political institutions and organized civil society. These are particularly important for the EU system because it is heavily dependent upon its exchanges with organized civil society for legitimacy-oriented goals, even with the case of the new European Citizens' Initiative (Chapter 6).

A key principle surrounding a number of the procedural measures surrounding exchanges between EU institutions and interest organizations involves transparency. The ETI, for instance, makes apparent the 'representativeness' of NGOs to those caring to look and to make a judgement, a softer instrument that the predecessor CONECCS database which make geographic representatives a criteria to access the database used by EU institutions to inform themselves of the groups to consult with (Chapter 3). While policy measures in pursuit of transparency are easy to champion, find ready constituency of supporters, and are generally irresistible in open public arenas, multi-level governance political systems do require bargaining to produce outcomes, which in turn is facilitated by some degree of opacity. Pursuing the point, Naurin shows how the mechanisms of member monitoring in trade associations come into play when transparency measures are introduced, in that they encourage general secretaries to play to the gallery of their member audiences rather than negotiating outcomes which may have wider distributional benefits. His data arises from a content analysis of letters written by trade associations before and after the 2001 Access to Documents regulation came into effect (Naurin 2005, 2007). A key point is retroactivity of the legislation in that that the authors of letters pre 2001 would not have known that their correspondence would be in the public domain, whereas the knowledge of this after the measure was introduced produced a marked increase in the use of self-interested references in letters, in the knowledge that trade association members (principals) would have the ability to monitor their agents. In this sense, 'full transparency' can produce self-interested, rather than deliberative, outcomes, and needs to be carefully managed to produce public interest outcomes.

The various procedures defining the 'rules of engagement' between EU institutions and civil society organizations have been defined primarily since the 2001 White Paper on Governance. They are in the process of extension and regular revision; the European Transparency Initiative and Expert Groups are measures which have already been upgraded during the relatively short time they have been in existence. Together with the European Citizens' Initiative, they have taken political will to establish, and once established, the detail tends to have followed; over time, these measures have been highly responsive to the detail of somewhat impatient public criticism delivered by 'watchdog' groups. There remain implementation gaps which are likely to be filled in the years to come. They cannot yet be expected to be at the level of maturation of comparable administrative instruments in other advanced democracies, but many of the procedures already exceed those in operation in a number of member states.

Interest group accreditation and the debates about group representativity and accountability

The 2002 Consultation Standards made a by-now renowned reference to the need to avoid the impression that 'Brussels is talking to Brussels' (European Commission 2002:12). This remains a key issue in the contemporary literature as well as for policy officials, with a number of authors making a distinction between 'Brussels groups' and (somewhat idealized and ill-defined) 'grass roots groups' (Chapter 6; Guiraudon 2001; Saurugger 2006, 2009). On the basis of his research among citizen interest groups in Brussels, Warleigh found little evidence of groups engaging citizens in their work, and argued that

> NGOs will be unable to act as agents of civil society Europeanisation unless they are internally democratic and willing and able to act as agents of political socialisation, with particular reference to EU decision making and policy ... NGOs are as yet simply not ready to play this role, and ... it cannot be assumed that their capacity to act in this way will be improved ... their internal governance is far too elitist to allow supporters a role in shaping policies, campaigns and strategies ... Moreover, most NGO supporters do not actually want to undertake such a role ... NGOs are no 'magic bullet' which will automatically hit the target of political socialisation. (Warleigh 2001:635)

Further evidence for this perspective is provided by Sudbery. A respondent from the European Environmental Bureau told her that

> while ideally it would be good to get people involved, time pressures mean that the most effective use of my time is to get on

with advocacy. In the end my role is not to encourage the most participatory governance, but to ensure the best results for the environment. (Sudbery 2003:90)

This succinctly captures the orientation towards 'output' rather than 'input' oriented legitimacy, and gives rise to a debate about what can reasonably be expected from NGOs. The 2001 WPG had floated the idea of 'extended partnership arrangements' in return for civil society organizations which could 'tighten up their internal structures, furnish guarantees of openness and representativity, and prove their capacity to relay information or lead debates in the Member States' (European Commission 2001a:17). While this brought rebuke from the European Parliament, some member states, and from some civil society organizations (Greenwood and Halpin 2007), on the grounds of elitism, it is to some extent reflected in continuing practice from the European Commission towards interest groups. The paradox is that, despite statements from the European Commission which formally reject de jure accreditation of groups, they have incorporated de facto accreditation practices. The formal position of the Commission on accreditation was first made explicit in 1992:

> The Commission has a general policy not to grant privileges to special interest groups, such as the issuing of entry passes and favoured access to information. Nor does it give associations an official endorsement by granting them consultative status. This is because the Commission has always wanted to maintain a dialogue which is as open as possible with all interested parties. (European Commission 1992:4)

This position has been periodically re-stated since. In the course of developing consultation standards in 2002, the Commission stated that it 'does not intend to create new bureaucratic hurdles in order to restrict the number of those that can participate in consultation processes' (European Commission 2002:11). Yet paradoxically, the same communication identified that 'openness and accountability are important principles for the conduct of organizations when they are seeking to contribute to EU policy development. It must be apparent which interests they represent, (and) how inclusive that representation is' (ibid.:17).

This preference for the representativity of interest groups was apparent from the public web-based database of interest groups

(CONECCS – Consultation, the European Commission, and Civil Society) which emerged from the WPG. CONECCS was

> a tool that can be used by the Commission itself to identify the appropriate mix of consultation partners who can offer the necessary geographical/sectoral/target group coverage. (CONECCS 2006)

The CONECCS database restricted entry to those groups which could meet criteria of geographic representativeness, and in particular members in at least three member/candidate states. Groups such as 'Statewatch' therefore found themselves unable to make an entry to the database; even if this did not carry practical consequences for them as an active group, the role of the database to identify consultation partners for the different Commission services meant that it had the potential for damage for less prominent organizations by linking representativeness to access.

This preference for representativeness has continued in the successor European Transparency Register, albeit with a much softer emphasis, by using the device of transparency to make it apparent which organizations do not have a geographic spread of members. This rule is particularly directed at NGOs (Chapter 3). Nonetheless, the mover of the register, Commissioner Kallas, continued to emphasize the 'no accreditation' line in a keynote speech in 2007: 'I have been very attentive to this danger of giving special privileges to an accredited group of lobbyists. There will be no accreditation' (Kallas 2007:4).

The paradox between statement and practice continues in a number of ways. The principal Social Partner organizations (Chapters 2, 3, and 5) have an elevated status based upon a formal evaluation of their representativity. The Social Platform has an elevated status (Chapter 6, and above). The European Consumer Consultative Group (Chapter 6) has access criteria based upon geographic representativeness and centrality of consumer mission. And unsurprisingly, the interest organizations standing to benefit from this elevated status have sought accreditation-based schemes. Business Europe did so during the debate on the White Paper on Governance (Jacobs 2003). The European Consumers Organisation did so in the case of the ECCG. And the Social Platform has consistently argued the case for an accreditation scheme based on criteria of representativity, applying a rule that prospective applicants for membership of it should themselves have members from at least half of EU member states (Chapter 6). A former Chair of the Civil Society Contact Group has argued when in office that

> I personally do believe that we will need to have a system of accreditation for NGOs ... I believe that NGOs need to establish criteria for transparency in relation to decision making, in relation to membership, accountability and funding. (Alhadeff 2003:103)

The dissenting voices in the Brussels NGO community about accreditation unsurprisingly come from those organizations whose legitimacy cannot be based upon their ability to represent a given 'who' constituency, but more advocate a 'what' cause in EU public policymaking. Such groups include those advocating for the interests of animals, the environment, victims of human rights abuses, prisoners, etc., but also 'niche' groups such as ECAS and the Permanent Forum of Civil Society who need to distinguish themselves from groups such as the Social Platform whose niche is representativeness (Chapter 6). As was discussed in Chapter 6, the process of representation always involves a disjuncture between the 'represented' and the 'representative', and the role of the representative can range from that of a 'mandated delegate' through to a 'trustee' (Pitkin 1967). The normative emphasis in policy practice of the European Commission upon groups to be 'representative' rather assumes the former role, whereas a trustee has greater freedom to interpret the interests of the subject under consideration rather than just a set of stated wishes. Similarly, the perspective that EU NGOs lack legitimacy because they are run by 'professionalized' staff suffers from the same misapprehension (Chapters 6 and 7). Rather, a trustee with expert knowledge may be in a better position to be able to identify which course of action to pursue, and in doing so provides a better service to the cause. This perspective also emerge in Chapter 4; a former Director General of the largest UK business association once told this author, 'if I represented my members opinions in discussions with government I'd be laughed at'. The 'trustees' in charge of the Brussels regional offices have developed activities with far greater potential for connecting with the citizens than have the mandated delegates from the Brussels offices of regional authorities, whose energies are taken up by the pursuit of domestic power struggles with domestic governments in another venue (Chapter 7).

The linkage between 'representativeness' and access seems to have been broken with the passing of the CONECCS database, although preference for it lives on through transparency application. The ETR regime represents something along the lines which Alhadeff had foreseen in 2003, with the use of transparency to illuminate membership and funding, and to some extent accountability. These principles had been stated clearly in the 2002 Commission Communication on consultation standards, which recorded that 'openness and accountability are important principles for the conduct of organisations when they are seeking to contribute to EU policy development' (European Commission 2002:17). These came downstream in the ETR, with Clause 4 of the code of conduct for interest representatives notable for assigning to them responsibility for information placed in the public domain. This concept also features in self-regulatory initiatives and in the content of 'compact' agreements to which NGOs have signed up to (Chapter 3), as well as in early versions of a draft 'European concordat' which has attempted to replicate 'compact' agreements at EU level. The accountability agenda had also made an appearance in the European Association Statute, an instrument which had been in preparation for over a decade between a constituency of NGOs and a section of the Commission, proposing a series of participative rights to structure the relationship between EU institutions and organized civil society (Kendall et al. 2009). While the Statute was abandoned in 2005 by the Barroso Commission under its 'cutting red tape' initiative, the compact seems to represent the next best thing for NGOs. While NGOs would like a legal basis for the consultation standards which emerged in 2002, the European Commission – like most comparable bureaucracies – has resisted tying its hands. A 'compact' raises the level of the agreement on consultation standards from that of a desirable target, to something more solemn (and in a small number of cases at the national level, gives it a legal foundation). For these reasons, the 'European Network of National Associations', comprising 15 national associations with experience of operating a compact, as well as the European Citizen Action Service, emerged in 2009 aiming to develop a European Concordat to the level of acceptance in practice by EU institutions. This network received start-up funding from the European Commission, of €440,000 (NCVO 2010), and at the time of writing had progressed to its third meeting by September 2010 and comparative research on compact standards.

These norms that internal standards should accompany decision-making roles now appear prominently in the literature (Cohen and Rogers 1995; Slim 2002; Edwards and Zadek 2003). Clearly, groups which simply articulate viewpoint should not be subject to regulation, but those which place information in the public domain have a responsibility, and therefore public accountability, for its accuracy (see Sikkink 2002). Bovens defines accountability as

> a relationship between an actor and a forum, in which the actor has an obligation to explain and to justify his or her conduct, the forum can pose questions and pass judgement, and the actor may face consequences. (Bovens 2007:447)

While this definition has recently attracted currency, a key question in operationalizing it is to meet the challenge of defining who the 'forum' is. Inevitably, the forum is diversely constituted, and no less so where organized civil society is a proxy for civil society. The ability to pose questions and pass judgement on organizations in this context resides in political institutions, in other civil society organizations, and among wider civil society. The same applies to sanctions, ranging from various degrees of exclusion and isolation. The challenge is to develop these concepts of accountability for use as regulatory devices. One aspect of the importance of Clause 4 of the ETR code of conduct lies in its deliberative capacity, considered below in that public reasoning depends upon the quality of information placed in the public domain.

Organized civil society in the EU and deliberative democracy

Deliberative approaches, drawing on the work of Habermas in advocating development through open exchanges based on the public use of reason, have been normatively applied to EU organized civil society by a number of authors (Joerges and Neyer 1997; Joerges 1999; Eriksen and Fossum 2000; Curtin 2003; Magnette 2006; Smismans 2010). A sympathetic hearing is also evident in the work of others (Warleigh 2003; Lord and Magnette 2004). While Eriksen sees the role of elites in EU policymaking as an obstacle to public deliberation, he also notes how the EU is more conducive to deliberation than other types of political systems because of the non-hierarchical nature of supranationality, and the involvement of a range of EU institutions (Eriksen 2000). Others share this perspective with an emphasis upon how the lack of majoritarian mechanisms leads to negotiated policy outcomes (Christiansen et al. 2004).

Whether interest groups can encompass deliberative standards involving a willingness to change demands in response to evidence and argument is doubtful. Some of the exchanges between interest groups and EU political institutions involve bargaining, which involves trying to get as much as possible of an original goal set, rather than deliberative participation. Christiansen and Piattoni see 'the network of well informed lobbies' at EU level as an anti-deliberative element through their elite nature and capacity to monopolize policy-making inputs. Nonetheless, they also identify circumstances when they can be agents of deliberation where extensive consultations arise through networks, and where they are involved in comitology (ibid.). Joerges and Neyer have likewise seen them as potential agents of democratic legitimation via deliberative politics, finding evidence from a study of food committees that the perspectives of differing interests and a wide variety of stakeholders are taken into account in a manner resembling deliberative processes (Joerges and Neyer 1997). Joerges cites the incredulity of Kohler-Koch: 'none other than comitology, that notorious system of inter-bureaucratic negotiation-diplomacy that even parliamentarians wish to abolish in the interest of democracy, is supposed to bring an element of democratically-legitimated politics into the Community' (Joerges 1999:336). In such committees in the foodstuffs domain, Joerges sees a high level of debate contributing to a high level of European protective standards: 'by virtue of its feedback links to Member States, comitology can, in principle, take all social concerns and interests into account while, at the same time, links with science (seen as a social body) can be shaped so as to allow for the plurality of scientific knowledge to be brought to bear' (ibid.:334). Joerges draws attention to the way in which the Scientific Committee on Food publishes its opinions and exposes them to wider public debate, and uses the internet to disseminate its findings, reflecting that 'the potential of this form of publication in terms of participatory democracy cannot be overestimated' (ibid.:336).

Aspects of the procedural regime which EU institutions have for engaging with organized civil society do present deliberative possibilities. In the main, the regime can be characterized as that of 'liberal democracy' (Kohler-Koch 2010b), where, as discussed earlier in this chapter, issues surrounding the connections which organized civil society has to civil society are raised. But where the aim is to achieve contributions to public discourse, it makes little sense to ask who is represented by the voice which speaks, and how the organization consulted its members so as to arrive at their position. Rather, it is the quality of the point raised, the discourse, the contribution to public debate, and a sufficient population of voices, which matters. In this latter environment, the approach is to 'let a thousand flowers bloom', and it makes little sense to place restrictions on those voices or to create standards for connections with civil society. Only certain kinds of interest groups ('who') might be equipped to do 'internal democracy' (Halpin and McLaverty 2010), but that may be an irrelevant standard to ask of 'what groups', particularly if the aim is to ensure that a wide plurality of interests and viewpoints are represented.

Even liberal democracy regimes have points within their procedures during which deliberative capacity is significant. Wherever 'ideas matter' to the formulation of public policies, so too do opportunities for deliberation. The 'advocacy coalition framework' focuses upon the ways in which iterated exchanges of competing ideas between different stakeholders over time result in changes to belief systems (Sabatier 1988). Deliberative mechanisms can operate through policy networks of varying degrees of integration. And they can arise in a number of categories of stakeholder consultations, whether private or public gatherings of people, or through written consultations, and contribute to the ideas which go into the formulation of public policy. The extent to which they do so is partly conditioned by the procedures through which ideas are channelled into policy-making, and whether these are mechanistic or otherwise. But they also depend upon general processes of the ways in which ideas are absorbed. This concept resonates with those used in the wider literature on sociological institutionalism, where belief systems arising from socialization effects of institutional participation help explain the behaviour of actors. In this tradition, Goehring sees deliberative elements of DG Trade's institutionalized dialogue with organized civil society (Goehring 2002), although there is some cynicism from civil society organizations that the forum is little more than a voice (ECORYS 2007). A number of authors have also assessed the presence and extent of deliberation by organized civil society interests in the context of the Open Method of Coordination, where 'grass roots' public deliberation among stakeholders has been identified (Eberlein and Kerwer 2002; Cohen and Sabel, in de la Porte and Nanz 2004; Smismans 2005).

Nonetheless, these latter authors take a guarded assessment from the results obtained from OMC, finding some wider development but relatively little evidence of anything resembling *deliberative* outcomes or practice (de la Porte and Nanz 2004).

The European Commission system of engaging with outside interests, while primarily a liberal democratic regime, does therefore have deliberative elements within it. It worries more about representativeness, but a little about diversity, as reflected in the European Commission's 2002 Communication on Consultation:

> Moreover, minority views can also form an essential dimension of open discourse on policies. On the other hand, it is important for the Commission to consider how representative views are when taking a political decision following a consultation process. (European Commission 2002:12)

The Commission system has more emphasis upon procedural participation than it does upon public reasoning, though its procedures are oriented towards delivery of public reasoning through impact assessments, etc. While the role of groups in traditions of liberal and deliberative democracy can be difficult to reconcile (Kohler-Koch 2010b; citing Steffek and Ferretti 2010 – 'watchdogs don't deliberate'), they can also be complementary. Developing norms of accountability based upon standards of behaviour in public discourse – is entirely consistent with a system founded upon liberal democracy, but with deliberative elements. The requirement upon organized civil society contained in Clause 4 of the ETI lobby registration scheme Code of Conduct, to ensure that information is unbiased, up to date, complete and not misleading, is deliberative in effect, and accountability oriented.

If deliberation involves the use of processes of dialogue which involve changing outlooks, then there may be a resonance with some of the earliest ideas of neo-functionalist theory. The advocacy coalition theory, however, segments belief systems into 'surface' and 'deeper' outlooks, suggesting that only the first type of these is affected by iterative dialogue.

Organized civil society and the development of EU competencies

A number of chapters have reviewed claims that civil society interests have contributed to the acquisition of new EU competencies.

These include the roles claimed for business interests in the expansion of the single market (Chapter 4), of social interests in the expansion of equality provisions, and more generally in seeking to expand competencies in the social field (Chapter 6), and some territorial interests in Treaty-based articles with specific applicability (Chapter 7).

The claimed role of the European Round Table of Industrialists in the achievement of the Single European Act (Chapter 4) has been widely used to challenge state-centric accounts of European integration, reviving echoes of neo-functionalist accounts of the process of European integration (Haas 1976). Separately, the ERT case is also frequently cited as a cause célèbre by activists seeking to illustrate an outlook which sees political decision-making as overwhelmingly driven by the preferences of business. These perspectives appear to be supported by some of the claims which ERT has in the past made about its impact. There is little doubt that the ERT did play a supporting role in the achievement of the single market, and that its relationship with the Commission and member states resembles some of the mechanisms of integration outlined by neo-functionalism. The ERT did, and does, include some of the most significant European industrial interests. A Commissioner is said to have played a role in the formation of the ERT, and in selecting and recruiting its members. Delors used the ERT extensively for political support to carry the message to member states and has publicly acknowledged its role in doing so, and a number of the messages conveyed by the organization have been well received by key decision-makers in domestic and EU politics. The ERT did imply that unless member states agreed to the Single European Act, its members would consider the viability of keeping their operational base within the EU.

But none of these factors, either by themselves or in combination, prove that the ERT was a causal mechanism in member states agreeing to the Single European Act. There was unanimous support for a well-functioning European single market among member state governments, whether by conviction or by promise of compensatory 'side payments' from regional funds. Whatever reservations individual member states may have harboured at the time about other aspects of the Single European Act were buried under their wider goal of achieving a single European market. 'Lobbying by big business organisations' was not a causal factor; member states knew that one home European market, where goods, services, people, and capital could flow almost unhindered across borders, was what they wanted, and the only long-term strategy of wealth creation and to secure Europe's competitiveness in the globe. Business voices may have played a supporting role in communicating the public case, but never a causal one.

While business outlooks may generally be taken into consideration in political decision-making, a world view that political decision-making is captured by business has a number of problems of a general nature, and those which are specific to EU level. A first, general problem, is that it is underpinned by a mistaken perspective that capital is homogenous. Enterprises may know markets, but when it comes to politics they have few bearings, often act clumsily (Hart 2010), have few means of co-ordinating between different product divisions, and may even be unaware that different parts of the business perceive different interests or are acting in different ways (Chapter 4). The detail of regulatory proposals tend to divide the interests of business (Lowi 1964), whether at the level of large enterprises, sectors, or across sectors. It either produces the politics of rival camps via competing interest groups (Wilson 1995) or the differences so divide business that collective agreement through established interest groups is impossible, and business breaks up into factions. Solidarity is often greater among trade unions, and certainly within environmental movements (Chapter 6; see, in particular, Long and Lörinczi 2009). Because the EU is a regulatory regime, competing politics between business interests is a feature of the EU system. And because EU decision-making is so fragmented between so many different elements, it is impossible for any one type of interest to routinely capture it.

Associations of business interests do not have the power to exercise monopolistic influences over matters of 'high politics' which are open public debate, such as a single European market, or European monetary integration (Chapter 4). Consequently, other factors may inform claims that the ERT, the Association for the Monetary Union of Europe, or other large firms, were causal agents in decision-making upon issues such as the course of monetary integration (van Apeldoorn 2000). And business interests in non-Euro member states continue to have diverging views about the desirability of adopting the Euro, largely depending upon where they do most of their business. Whatever role civil society interests did play can be easily accommodated by accounts which posit these as no more than contributory background factors to the positions adopted by member states. Business associations have a variety of reasons for propaganda which has the effect of exaggerating their influence, ranging from organizational survival to reputational factors.

Thus, there may therefore be reasons to doubt the 'most-likely' case cited in support of neo-functionalist accounts of the integration process. Yet, outside of producer fields something has emerged which bears very close resemblance to neo-functionalist accounts of competencies arising from the relationship between the European Commission and interest groups, with the addition of a few elements (Chapter 6). DG V/DG Employment and Social Affairs has been the key Commission service creating and nurturing interest groups as agents of political demands to the member states. It would first select a relatively uncontentious policy arena, such as actions against discrimination. It would fund a conference on the subject designed to attract a wide range of stakeholders, perhaps linked to the designation of a thematic European action year. Once together, the activists agree to form an interest group, and the group is sustained by EU funding. The Commission then finds things for the transnational interest group to do to help sustain it, such as designating 'observatory' status to collect and supply it with information. Alternatively, the Commission will act as broker to help organize the most effective transnational interest group structure. The Commission and the newly formed interest group then engage in 'activity noise', generating action programmes and activities in the interest arena, with relatively symbolic funding. Action programmes against poverty, and racism, have emerged in this way. In the latter case, the Commission took the lead in the absence of specific interest groups in the field, in the knowledge that the action programmes and its funding would stimulate the formation of transnational interest groups. These activities generate requests for EU competencies to which member states find hard to openly resist.

The campaign run by the European Women's Lobby aimed at the expansion of equality provision in the Treaty of Amsterdam seems to provide a classic neo-functionalist case (Chapter 6). Here was a group which had been nurtured by the Commission until it was strong enough to carry the campaign to the member states, running a road show to gather popular support, and using the relationship between one of its national members and the corresponding government as the key agent. Framing the issue around the need for the EU to find legitimacy from its citizens and using public opinion surveys to demonstrate that the EU was generally less popular among women, the campaign proved irresistible. While some caution needs to be exercised in drawing wider conclusions based upon a story of triumph told by a former General Secretary of the apparently successful organization, it has a ring of plausibility about it. Here, the mixture of the EU labour market focus, an irresistible policy frame of equality, a committed patron, a strong network of grassroots organizations with a well-resourced hub, and the ability to work in institutionalized politics, all combined to create a favourable set of circumstances for EU women's organizations. The Commission and the ECJ have become powerful institutional advocates of EU equal opportunities policies (Mazey 2000), and the women's movement have become embedded within the Equal Opportunities Unit of DG Employment and Social Affairs (Pollack 1997; Mazey and Richardson 1999).

Such a process is by no means a linear pattern with an inevitable consequence of further integration, and there are other cases in which similar mechanisms have been at work, but with mixed impact. The formation of the Social Platform was stimulated by EU institutions with the aim of achieving a 'civil dialogue'; participatory rules are certainly in place, but some of the key demands of the Social Platform remain unfulfilled, such as a legal basis for consultation standards. The Commission now funds another network of civil society organizations to develop an alternative, softer, 'compact' model. Other social fields have no apparent outcomes in terms of new Treaty competencies (see, for instance, the case of FEANTSA and homelessness in Chapter 6). Most of the development of EU competencies in the consumer protection field seems to have emerged from crisis events unrelated to the work of consumer groups, such as food safety issues (Chapter 6). Nonetheless, groups are used by the Commission as agents of political demand to the member states. The EWL case shows how it needs the right relationship between a corresponding interest group in the member states, and a member state government, together with the other type of circumstances outlined, to reach the conclusion of an expansion of EU competencies.

The common elements to the ERT and EWL cases help to identify the circumstances in which groups do play the role cast for them in institutionalist accounts of the integration process. Both involved groups in which the Commission had played a critical role in group formation and nurturing. Both pushed the right buttons at the right time so that they were framed in the critical discourse – the ERT of wealth creation at a time when market-oriented governments had come to power across the member states, and the EWL at a time of critical concern. This resulted in unopposed 'campaign messages' in both cases, although the ERT campaign would always be secondary given the enthusiasm among member state governments for the cause, whereas the extension of equality campaign seemed to require the EWL as an agent to make something happen which would be politically impossible for member states to resist. Member states do indulge in 'cheap talk' at times, with the result that they are required to deliver on it when called to do so, such that 'there is no such thing as cheap talk' (Lange 1992). Once member states have set the parameters for EU policymaking through Treaties, the playing field seems to be left open for networks of interests and supranational institutions to progress integration. The role of territorial interests in expanding the structural funds, and particularly Community initiatives such as URBAN and INTERREG, seems to provide such a case. Eurocities, and some of the 'Commissions' of the Conference of Peripheral Maritime Regions, seem to have been particularly influential in this respect (Chapter 7).

Conclusions: organized civil society and the EU

The systemic features of organized civil society in any system arise primarily from its structural components. The EU system will, therefore have features which are to be found elsewhere, but which vary because of the degree of intensity of those properties in the EU system. The structural components underlying the EU system mainly produce pluralistic effects.

First, the sheer multiplicity of elements means that the EU has to have a consensual-oriented decision-making system designed to accommodate the diversity of interests it contains rather than a majoritarian one in which a majority is empowered to routinely impose their will (Lijphart 1999). Majoritarian systems create 'winner takes all' politics, whereas consensual-oriented decision-making systems do not create outright 'winners' and 'losers' over time, and even single legislative acts mostly tend towards compromise. This involves a corresponding need among civil society actors to dilute expectations as well as interests. The EU's multi-level governance is a consensus-oriented decision-making system par excellence, and no one type of civil society interest can routinely dominate it. The behaviour of civil society organizations is therefore oriented towards finding common cause and building alliances. It is common, for example, for a company public affairs manager to spend more of their time talking to NGOs than to EU institutions, in the hope of finding a broadly based alliance which will carry the day, and obeying the practitioner law to 'position yourself as part of the solution rather than part of the problem'. In turn, this can change the behaviour of actors, and even their very perceptions as to what their interests are.

Second is Lowi's classic formulation that 'policies make politics', and in particular that regulatory policies produce underlying competitive interest group politics because their effects are intensely concentrated upon relatively narrow constituencies of interests (Lowi 1964). In such circumstances, business interests are factional, rather than homogenous, both across sectors and often within a single sector, because firms are differentially affected by regulation. Because the EU is primarily a regulatory regime, it will be marked by such politics. Levy and Prakash (2003) note how changing preferences across issues and forums, together with the multiplicity of players in bargaining, result in indeterminate outcomes upon governance. And collective EU business associations are often paralysed through the inability of their members to reach common positions, except in specific types of circumstances. Membership of such associations is often driven more by the 'costs of non-membership' than by any expectation that the association will be able to reach common positions (Chapter 4). Solidarity is greater among NGOs and Trade Unions than among business interests. And relatedly, 'the behavioural theory of the firm' (Cyert and March 1992) explains why companies are often poorly equipped to undertake political action. Large organizations are by nature incoherent, and decentralized companies in particular have immense difficulties co-ordinating regulatory preferences across product divisions. The world of political decision-making is unchartered territory for many, and they often act clumsily (Chapter 4).

Third is the extent of accountability levers (Mahoney 2008). The lack of direct connections between EU politics and its citizens means that it is relatively insulated from pressures from civil society. The positive outcome is that the system cannot be captured by any one type of interest. The negative side to a lack of connecting mechanisms to civil society is a lack of popular legitimacy, and particularly arising from a lack of popular participation. Because of this, the EU political institutions have needed to construct participatory regimes, built upon organized civil society, that is, elite interest groups. The main task is to ensure a sufficient population of interest groups in which a wide variety of interests are represented, and which are sufficiently resourced so as to be able to act as checks and balances upon each other, and upon EU political institutions. A series of procedures ensures: funding for NGOs sufficient for them to be able to undertake these tasks; formal equality of access (such as consultation standards and regimes) for all; and that interest groups are equipped with the tools to act as watchdogs, by dedicated transparency tools which produce all important symmetries of information flows (Parks 2009b) (such as rights of access to information and a transparency register). In effect, interest groups are used as surrogate democratic mechanisms. The population of Brussels NGOs is notably well resourced and professionalized, with mature features of inter-locking coalitions well capable of political action, and in some cases with outlooks so broad as to resemble political parties (Chapter 6). This population has expanded to include traditionally 'outsider' organizations, both as established players in purpose-designed buildings in Brussels drawing upon a wide range of wealthy donor foundations, and through such organizations acting as 'bridges' to social movement activist networks (Chapter 6). This raises the issue as to whether any type of participation, no matter how apparently hostile, can be regarded as positive for the EU system in that it is open to interpretation as a contribution to the public sphere. Somehow, even anti-globalization organizations manage to flourish in the Brussels paradox of institutionalization within the embrace of a liberal regime. For those which remain outside Brussels, the key issue is whether their engagement with the EU has a de-legitimizing effect (Hadden 2009), or as 'norm entrepreneurs' social movement actors contribute ideas, voices, and otherwise pluralistic effects of checks and balances, as well as a voice for the marginalized (Ruzza 2011).

An established way of accounting for the impact of interests in political systems is to focus upon the resources exchanged between political institutions and outside interests. At the EU level, this has been applied in an exploration of the presence of corporatism at EU level (Greenwood et al. 1992), by Pappi and Henning to the Common Agricultural Policy (Pappi and Henning 1999), in a much more developed form by Bouwen a decade later (Bouwen 2002), and most recently stated by Persson:

> The Commission has regarded external advice as a way to improve the quality of policies: in exchange, interest groups get an opportunity to influence policy and to defend and promote the interests of their members. (Persson 2009:143)

As an explanatory device this may have been weakened by the extensive participatory regimes developed since the White Paper on Governance. While these have essentially pluralistic impacts, the key question is the extent to which consultative regimes can be dominated by elites. In one account, the first tier is formally open to all, and therefore has little impact. A second tier has restricted access but the legitimacy of the system depends upon this access being carefully balanced between producer and other types of interests. The cleavage of access is not therefore between 'privileged' business organizations which overpower the 'small voices' of NGOs but between the institutionalized world of Brussels 'insider' organizations and 'outsider' organizations. The population of institutionalized insiders is composed just as significantly by producer interests as well as by non-producer interests. Alongside fragmented producer interests in the institutionalized world of Brussels organized civil society are NGOs which are primarily federations (associations of associations) and even confederations ('families' of associations). In this environment, even anti-globalization/capitalist organizations can become insider lobbyists, paradoxically illustrated by a case involving 'lobbying against lobbying' (Chapter 3). A first tier of consultation is widely open and attracting widespread participation. The second tier is focused upon the detail of public policies, but in this second tier NGOs have good access, and are well equipped to satisfy the technical needs of political institutions (Chapter 6; Richardson and Coen 2009).

Another recognized tool from comparative politics with the capability for universal application lies in the extent of 'fit' between the agendas of political institutions and civil society interests converge (Kingdon 1995). Where these converge, the combined players become powerful forces. The anti-globalization/capitalist organization lobbying against lobbying seemed to achieve elite access to the Cabinet of a Commissioner, and acted as a political agent for it in the establishment of the concept of the European Transparency Register (Chapter 3). Eising (2009) and Woll (2009) separately demonstrate how the EU political institutions use interest groups for their own policy-related ends, and how civil society organizations are willing to completely re-evaluate their entire outlook so as to avoid being frozen out by the European Commission. And Bouza Garcia (2010) shows how civil society organizations limit their agendas by first establishing the parameters of acceptability within the Commission. In this account, EU institutions become the driver.

This account carries echoes of early neo-functionalist theory, in which a purposeful Commission establishes interest groups as political agents to act upon member states, ending in the creation of Treaty competencies. The most cited case of the European Round Table of Industrialists and the creation of the European single market is a rather weak one because member states would have done it anyway. But the role of the European Women's Lobby in the establishment of equality competencies in the Treaty of Amsterdam looks just like the early neo-functionalist literature predicted (Haas 1976). And the pattern of establishment of NGOs has often included the Commission as the key agent in stimulating group formation. Where the climate of ideas is irresistible, integration results.

Deliberative concepts are also founded on the premise that ideas matter. While the EU's regimes are 'liberal' in nature, they become discursive when they are built upon the exchange of evidence in support of competing positions, such as impact assessments. While the emphasis upon stakeholder accountability is liberal democratic in nature, where these accountability standards relate to responsibility for information placed in the public domain they have deliberative overtones. These become particularly important in participatory models because of the difficulties of mediating between competing claims. Otherwise, the traditional critiques of participatory models based around interest groups can be met; an extensive population of interest groups, together with the design of procedural regimes, ensures sufficient checks and balances, particularly in a multi-level governance system founded on regulation.

What, then, is unique about the EU system of interest intermediation? The answer lies in its extent of dependence upon organized interests to secure routine democratic outcomes, for policy-related tasks, and as political agents of EU institutions in the battles over European integration. The federated structure of EU level interest groups seems to limit the democratizing potential of groups. But even then, professionalized 'trustees' of civil society interests seem to develop the activities of organizations in ways which carry potential for democratically oriented outcomes.

Bibliography

Ager, B. (2002) 'The Challenge of Change in EU Business Associations', paper presented at the conference on 'The Challenge of Change in EU Business Associations', Brussels, 7–10 May 2002.

Ales, E., Englblom, S., Jaspers, T., Laulom, S., Sciarra, S., Sobczak, A. and Valdés Dal-Ré (2006) 'Transnational Collective Bargaining: Past, Present and Future', Final Report to the European Commission from tender invitation VT/2004/100.

Alhadeff, G. (2003) 'International Regulation of NGOs', in European Policy Forum (eds), *NGOs, Democratisation and the Regulatory State* (London: EPF).

AMCHAM-EU (2008) Annual Report (Brussels: AMCHAM-EU).

AMCHAM-EU (2009a) Amcham-EU Profile (Brussels: AMCHAM-EU).

AMCHAM-EU (2009b) 'Annual Report', http://www.amchameu.eu/Portals/0/videos/annual_report_2009/index.html, accessed on 1 September 2010.

AMCHAM-EU (2011) 'About AMCHAM-EU: Overview, Mission and Vision', http://www.amchameu.eu/AboutUs/tabid/61/Default.aspx, accessed on 17 January 2011.

Armingeon, K. (1994) 'The Regulation of Trade Unions and Collective Labour Relations in the European Union', paper prepared for presentation at the 'Joint Sessions of the European Consortium for Political Research', Madrid, 17–22 April.

Armstrong, H. (1995) 'The Role and Evolution of European Community Regional Policy', in B. Jones and M. Keating (eds), *The European Union and the Regions* (Oxford: Clarendon Press): 23–64.

Armstrong, K. (2003) 'Tackling Social Exclusion through OMC: Reshaping the Boundaries of European Governance', in T. Borzel and R. Cichowski (eds), *The State of the European Union* (Oxford: Oxford University Press): 170–94.

Averyt, W. (1977) *Agro Politics in the European Community: Interest Groups and the Common Agricultural Policy* (New York: Praeger).

Bache, I. (1999) 'The Extended Gatekeeper: Central Government and the Implementation of EC Regional Policy in the UK', *Journal of European Public Policy*, 6 (1): 28–49.

Badiello, L. (1998) 'Regional Offices in Brussels: Lobbying from the Inside', in P-H. Claeys, C. Gobin, I. Smets and P. Winand (eds), *Lobbying, Pluralism and European Integration* (Brussels: European Interuniversity Press).

Balanya, B., Doherty, A., Hoederman, O., Ma'anit, A. and Wesselius, E. (2003) *Europe Inc: Regional & Global Restructuring & the Rise of Corporate Power* (London: Pluto Press).

Balme, R. (1991) 'EEC Regional Policies and Policy Networks in the Member States', paper prepared for presentation at the 'Joint Sessions of the European Consortium for Political Research', University of Essex, 22–28 March.

Balme, R. and Chabanet, D. (2008) *European Governance and Democracy: Power and Protest in the EU* (Lanham, MD: Rowman and Littlefield).

Bartle, I. (1999) 'Transnational Interests in the European Union: Globalization and Changing Organization in Telecommunications and Electricity', *Journal of Common Market Studies*, September, 37 (3): 363–83.

Bauer, M. (2002) 'Limitations to Agency Control in European Union Policy-Making: The Commission and the Poverty Programmes', *Journal of Common Market Studies*, 40 (3): 389.

Bavarian State Ministry of the Environment, Public Health and Consumer Protection (2006) 'Cooperation in the Field of European Policy', http://www.stmugv.bayern.de/en/eu/zus_allgem.htm, accessed on 6 September 2006.

BBC (2006) 'Big Rise in Air Travel Complaints', http://news.bbc.co.uk/1/hi/business/5197902.stm, last accessed on 26 April 2011.

Benington, J. (1994) *Local Democracy and the European Union: The Impact of Europeanisation on Local Government* (London: Commission for Local Democracy).

Bennett, R. (1997) 'Trade Associations: New Challenges, New Logic?' in R. Bennett (ed.), *Trade Associations in Britain and Germany* (London: Anglo-German Foundation): 1–11.

Bennett, R. (2000) 'Business Routes of Influence in Brussels: Exploring the Choice of Direct Representation', paper prepared for presentation at the conference on 'The Impact of Europeanisation on Domestic Business Interest Associations', Florence, 31 May–2 June.

Berkhout, J. and Lowery, D. (2008) 'Counting Organized Interests in the European Union: A Comparison of Data Sources', *Journal of European Public Policy*, 15 (4): 489–513.

Berkhout, J. and Lowery, D. (2010) 'The Changing Demography of the EU Interest System since 1990', *European Union Politics*, 11 (3): 447–61.

Betts, P. (2001) 'The Quiet Knights of Europe's Round Table', *Financial Times*, 20 March: 16.

BEUC (2002) BEUC in Brief Issue n. 39 (Brussels: BEUC).

Bieler, A. (2005) 'European Integration and the Transnational Structuring of Social Relations: The Emergence of Labour as a Regional Actor?', *Journal of Common Market Studies*, 43 (3): 461–84.

Boleat, M. (2002) 'Trade Association Effectiveness at the European Level', report for the CBI Trade Association Forum (London: Trade Association Forum).

Borrás, S., Koutalakis, C. and Wendler, F. (2007) 'European Agencies and Input Legitimacy: EFSA, EMEA and EPO in the Post-Delegation Phase', *Journal of European Integration*, 29 (5): 583–600.

Boucké, T., Blomme, W., Devos, C. and Staelraeve, S. (2005) 'Will the Coordination of Collective Bargaining Smooth the Path for a European "Social Dimension?"' paper prepared for presentation at the General Conference of the European Consortium for Political Research, Budapest, September 2005, section 8.4.

Bouwen, P. (2002) 'Corporate Lobbying in the EU: The Logic of Access', *Journal of European Public Policy*, 9 (3): 365–90.

Bouwen, P. (2006) 'Business Interest Representation and Legitimate European Governance', in S. Smismans (ed.), *Civil Society and Legitimate European Governance* (Cheltenham: Edward Elgar): 277–96.

Bouza Garcia, L. (2010) 'Civil Society Expectations on Article 11 TUE; More Democracy or Better Access?' paper prepared for presentation at the UACES Annual Conference, Bruges, 5–7 September 2010.

Bouza Garcia, L. (2011) 'Democratic Innovations of the EU: How Could the New Article 11 TEU Contribute to Reduce the EU's Democratic Malaise', paper prepared for the joint sessions of the European Consortium for Political Research, St Gallen, Switzerland, 12–17 April.

Bovens, M. (2007) 'Analysing and Assessing Accountability: A Conceptual Framework', *European Law Journal*, 13 (4): 447–68.

Bozzini, E. (2008) 'Democracy, Participation and Consultation: An Empirical Analysis of EU Consultation Processes', paper prepared for presentation at the SISP meeting in Rome, 2009, www.sisp.it/files/papers/2009/emanuela-bozzini-501.pdf, accessed on 7 November 2010.

Branch, A. and Greenwood, J. (2001) 'European Employers: Social Partners?' in H. Compston and J. Greenwood (eds), *Social Partnership in the European Union* (Basingstoke: Palgrave Macmillan): 41–70.

Brodscheid, A. and Coen, D. (2003) 'Insider and Outsider Lobbying of the European Commission: An Informational Model of Forum Politics', *European Union Politics*, 4 (2): 165–91.

Brodscheid, A. and Coen, D. (2007) 'Lobbying Activity and Fora Creation in the EU: Empirically Exploring the Nature of the Public Good', *Journal of European Public Policy*, 14 (3): 346–65.

Browne, W. (1990) 'Organized Interests and Their Issue Niches: A Search for Pluralism in a Policy Domain', *Journal of Politics*, 52 (2), May: 477–509.

Brussels European Liaison Office (BELO) (2009) 'Local and Regional Representations: A Recent Development', http://www.blbe.be/default.asp?V_DOC_ID=1867, accessed on 2 February 2010.

Buitendijk, G. J. and van Schendelen, M. P. C. M. (1995) 'Brussels Advisory Committees: A Channel for Influence?' *European Law Review*, 20 (1), February: 37–57.

Bullmann, U. (1997) 'Introductory Perspectives: The Politics of the Third Level', in C. Jeffery (ed.), *The Regional Dimension of the European Union* (London: Frank Cass).

Burson Marsteller (2001) *A Guide to Effective Lobbying of the European Parliament* (Brussels: Burson Marsteller).

Burson Marsteller (2009) 'A Guide to Effective Lobbying in Europe', http://www. burson-marsteller.com/Innovation_and_insights/blogs_and_podcasts/BM_ Blog/Lists/Posts/Post.aspx?ID=143, accessed on 17 January 2011.

Butt Philip, A. (1985) 'Pressure Groups in the European Community', Working Paper no. 2 (London: University Association for Contemporary European Studies).

Butt Philip, A. and Porter, M. (1995) 'David versus Goliath? The Challenge for Environmentalists in the Making and Implementation of EU Environmental Policy', paper prepared for presentation at the Fourth Biennial International Conference of the European Community Studies Association, Charleston, SC, 11–14 May.

Butt Philip, A. and Porter, M. (1997) 'Business Alliances, Network Construction and Agenda Definition: Recent Development in Lobbying Activities in Brussels and Strasbourg', paper prepared for delivery at the Fifth Biennial International Conference of the European Community Studies Association, Seattle, 29 May–1 June.

Calingaert, M. (1993) 'Government-Business Relations in the European Community', *California Management Review*, 35 (2): 118–33.

Caporaso, J. (1974) *The Structure and Function of European Integration* (Pacific Palisades: Goodyear).

Case, R. and Givens, T. (2010) 'Re-Engineering Legal Opportunity Structures in the European Union? The Starting Line Group and the Politics of the Racial Equality Directive', *Journal of Common Market Studies* (48): 221–41.

Chabanet, D. (2006) 'The Regulation of Interest Groups in the EU', CONNEX Research Group 4 Work Package A1, http://www.mzes.uni-mannheim.de/ projekte/typo3/site/index.php?id=71, accessed on 23 September 2010.

Chabanet, D. (2007) 'The Regulation of Interest Groups in the European Union', paper prepared for presentation at CONNEX Thematic Conference on Accountability, Robert Schuman Centre, European University Institute, Florence, Italy, 29–30 June 2007.

Chalmers, A. (2010) 'Sub-National Network Associations in the European Union', http://web.me.com/adamchalmers1/Site/Academic_Work.html, accessed on 9 November 2010.

Chalmers, A. (2011) 'Interests, Influence and Information: Comparing the Influence of Interest Groups in the European Union', *Journal of European Integration*, 33 (4).

Christiansen, T., Føllesdal, A. and Piattoni, S. (2004) 'Informal Governance in the EU: An Introduction', in T. Christiansen and S. Piattoni (eds), *Informal Governance in the European Union* (Cheltenham: Edward Elgar).

Cichowski, R. (2008) *The European Court and Civil Society* (Cambridge: Cambridge University Press).

Cini, M. (1996) *The European Commission: Leadership, Organisation and Culture in the EU Administration* (Manchester: Manchester University Press).

Cini, M. (2008) 'European Commission Reform and the Origins of the European Transparency Initiative', *Journal of European Public Policy* (15): 743–60.

Civil Society Contact Group (CSCG) (2006) 'Making your Voice Heard in the EU: A Guide for NGOs', http://www.avrupa.info.tr/Files/File/NGOGuide_EN.pdf, accessed on 26 April 2011.

Coen, D. (1997) 'The Evolution of the Large Firm as a Political Actor in the European Union', *Journal of European Public Policy*, 14 (3): 346–65.

Coen, D. (1999) 'The Impact of US Lobbying Practice on the European Business-Government Relationship', paper prepared for presentation at the Fifth Biennial International Conference of the European Community Studies Association, Pittsburgh, 2–5 June.

Coen, D. (2009) 'Business Lobbying in the European Union', in D. Coen and J. Richardson (eds), *Lobbying the European Union: Institutions, Actors and Issues* (Oxford: Oxford University Press): 277–97.

Coen, D. (2010) 'European Business-Government Relations', in D. Coen, W. Grant and G. Wilson (eds), *The Oxford Handbook of Business and Government* (Oxford: Oxford University Press): 285–306.

Coen, D. and Grant, W. (2001) 'Corporate Political Strategy and Global Policy', *European Business Journal*, 13 (1): 37–44.

Cohen, J. and Rogers, J. (1995) *Associations and Democracy* (London: Verso).

Coleman, W. (1988) *Business and Politics: A Study of Collective Action* (Kingston: McGill-Queen's University Press).

Collins, M. (1993, 2nd edn) *A Complete Guide to European Research Technology and Consultancy Funds* (London: Kogan Page).

Commission of the European Communities (1992) *An Open and Structured Dialogue between the Commission and Special Interest Groups* (Brussels) CEC: SEC (92) 2272 final.

Committee of the Regions (2009) 'Associations/Bureaux de Representation Regionale et Commuale a Bruxelles: Repertoire' (Brussels: Committee of the Regions) (available as pdf via Google title search; accessed on 1 February 2010).

Compact (2000) 'Consultation and Policy Appraisal: A Code of Good Practice', http://www.thecompact.org.uk/information/100023/100219/publications/, accessed on 13 November 2010.

Compass Partnership (1997) *Trade Association Performance: Report of a Benchmarking Exercise of Trade Associations* (London: ABI).

Compston, H. (1992) 'Trade Union Participation in EC Economic Policy Making', Strathclyde Papers on Government and Politics no. 90 (Glasgow: University of Strathclyde).

CONECCS (2006) 'Questions and Answers', http://www.europa.eu.int/comm/civil_society/coneccs/question.cfm?CL=en, accessed on 5 September 2006.

Corbett, R., Jacobs, F. and Shackleton, M. (2005, 6th edn) *The European Parliament* (London: John Harper Publishing).

Corbett, R., Jacobs, F. and Shackleton, M. (2007, 7th edn) *The European Parliament* (London: John Harper).

Corporate Europe Observatory (2004) 'European Commission Must Act to Curb Excessive Corporate Lobbying Power', http://www.archive.corporateeurope.org/barroso.html, accessed on 27 July 2010.

Crespy, A. (2009) 'Resisting "Neo-Liberal Europe": National and Transnational Mobilisation against the Bolkestein Directive', paper prepared for presentation at the conference on 'Bringing Civil Society in: The European Union and the Rise of Representative Democracy', Robert Schuman Centre, European University Institute, Florence, 13–14 March.

Crombez, C. (2002) 'Information, Lobbying and the Legislative Process in the European Union', *European Union Politics*, 3 (1): 7–32.

Cullen, P. (1999) 'Pan European NGOs: EU Sponsored Mobilisation and Activism for Social Rights', paper prepared for presentation at the 6th Biennial Conference of the European Community Studies Association, Pittsburgh, 2–5 June.

Cullen, P. (2005) 'Revisiting the Civil Dialogue: EU NGOs, Ratification of the Constitutional Treaty and Participatory Democracy', paper prepared for presentation at the 9th Biennial Conference of the European Union Studies Association, Austin, 31 March–2 April.

Curtin, D. (2003) 'Private Interest Representation or Civil Society Deliberation? A Contemporary Dilemma for European Union Governance', *Social and Legal Studies*, 21 (1): 55–75.

Cyert, R. and March, J. (1992, 2nd edn) *A Behavioural Theory of the Firm* (Cambridge: Blackwell Business).

Dankelman, S. (1996) 'The Europeanisation and Transformation of National Professional Institutions', paper for the 24th joint sessions of the European Consortium for Political Research, Oslo, 29 March–3 April.

Davis, J. (2003) 'This is My Life: Tony Long', *E!Sharp*, April: 64–8.

De Clerck-Sachsse, J. (2010) 'Civil Society and Democracy in the EU: The Paradox of the European Citizens' Initiative', paper prepared for presentation at the Annual Conference of the University Association of Contemporary European Studies (UACES), Bruges, 6–8 September.

Deeken, J. (1993) 'Regional Policy and the European Commission: Policy Entrepreneur or Brussels Bureaucracy', paper prepared for presentation at the Third Biennial International Conference of the European Community Studies Association, Washington, DC, 27–29 May.

Deighton, W. (2011) 'Agri-Business Fortune behind Spin Watch', http://spinwatchwatch.wordpress.com/2010/05/28/agri-business-fortune-behind-spinwatch/, accessed on 17 November 2010.

De la Porte, C. and Nanz, P. (2004) 'The OMC – A Deliberative-Democratic Mode of Governance? The Cases of Employment and Pensions', *Journal of European Public Policy*, 11 (2), April: 267–88.

della Porta, D. (2007) 'The Europeanization of Protest: A Typology and Empirical Evidence', in B. Kohler-Koch and B. Rittberger (eds), *Debating the Democratic Legitimacy of the European Union* (Lanham, MD: Rowman and Littlefield).

Dods (2011) *The European Union and Public Affairs Directory* (London: Dods).

Doerr, N. (2009) 'Democracy, Language and Transnational Civil Society Dialogues "From Below"? Lessons from Deliberative Experiments in the European Social Forums', paper prepared for the conference on 'Bringing Civil Society in: The European Union and the Rise of Representative Democracy', European University Institute, Florence, 14 March.

Dølvik, J. E. and Visser, J. (2001) 'ETUC and European Social Partnership: A Third Turning-Point', in H. Compston and J. Greenwood (eds), *Social Partnership in the European Union* (Basingstoke: Palgrave Macmillan): 11–40.

Dorey, P. (2005) *Policy Making in Britain* (London: Sage).

Eberlein, B. and Kerwer, D. (2002) 'Theorising the New Modes of European Union Governance', European Integration Online Papers, 6, 5, April, http://eiop.or.at/eiop/texte/2002-005a.htm, accessed on 13 November 2010.

ECORYS (2007) 'A Voice, Not a Vote: Evaluation of the Civil Society Dialogue at DG Trade', http://trade.ec.europa.eu/doclib/docs/2007/march/tradoc_133527.pdf, accessed on 23 June 2010.

Edelman, M. (1971) *Politics as Symbolic Action* (New York: Academic Press).

Edwards, M. and Zadek, S. (2003) 'Governing the Provision of Global Goods: The Role and Legitimacy of Nonstate Actors', in I. Kaul, P. Conceiçã, K. Goulven and R. Mendoza (eds), *Providing Global Public Goods: Managing Globalisation* (Oxford: Oxford University Press).

EEB (European Environmental Bureau) (2010) *Spring Alliance: Who We Are, What We Want* (Brussels: EEB).

Egan, M. (2001) *Constructing a European Market* (Oxford: Oxford University Press).

Eising, R. (2001a) 'Associative Democracy in the EU', paper prepared for presentation at the 7th Biennial Conference of the European Community Studies Association, Madison, WI, 31 May–2 June.

Eising, R. (2001b) 'The Access of Business Associations to the European Commission: French, German, British and EU Associations in a Multilevel System', paper prepared for presentation at the 7th Biennial Conference of the European Community Studies Association, Madison, WI, 31 May–2 June.

Eising, R. (2009) *The Political Economy of State-Business Relations in Europe* (London: Routledge).

ELISAN (European Local Inclusion and Social Action Network) (2011) 'Presentation', http://www.elisan.eu/presentation.asp?lg=en, accessed on 18 January 2011.

EPE (European Partners for the Environment) (2006) 'European Partners for the Environment: A Multi Stakeholder Network of Excellence', http://www.epe.be/menutexts/aboutepe.html#Mission, accessed on 13 November 2010.

Eriksen, E. (2000) 'Deliberative Supranationalism in the EU', in E. Eriksen and J. Fossum (eds), *Democracy in the European Union: Integration through Deliberation* (London: Routledge): 42–64.

Eriksen, E. and Fossum, J. (2000) 'Post National Integration', in E. Eriksen and J. Fossum (eds), *Democracy in the European Union: Integration through Deliberation* (London: Routledge): 1–28.

Erne, R. (2008) *European Unions: Labor's Quest for a Transnational Democracy* (Ithaca: Cornell University Press).

Erne, R. (2009) 'European Unions: Labour's Quest for a Transnational Democracy', paper prepared for presentation at the conference on 'Bringing Civil Society in: The European Union and the Rise of Representative Democracy', European University Institute, Florence, 14 March.

ERT (European Round Table of Industrialists) (2001) 'Achievements: Highlights of ERT Activities', http://www.ert.be/pg/eng_frame.htm, last accessed in 2002.

ERT (2010) 'ERT Origins: Providing the Wake Up Call', http://www.ert.be/origins.aspx, accessed on 1 September 2010.

ETUC (European Trade Union Confederation) (2007) 'Constitution of the European Trade Union Confederation', http://www.etuc.org/r/960, accessed on 12 November 2010.

ETUC (2011a) 'The In-Depth Modification of the Services Directive is a Success', http://www.etuc.org/a/3058, accessed on 17 January 2011.

ETUC (2011b) 'European Works Councils', http://www.etuc.org/r/57, accessed on 17 January 2011.

EurActiv (2008) 'EU Lobbyists Scramble over Their Exact Numbers', http://www.euractiv.com/en/pa/eu-lobbyists-scramble-exact-numbers/article-173152, accessed on 2 June 2010.

EurActiv (2009a) 'Chemicals Group Suspended from EU Lobby Register', http://www.euractiv.com/en/pa/chemicals-group-suspended-eu-lobby-register/article-184291, accessed on 27 August 2010.

EurActiv (2009b) 'Transparency Initiative', http://www.euractiv.com/en/pa/transparency-initiative/article-140650, accessed on 27 August 2010.

EUREGHA (European Regional and Local Health Authorities) (2011) 'About Us', http://www.euregha.net/home/index.php?option=com_content&task=section&id=4&Itemid=28, accessed on 19 January 2011.

EUR-Lex (2002) Official Journal of the European Communities, series C, C110 E/27 of 7.5.2002.

Europa (2011a) *Staff Regulations for Officials of the European Communities*, http://ec.europa.eu/civil_service/docs/toc100_en.pdf, accessed on 12 January 2011.

European Commission (1992) 'An Open and Structured Dialogue between the Commission and Special Interest Groups', http://ec.europa.eu/civil_society/interest_groups/docs/v_en.pdf, accessed on 7 January 2011.

European Commission (1997) 'Communication from the Commission on Promoting the role of Voluntary Organizations and Foundations in Europe', http://europa.eu/legislation_summaries/employment_and_social_policy/social_inclusion_fight_against_poverty/c10714_en.htm, accessed on 16 May 2011.

European Commission (2000a) 'Code of Good Administrative Behaviour: Relations with the Public', http://ec.europa.eu/civil_society/code/_docs/code_en.pdf, accessed on 27 August 2010.

European Commission (2000b) 'The Commission and Non-Governmental Organisations: Building a Stronger Partnership', discussion paper presented by President Prodi and Vice President Kinnock, http://ec.europa.eu/civil_society/ngo/index_en.htm, accessed on 12 November 2010.

European Commission (2001a) 'European Governance: A White Paper', COM(2001) 428 final, http://ec.europa.eu/governance/index_en.htm, accessed on 12 November 2010.

European Commission (2001b) 'Report from the Commission on the "Action Plan for Consumer Policy 1999–2001" and on the "General Framework for Community Activities in Favour of Consumers 1999–2003"', COM(2001) 486 final.

European Commission (2001c) Draft Memorandum to the Commission, Approaches to European Governance: For Democratic European Governance, Brussels, 10 March 2001.

European Commission (2002) 'Towards a Reinforced Culture of Consultation – General Principles and Minimum Standards and Dialogue for Consultation of Interested Parties by the Commission', COM(2002) 704 final.

European Commission (2005a) 'Impact Assessment Guidelines, SEC(2005) 791', http://europa.eu.int/comm/secretariat_general/impact/key_en.htm last accessed on 6 September 2006.

European Commission (2005b) 'EU Forum Science in Society: Report of the Specific Session "Civil Society and Science: an increased role for NGOs?"', Brussels, 10 March 2005, RTD-C2/VWM, http://europa.eu.int/comm/research/conferences/2005/forum2005/docs/library_report_ong_en.pdf, last accessed on 5 September 2006.

European Commission (2006a) 'Green Paper: European Transparency Initiative, Brussels, 3.5.2006, COM(2006) 194 final', http://ec.europa.eu/transparency/eti/index_en.htm, accessed on 27 August 2010.

European Commission (2006b) 'Amended Proposal for a Decision of the European Parliament and of the Council Establishing a Programme of Community Action in the Field of Consumer Policy (2007–2013), COM(2006) 235 final', http://ec.europa.eu/consumers/overview/programme_2007-2013_en.htm, accessed on 13 November 2010.

European Commission (2006c) 'European Governance: Better Lawmaking', http://ec.europa.eu/governance/law_making/law_making_en.htm, last accessed on 6 September 2006.

European Commission (2006d) 'The European Commission and Civil Society: General Overview', http://ec.europa.eu/civil_society/apgen_en.htm, last accessed on 26 April 2010.

European Commission (2007) Report from the Commission 'Better Lawmaking 2006', COM(2007)286 final of 6.6.2007.

European Commission (2010a) Communication from the President to the Commission: Framework for Commission Expert Groups: Horizontal Rules and Public Register, Brussels, 10.11.2010, C(2010) 7649 final.

European Commission (2010b) Report from the Commission on the Application in 2009 of Regulation (EC) No 1049/2001 Regarding Public Access to European Parliament, Council and Commission documents, Brussels, 30.6.2010, COM(2010)351 final.

European Commission (2011a) 'Who We Are', http://ec.europa.eu/civil_service/about/who/index_en.htm, accessed on 6 January 2011.

European Commission (2011b) 'The Co-Decision or Ordinary Legislative Procedure', http://ec.europa.eu/codecision/procedure/index_en.htm, accessed on 6 January 2011.

European Commission (2011c) 'European Business Test Panel', http://ec.europa.eu/yourvoice/ebtp/faqs/index_en.htm, accessed on 9 January 2011.

European Commission (2011d) 'Register of Expert Groups and Other Similar Entities', http://ec.europa.eu/transparency/regexpert/faq.cfm?aide=1, accessed on 9 January 2011.

European Commission (2011e) 'Social Dialogue', http://ec.europa.eu/social/main.jsp?catId=329&langId=en, accessed on 9 January 2011.

European Commission (2011f) 'Code of Conduct for Interest Representatives', https://webgate.ec.europa.eu/transparency/regrin/infos/codeofconduct.do, accessed on 12 January 2011.

European Commission and Council of the European Communities (1997) Communication from the Commission on Promoting the Role of Voluntary Organisations and Foundations in Europe, COM(97)241 final, Luxembourg, Office for Official Publications of the European Communities.

European Commission Financial Transparency System (2010), http://ec.europa.eu/beneficiaries/fts/index_en.htm, accessed on 27 September 2010.

European Commission Register of Interest Representatives (2010), https://webgate.ec.europa.eu/transparency/regrin/welcome.do?locale=en#, accessed on 27 September 2010.

European Economic and Social Committee (2004) 'Opinion on Improving the Implementation of the Lisbon Strategy, CESE 153 1438/2004', http://eescopinions.esc.eu.int/EESCopinionDocument.

aspx?identifier=ces\eco\eco153\ces1438-2004_ac.doc&language=EN, accessed on 5 September 2006.

European Foundation (for the Improvement of Living and Working Conditions) (2005) 'Industrial Relations Developments in Europe 2004', http://www.eurofound.eu.int/publications/bysubject/listIndustrialrelations2005.htm, last accessed on 5 September 2006.

European Foundation (2008) 'European Works Councils in Practice: Key Research Findings', http://www.eurofound.europa.eu/pubdocs/2008/28/en/1/ef0828en.pdf, accessed on 20 September 2010.

European Foundation (2009) 'Trade Union Strategies to Recruit New Groups of Workers', http://www.eurofound.europa.eu/eiro/studies/tn0901028s/tn0901028s.htm, accessed on 16 September 2010.

European Ombudsman (2010a) 'Overview 2009', http://www.ombudsman.europa.eu/activities/annualreports.faces, accessed on 6 November 2010.

European Ombudsman (2010b) 'Ombudsman Criticises Commission for Failure to Cooperate Sincerely with Him', http://europa.eu/rapid/pressReleasesAction.do?reference=EO/10/7&format=HTML&aged=0&language=EN&guiLanguage=en, accessed on 13 November 2010.

European Parliament (2001) 'Committee on Constitutional Affairs: Final Report on the Commission White Paper on European Governance, A5-0399/2001', http://www2.europarl.eu.int/omk/sipade2?PUBREF=-//EP//NONSGML+REPORT+A5-2001-0399+0+DOC+PDF+V0//EN&L=EN&LEVEL=2&NAV=S&LSTDOC=Y, accessed on 5 September 2006.

European Parliament (2003) 'Lobbying in the European Union: Current Rules and Practices, Working Paper Directorate General for Research, Constitutional Affairs Series AFCO 104', http://ec.europa.eu/civil_society/interest_groups/docs/workingdocparl.pdf, accessed on 12 November 2010.

European Parliament (2010a) 'Rules of Procedure of the European Parliament', http://www.europarl.europa.eu/sides/getLastRules.do?language=EN&reference=TOC, accessed on 12 January 2011.

European Parliament (2010b) 'Rules of Procedure of the European Parliament, Annex X', http://www.europarl.europa.eu/sides/getDoc.do?pubRef=-//EP//TEXT+RULES-EP+20100705+ANN-10+DOC+XML+V0//EN&language=EN&navigationBar=YES, accessed on 12 January 2011.

European Parliament, Council and Commission (2003) 'Joint Practical Guide of the European Parliament, the Council and the Commission for persons involved in the drafting of legislation', http://eur-lex.europa.eu/en/techleg/index.htm, last accessed on 27 April 2011.

European Partners for the Environment (2010) 'About Us', http://www.epe.be/Default.aspx?p=100&n=101, accessed on 26 April 2011.

European Transparency Register (2010) 'Register of Interest Representatives', https://webgate.ec.europa.eu/transparency/regrin/welcome.do?locale=en, accessed on 16 May 2011.

European Youth Forum (2011) 'Secretariat', http://www.youthforum.org/index.php?option=com_content&view=article&id=448&Itemid=96&lang=en, accessed on 11 April 2011.

European Women's Lobby (EWL) (2010) 'New EU Strategy for Gender Equality Has Potential to Deliver Results, Says European Women's Lobby', http://ewl.horus.be/site/hp.asp, accessed on 31 October 2010.

Evetts, J. (1995) 'International Professional Associations: The New Context for Professional Projects', *Work, Employment and Society*, 9 (4): 763–72.

Evetts, J. (2000) 'Professions in European and UK Markets: The European Professional Federations', *International Journal of Sociology and Social Policy*, 20 (11/12): 1–30.

Falkner, G. (1998) *EU Social Policy in the 1990s: Towards a Corporatist Policy Community* (London: Routledge).

Fazi, E. and Smith, J. (2006) 'Civil Dialogue: Making It Work Better', http://www.act4europe.org/code/en/materials.asp?Page=222&menuPage=222, accessed on 31 October 2010.

Fielder, N. (2000) 'The Origins of the Single Market', in V. Bornschier (ed.), *State-Building in Europe: The Revitalization of Western European Integration* (Cambridge: Cambridge University Press): 75–92.

Financial Times (1994) 'Business and the Environment: Same Journey, Different Routes', *Financial Times*, 13 July: 20.

Fleurke, F. and Willemse, R. (2006) 'The European Union and the Autonomy of Sub-National Authorities: Towards an Analysis of Constraints and Opportunities in Sub-National Decision-Making', *Regional and Federal Studies*, 16 (1): 83–98.

Friends of the Earth Europe (2006) 'Transparency in EU Decision Making: Reality or Myth?' http://www.foeeurope.org/publications/publications2006.htm, accessed on 12 November 2010.

Friends of the Earth Europe (2008) 'Whose Views Count? Business Influence and the European Commission's High Level Groups', http://www.foeeurope.org/publications/publications2008.html, accessed on 12 November 2010.

G8 (2002) 'Introducing European Environmental NGOs: Their Role and Importance in European Union Decision Making', www. t-e.nu, last accessed September 2002.

G10 (2010) 'About the Green 10', http://green10.org/, accessed on 27 October 2010.

G10 (2011) 'What is the Green 10?', http://www.foeeurope.org/links/green10.htm, accessed on 16 May 2011.

Gardner, J. (1991) *Effective Lobbying in the European Community* (Dordrecht: Kluwer).

Geddes, A. (2000) 'Lobbying for Migrant Inclusion in the European Union: New Opportunities for Transnational Advocacy', *Journal of European Public Policy*, 7 (4), October: 632–49.

Gehlen, C. (2006) *Lobbying in Brussels: The EU Directive on the Patentability of Computer-Implemented Inventions* (Cranfield: European Case Clearing House).

Gehring, T. and Krapohl, S. (2007) 'Supranational Regulatory Agencies between Independence and Control: The EMEA and the Authorization of Pharmaceuticals in the European Single Market', *Journal of European Public Policy*, 14 (2): 208–26.

Georgiev, V. (2011) 'Commission on the Loose? Delegated Lawmaking and Comitology After Lisbon', paper prepared for presentation to the 12th Biennial Conference of the European Union Studies Association, Boston, 3–5 March.

Geyer, R. (2001) 'Can EU Social NGOs Co-operate to Promote EU Social Policy?', *Journal of Social Policy*, 30 (3): 477–94.

Gillies, D. (1998) 'Lobbying and European Community Environmental Law', *European Environment*, 8 (6), November–December: 175–83.

Goehring, R. (2002) 'Interest Representation and Legitimacy in the European Union: The New Quest for Civil Society Formation', in A. Warleigh and J. Fairbrass (eds), *Influence and Interests in the EU: The New Politics of Persuasion and Advocacy* (London: Europa): 118–37.

Gornitzka, A. and Sverdrup, U. (2010) 'Access of Experts: Information and EU Decision Making', *West European Politics*, 34 (1): 48–70.

Gouldner, A. (1979) *The Future of Intellectuals and the Rise of the New Class* (London: Continuum).

Grande, E. (1996) 'The State and Interest Groups in a Framework of Multi-Level Decision Making: The Case of the European Union', *Journal of European Public Policy*, 3 (3), September: 318–38.

Grant, W. (1990) 'Organised Interests and the European Community', paper prepared for presentation at the 6th International Colloquium of the Feltrinelli Foundation, Corton, 29–31 May.

Grant, W. (1993) 'Pressure Groups and the European Community: An Overview', in S. Mazey and J. Richardson (eds), *Lobbying in the European Community* (Oxford: Oxford University Press): 27–46.

Grant, W. (1997) 'Perspectives on Globalisation and Economic Coordination', in J. R. Hollingsworth and R. Boyer (eds), *Contemporary Capitalism: The Embeddedness of Institutions* (Cambridge: Cambridge University Press): 319–36.

Graziano, L. (1999) 'Lobbying and Interest Representation in Brussels', paper prepared for presentation at the Annual Conference of the American Political Science Association, Boston, 3–6 September.

Graziano, P. (2010) 'Europeanization and Consumer Interests: A Framework of Analysis (with Evidence from the Italian Case)', paper prepared for presentation at the 40th Annual Conference of the University Association for Contemporary European Studies (UACES), Bruges, 6–8 September 2010, http://www.uaces.org/pdf/papers/1001/graziano.pdf, accessed on 27 October 2010.

Green-Cowles, M. (1995) 'The European Round Table of Industrialists: The Strategic Player in European Affairs', in J. Greenwood (ed.), *European Casebook on Business Alliances* (Hemel Hempstead: Prentice-Hall): 225–36.

Green-Cowles, M. (1996) 'The EU Committee of AmCham: The Powerful Voice of American Firms in Brussels', *Journal of European Public Policy*, 3 (3): 339–58.

Green-Cowles, M. (1997) 'The Changing Architecture of Big Business', paper prepared for presentation at the 5th Biennial Conference of the European Community Studies Association, Seattle, 29 May.

Greenwood, J. (1997) *Representing Interests in the European Union* (Basingstoke: Palgrave Macmillan).

Greenwood, J. (2002a) *Inside the EU Business Associations* (Basingstoke: Palgrave Macmillan).

Greenwood, J. (2002b) 'Electricity Liberalisation', in R. Pedler (ed.), *European Union Lobbying: Changes in the Arena* (Basingstoke: Palgrave Macmillan).

Greenwood, J. (2003) *Interest Representation in the European Union* (Basingstoke: Palgrave Macmillan).

Greenwood, J. (2011) 'Actors of the Common Interest? The Brussels Offices of the Regions', *Journal of European Integration*, 33 (4).

Greenwood, J., Grote, J. and Ronit, K. (1992) *Organised Interests and the European Community* (London: Sage).

Greenwood, J. and Halpin, D. (2007) 'The Public Governance of Interest Groups in the European Union', *Perspectives on European Politics and Society*, 8 (2), June: 189–210.

Greenwood, J., Levy, R. and Stewart, R. (1995) 'The European Union Structural Fund Allocation: Lobbying to Win or Recycling the Budget', *European Urban and Regional Studies*, 2 (4): 317–38.

Greenwood, J. and Ronit, K. (1994) 'Interest Groups in the European Polity: Newly Emerging Dynamics and Forms', *West European Politics*, 17 (1): 31–56.

Greer, S., da Fonseca, E. and Adolph, C. (2008) 'Mobilizing Bias in Europe: Lobbies, Democracy and EU Health Policy-Making', *European Union Politics*, 9 (3): 403–33.

Guiraudon, V. (2001) 'Weak Weapons of the Weak? Transnational Mobilization around Migration in the European Union', in D. Imig and S. Tarrow (eds), *Contentious Europeans* (Lanham, MD: Rowman and Littlefield): 163–83.

Haas, E. (1958) *The Uniting of Europe: Political, Economic and Social Forces, 1950–1957* (Stanford, CA: Stanford University Press).

Haas, E. (1976) *The Obsolescence of Regional Integration Theory* (Berkeley, CA: Institute of International Studies).

Hadden, J. (2009) 'Two Worlds of European Collective Action?: Civil Society Spillover(s) in European Climate Change Networks', paper prepared for the conference on Bringing Civil Society in: The European

Union and the Rise of Representative Democracy, European University Institute, Florence, 14 March.

Hall, I. (2010) 'Commissioner Barnier Moves to Achieve "Fair Balance" in Composition of Expert Groups, Public Affairs News', http://www.publicaffairsnews.com/no_cache/home/european-news/news-detail/newsarticle/commissioner-barnier-moves-to-achieve-fair-balance-in-composition-of-expert-groups/10/, accessed on 18 January 2011.

Hall, R. and Deardorff, A. (2006) 'Lobbying as Legislative Subsidy', *American Political Science Review*, 100 (1): 69–84.

Halpin, D. and McLaverty, P. (2010) 'Legitimating INGO Advocacy: The Case of Internal Democracies', in J. Steffek and K. Hahn (eds), *Evaluating Transnational NGOs: Legitimacy, Accountability, Representation* (Basingstoke: Palgrave Macmillan).

Harlow, C. (1992) 'A Community of Interests? Making the Most of European Law', *Modern Law Review*, 55 (3): 331–50.

Harlow, C. (2002) *Accountability in the European Union* (Oxford: Oxford University Press).

Harlow, C. and Rawlings, R. (1992) *Pressure through Law* (Routledge: London).

Hart, D. (2010) 'The Political Theory of the Firm', in D. Coen, W. Grant and G. Wilson (eds), *The Oxford Handbook of Business and Government* (Oxford: Oxford University Press): 173–90.

Harvey, B. (1995) *Networking in Europe: A Guide to European Voluntary Organisations* (London: NCVO Publications).

Hayes-Renshaw, F. (2009) 'Least Accessible but Not Inaccessible: Lobbying the Council and the European Council', in D. Coen and J. Richardson (eds), *Lobbying the European Union: Institutions, Issues and Actors* (Oxford: Oxford University Press): 70–88.

Hayes-Renshaw, F. and Wallace, H. (2006, 2nd edn) *The Council of Ministers* (Basingstoke: Palgrave Macmillan).

Helfferich, B. and Kolb, F. (2000) 'Multilevel Action Coordination in European Contentious Politics: The Case of the European Women's Lobby', in D. Imig and S. Tarrow (eds), *Contentious Europeans: Protest and Politics in an Integrating Europe* (Lanham, MD: Rowman and Littlefield): 143–62.

Hillman, A. J., Keim, G. D. and Schuler, D. (2004) 'Corporate Political Activity: A Review and Research Agenda', *Journal of Management*, 30: 837–57.

Hood, L. (2009) 'Critics Say Commission's Lobbying Register Must Be Mandatory to Make a Difference', Research Research.com, issue 282, 6 August 2009.

Hooghe, L. (1994) 'Political-Administrative Adaptation in the EU and Regional Mobilization: The European Commission and the Structural Funds', paper prepared for presentation at the IXth International Conference of Europeanists, Council for European Studies, Chicago, 30 March–1 April 1994.

Hooghe, L. (1995) 'Subnational Mobilisation in the European Union', *West European Politics*, 18 (3), July: 175–98.

Hooghe, L. (2002) 'The Mobilisation of Territorial Interests and Multilevel Governance', in R. Balme and D. Chabanet (eds), *Collective Action in Europe* (Paris: Presses de Sciences Po): 347–74.

Hooghe, L. and Marks, G. (1996) '"Europe with the Regions": Channels of Regional Representation in the European Union', *Publius*, 26 (1), Winter: 1–20.

Hooghe, L., Marks, G. and Schakel, A. (2010) *The Rise of Regional Authority: A Comparative Study of 42 Democracies (1950–2006)* (London: Routledge).

Hoskyns, C. (1996) *Integrating Gender: Women, Law and Politics in the European Union* (London: Verso).

Hrbek, R. (1995) 'Federal Balance and the Problem of Democratic Legitimacy in the European Union', *Aussenwirtschaft*, 50: 43–66, 64.

Hüller, T. and Quittkat, C. (2009) 'Democratising the European Union via Civil Society Involvement? The Case of the Commission's On-line Consultations', paper prepared for presentation at the workshop on Bringing Civil Society in: The European Union and the Rise of Representative Democracy, European University Institute, Florence, 13–14 March.

Huysseune, M. and Jans, T. (2008) 'Brussels as the Capital of a Europe of the Regions? Regional Offices as European Policy Actors, Brussels Studies, 16, 25 February', http://www.brusselsstudies.be/PDF/EN_57_BruS16EN.pdf, accessed on 2 February 2010.

Imig, D. and Tarrow, S. (1999) 'The Europeanisation of Movements? A New Approach to Transnational Contention', in D. della Porta, H. Kriesi and D. Rucht (eds), *Social Movements in a Globalizing World* (London: Routledge).

INGO (International Non Governmental Organisations) (2011) 'International Non Governmental Organisations Charter for Accountability', http://www.ingoaccountabilitycharter.org/, accessed on 12 January 2011.

Institut des Sciences du Travail (1999) 'Report on the Representativeness of European Social Partner Organisations', Part 1, http://www.europa.eu.int/comm/employment_social/soc-dial/social/index_en.htm, accessed on 5 September 2006.

Jacobs, G. (2003) 'Suggestion for Amendment of Article 34', presented to European Convention 2003/4, http://european-convention.eu.int/Docs/Treaty/pdf/34/Art34JacobsEN.pdf, accessed on 13 November 2010.

Jarman, H. (2011) 'Collaboration and Consultation: Functional Representation in EU Stakeholder Dialogues', *Journal of European Integration*, 33 (4).

Jefferies, D. and Evetts, J. (2000) 'Approaches to the International Recognition of Professional Qualifications in Engineering and the Sciences', *European Journal of Engineering Education*, 25 (1): 99–107.

Jeffery, C. (2000) 'Sub-National Mobilization and European Integration: Does It Make Any Difference?' *Journal of Common Market Studies*, 38 (1): 1–23.

Joerges, C. (1999) '"Good Governance" through Comitology?' in C. Joerges and E. Vos (eds), *EU Committees: Social Regulation, Law and Politics* (Oxford: Hart): 311–38.

Joerges, C. and Neyer, J. (1997) 'Transforming Strategic Interaction into Deliberative Problem-Solving: European Comitology in the Foodstuffs Sector', *Journal of European Public Policy*, 4 (4): 609–25.

John, P. (1996) 'The Presence and Influence of UK Local Authorities in Brussels', *Public Administration*, 74 (2): 293–313.

John, P. (2000a) 'The Europeanisation of Sub-National Governance', *Urban Studies*, 37 (5–6): 877–94.

John, P. (2000b) 'A Europe of Regimes? Urban Collective Action in the Global Era', paper prepared for presentation at the XVIIIth World Congress of the International Political Science Association, Quebec City, 1–5 August.

John, P. and McAteer, M. (1998) 'Sub-National Institutions and the New European Governance: UK Local Authority Lobbying Strategies for the IGC', *Regional and Federal Studies*, 8 (3): 104–24.

Jordan, A. G. and Maloney, W. (1997) *The Protest Business* (Manchester: Manchester University Press).

Kallas, S. (2005) 'The Need for a European Transparency Initiative', speech in Nottingham of 3 March 2005, speech no.:05/130, http://europa.eu/rapid/pressReleasesAction.do?reference=SPEECH/05/130&format=HTML&aged=0&language=EN&guiLanguage=en, accessed on 13 November 2010.

Kallas, S. (2007) 'Lobbying: What Europe Can Learn from the US', speech to the EU Committee of the American Chamber of Commerce, 18.9.2007, http://europa.eu/rapid/pressReleasesAction.do?reference=SPEECH/07/544&format=HTML&aged=0&language=EN&guiLanguage=en, accessed on 9 November 2010.

Kamm, O. (1995) 'Greenpeace and the Politics of Honesty', *The Independent*, 8 September 1995, http://www.independent.co.uk/opinion/letter–greenpeace-and-the-politics-of-honesty-1600021.html, accessed on 5 November 2010.

Kaufmann B., Lamassoure, A. and Meyer, J. (2004) *Transnational Democracy in the Making* (Amsterdam: Initiative & Referendum Europe).

Kautto, P. (2009) 'Nokia as an Environmental Policy Actor: Evaluation of Collaborative Corporate Political Activity in a Multinational Company', *Journal of Common Market Studies*, 47 (1): 103–25.

Keating, M. (1995) 'Europeanism and Regionalism', in B. Jones and M. Keating (eds), *The European Union and the Regions* (Oxford: Clarendon Press): 1–22.

Keating, M. and Hooghe, L. (2006) 'Bypassing the Nation-State? Regions and the EU Policy Process', in J. Richardson (ed.), *European Union: Power and Policy Making* (Oxford: Oxford University Press): 239–58.

Keating, M. and Waters, N. (1985) 'Scotland in the European Community', in M. Keating (ed.), *Regions in the European Community* (Oxford: Clarendon Press).

Kendall, J. and Fraisse, L. (2005) 'The European Statute of Association: Why an Obscure but Contested Symbol in a Sea of Indifference and Scepticism?' Third Sector European Partnership, Third Sector European Partnership Working Paper no. 11 Department of Social Policy, London School of Economics, www.lse.ac.uk/collections/ TSEP/ OpenAccessDocuments/11%20TSEP.pdf, accessed on 10 July 2010.

Kendall, J., Will, C. and Brandsen, T. (2009) 'The Third Sector and the Brussels Dimension: Trans-EU Governance Work in Progress', in J. Kendall (ed.), *Handbook on Third Sector Policy in Europe: Multi-Level Processes and Organized Civil Society* (Cheltenham: Edward Elgar).

Kingdon, J. (1995, 2nd edn) *Agendas, Alternatives and Public Policy* (New York: Harper Collins).

Kirchner, E. and Schweiger, H. (1981) *The Role of Interest Groups in the European Community* (Aldershot: Gower).

Kirchner, T. (2006) 'Interest Groups and the Legitimation of Governance in the European Union', M.Phil. thesis, University of Cambridge.

Kirk, L. (2005) 'Brussels Lobbyists to Come under Stricter Monitoring', http://euobserver.com/?aid=18597&rk=1, accessed on 27 August 2010.

Knill, C. (2001) 'Private Governance across Multiple Arenas: European Interest Associations as Interface Actors', *Journal of European Public Policy*, 8 (2), April: 227–46.

Knodt, M. (2002) 'Regions in Multilevel Governance Arrangements: Leadership versus Partnerships', in J. Grote and B. Gbikpi (eds), *Participatory Governance: Political and Societal Implications* (Opladen: Leske & Budrich).

Kohler-Koch, B. (2007) 'The Organization of Interests and Democracy in the European Union', in B. Kohler-Koch and B. Rittberger (eds), *Debating the Democratic Legitimacy of the European Union* (Plymouth: Rowman and Littlefield): 255–71.

Kohler-Koch, B. (2008) 'Efficient and Democratic Governance in a Multi-Level Europe: Final Activity Report', http://www.mzes.uni-mannheim. de/projekte/typo3/site/fileadmin/reports/Publishable_Final_Report.pdf, accessed on 3 September 2010.

Kohler-Koch, B. (2010a) 'How to Put Matters Right? Assessing the Role of Civil Society in EU Accountability', *West European Politics*, 33 (5): 1117–41.

Kohler-Koch, B. (2010b) 'Civil Society and EU Democracy: Astroturf Representation', *Journal of European Public Policy*, 17 (1): 100–16.

Kohler-Koch, B. and Quittkat, C. (2011) *The Disenchantment of Participatory Democracy: The Role of Civil Society in the Democratisation of EU Governance* (Frankfurt/Main: Campus Verlag).

Kok, W. (2004) 'Facing the Challenge: The Lisbon Strategy for Growth and Employment', report from the High Level Group Chaired by Wim Kok, ec.europa.eu/growthandjobs/pdf/kok_report_en.pdf, accessed on 5 September 2006.

Lahusen, C. (2002) 'Professional Consultancies in the European Union: Findings of a Survey on Commercial Interest Intermediation', typescript, Otto-Friedrich-Universität Bamberg.

Lahusen, C. (2003) 'Moving into the European Orbit: Commercial Consultants in the European Union', *European Union Politics*, 4 (2): 191–218.

Landmarks Publications (2001) *European Public Affairs Directory 2002* (Brussels: Landmarks).

Landmarks Publications (2007) *European Public Affairs Directory 2006* (Brussels: Landmarks).

Lange, P. (1992) 'The Politics of the Social Dimension', in A. M. Sbragia (ed.), *Euro Politics: Institutions and Policymaking in the "New" European Community* (Washington, DC: Brookings): 225–56.

Laslett, J. (1991) 'The Mutual Recognition of Diplomas, Certificates and Other Evidence of Formal Qualifications in the European Community', *Legal Issues of European Integration 1990/1*, Amsterdam.

Leblond, P. (2008) 'The Fog of Integration: Reassessing the Role of Economic Interests in European Integration', *British Journal of Politics and International Relations*, 10: 9–26.

Lehmann, W. (2009) 'The European Parliament', in D. Coen and J. Richardson (eds), *Lobbying the European Union: Institutions, Actors and Issues* (Oxford: Oxford University Press): 39–69.

Lehmkuhl, D. (2000) 'Under Stress: Europeanisation and Trade Associations in the Member States', European Integration online Papers (EIoP) Vol. 4 (2000) N° 14; http://eiop.or.at/eiop/texte/2000-014a.htm, accessed on 13 November 2010.

Leigh, C. (2009) 'Independence and Transnational Activism: Lessons from Gleneagles, Cosmopolis, 1', http://agora.qc.ca/cosmopolis.nsf/Archives, accessed on 12 November 2010.

Lenschow, A. (1996) 'The Nature and Transformation of Governance in European Environmental Policy', paper prepared for presentation at the 'Joint Sessions of the European Consortium for Political Research', Oslo, 29 March–3 April.

Lenschow, A. (1999) 'Transformation in European Environmental Governance', in B. Kohler-Koch and R. Eising (eds), *The Transformation of Governance in the European Union* (London: Routledge): 39–60.

Leonardi, R. (1993) *The Regions and the European Community* (London: Frank Cass).

Leonardi, R. and Nanetti, R. (1990) *The Regions and European Integration: The Case of Emilia Romagna* (London: Pinter).

Levy, D. and Prakash, A. (2003) 'Bargains Old and New: Multinational Corporations in Global Governance', *Business and Politics*, 5 (2): 131–50.

Lijphart, A. (1999) *Patterns of Democracy: Government Forms and Performance in Thirty-Six Countries* (New Haven: Yale University Press).

Lindberg, L. (1963) *The Political Dynamics of European Economic Integration* (Stanford: Stanford University Press).

Lindblom, C. (1977) *Politics and Markets* (New York: Basic Books).

Long, T. (1995) 'Shaping Public Policy in the European Union: A Case Study of the Structural Funds', *Journal of European Public Policy*, 2 (4): 672–9.

Long, T. and Lörinczi, L. (2009) 'NGOs as Gatekeepers: A Green Vision', in D. Coen and J. Richardson (eds), *Lobbying the European Union: Institutions, Issues and Actors* (Oxford: Oxford University Press): 169–88.

Long, T., Salter, L. and Singer, S. (2002) 'WWF: European and Global Climate Policy', in R. Pedler (ed.), *Lobbying the European Union: Changes in the Arena* (Basingstoke: Palgrave Macmillan): 87–103.

Lord, C. and Magnette, P. (2004) 'E Pluribus Unum? Creative Disagreement about Legitimacy in the EU', *Journal of Common Market Studies*, 42 (1): 183–202.

Lovecy, J. (1993) 'Regulating Professional Services in the Single European Market: The Cases of Legal and Medical Services in France and the United Kingdom', paper prepared for presentation at the Third Biennial International Conference of the European Community Studies Association, Washington, DC, 27–29 May.

Lovecy, J. (1999) 'Governance Transformation in the Professional Services Sector: A Case of Market Integration by the Back Door', in B. Kohler-Koch and R. Eising (eds), *The Transformation of Governance in the European Union* (London: Routledge): 135–52.

Lowery, D. (2007) 'Why Do Organized Interests Lobby? A Multi-Goal, Multi-Context Theory of Lobbying', *Polity*, 39 (1): 29–54.

Lowi, T. (1964) 'American Business, Public Policy, Case-Studies and Political Theory', *World Politics*, 16 (4), July: 677–715.

Magnette, P. (2006) 'Democracy in the European Union: Why and How to Combine Representation and Participation', in S. Smismans (ed.), *Civil Society and Legitimate European Governance* (Cheltenham: Edward Elgar): 23–41.

Mahoney, C. (2004) 'The Power of Institutions: State and Interest Group Activity in the European Union', *European Union Politics*, 5 (4): 441–66.

Mahoney, C. (2008) *Brussels versus the Beltway: Advocacy in the United States and the European Union* (Washington DC: Georgetown University Press).

Mahoney, C. and Beckstrand, M. (2009) 'Following the Money: EU Funding of Civil Society Organisations', paper prepared for presentation at the 11th Biennial European Union Studies Association (EUSA) Conference, Los Angeles, 23–25 April 2009.

Majone, G. (1996) *Regulating Europe* (London: Routledge).

Mamadouh, V. (2001) 'The Regions in Brussels: Subnational Actors in the Supranational Arena', *Tijdscrift voor Economische en Sociale Geografie*, 92 (4): 478–87.

Marginson, P. and Sisson, K. (1998) 'European Collective Bargaining: A Virtual Prospect?' *Journal of Common Market Studies*, December, 36 (4): 505–28.

Marks, G. (1992) 'Structural Policy in the European Community', in A. Sbragia (ed.), *Euro Politics: Institutions and Policy Making in the 'New' European Community* (Washington, DC: Brookings): 191–224.

Marks, G. (1993) 'Structural Policy and Multilevel Governance in the EC', in A. Cafruny and G. Rosenthal (eds), *The State of the European Community*, vol. 2 (Boulder, CO: Lynne Rienner): 391–410.

Marks, G., Haesley, R. and Mbaye, H. (2002) 'What Do Subnational Offices Think They Are Doing in Brussels?' *Regional and Federal Studies*, 12 (3): 1–23.

Marks, G. and McAdam, D. (1996) 'Social Movements and the Changing Structure of Political Opportunity in the European Union,' *West European Politics*, 19 (2): 349–78.

Marks, G. and McAdam, D. (1999) 'On the Relationship of Political Opportunities to the Form of Collective Action: the Case of the European Union', in D. della Porta, H. Kriesi and D. Rucht (eds), *Social Movements in a Globalizing World* (London: Routledge).

Marshall, D. (2010) 'Who to Lobby and When: Institutional Determinants of Interest Group Strategies in European Parliament Committees', *European Union Politics*, 11 (4): 533–52.

Martin, S. (1993) 'The Europeanisation of Local Authorities: Challenges for Rural Areas', *Journal of Rural Studies*, 9 (2): 153–61.

Martin, A. and Ross, G. (2001) 'Trade Union Organizing at the European Level', in D. Imig and S. Tarrow (eds), *Contentious Europeans* (Lanham, MD: Rowman and Littlefield): 53–76.

Mattli, W. (1999) *The Logic of Regional Integration* (Cambridge: Cambridge University Press).

Mazey, S. (2000) 'Introduction: Integrating Gender-Intellectual and "Real World" Mainstreaming', *Journal of European Public Policy*, 7 (3): 333–45.

Mazey, S. and Richardson, J. (1999) 'Interests', in L. Cram, D. Dinan and N. Nugent (eds), *Developments in the European Union* (Basingstoke: Macmillan): 105–29.

Mazey, S. and Richardson, J. (2005) 'Environmental Groups and the European Community: Challenges and Opportunities', in A. Jordan (ed.), *Environmental Policy in the European Union* (London: Earthscan): 106–21.

McAleavy, P. (1994) *The Political Logic of the European Community Structural Funds Budget: Lobbying Efforts by Declining Industrial Regions*, EUI Working Paper Robert Schuman Centre no. 94/2 (Florence: European University Institute).

McCann, K. (2010) 'MEPs: Banking Lobby "Danger to Democracy"', *Public Affairs News*, August: 12.

McGown, M. (2009) 'Interest Groups and the European Court of Justice', in D. Coen and J. Richardson (eds), *Lobbying the European Union: Institutions, Issues and Actors* (Oxford: Oxford University Press): 89–104.

McLaughlin, A. M. (1992) 'Underfed Euro Feds', paper prepared for presentation at the Annual Conference of the Political Studies Association, Queens University, Belfast, 21 April.

McLaughlin, A. M. and Greenwood, J. (1995) 'The Management of Interest Representation in the European Union', *Journal of Common Market Studies*, 33 (1) March: 143–56.

Metcalfe, L. (2001) 'More Green than Blue: Positioning the Governance White Paper', *EUSA Review*, 14 (4): 3–4.

Moore, C. (2006) '"Schloss Neuwhahnstein"? Why the Länder Continue to Strengthen Their Representations in Brussels', *German Politics*, 15 (2): 192–205.

Moravcsik, A. (1993) 'Preferences and Power in the European Community: A Liberal Intergovernmentalist Approach', *Journal of Common Market Studies*, 31 (4), December: 473–524.

Moravcsik, A. (1998) *The Choice for Europe: Social Purpose and State Power from Messina to Maastricht* (Ithaca: Cornell University Press).

Moravcsik, A. (2002) 'In Defence of the Democratic Deficit: Reassessing Legitimacy in the European Union', *Journal of Common Market Studies*, 40 (4): 603–24.

Müller, H. W. (1997) 'Thinking Small, Acting Big', *European Voice*, 3 (20), 22–28 May: 14.

Murgado, R. (2010) 'Explaining Transnational NGOs Evolution within European Governance', Ph.D. proposal (Mons: Les Facultés Universitaires Catholiques de Mons (FUCaM)).

Naurin, D. (2005) 'Why Increasing Transparency in the European Union Will Not Make Lobbyists Behave Any Better Than They Already Do', paper prepared for presentation at the 9th Biennial Conference of the European Union Studies Association, Austin, 31 March–2 April.

Naurin, D. (2007) *Deliberation behind Closed Doors: Transparency and Lobbying in the European Union* (Colchester: ECPR Press).

NCVO (National Council for Voluntary Organisations) (2010) '20 Civil Society Organisations Begin Work on European "Compact"', http://www.ncvo-vol.org.uk/documents/press-releases/20-civil-society-organisations-begin-work-european-compact, accessed on 9 November 2010.

Neale, P. (1994) 'Expert Interest Groups and the European Commission: Professional Influence on EC Legislation', *International Journal of Sociology and Social Policy*, 14 (6/7): 1–24.

Nicoll, W. and Salmon, T. (1990) *Understanding the European Communities* (Hemel Hempstead: Harvester Wheatsheaf).

Nollert, M. and Fielder, N. (2000) 'Lobbying for a Europe of Big Business: The European Roundtable of Industrialists', in V. Bornschier (ed.), *State-Building in Europe: The Revitalization of Western European Integration* (Cambridge: Cambridge University Press): 187–209.

Nugent, N. (2010, 7th edn) *The Government and Politics of the European Union* (Basingstoke: Palgrave Macmillan).

Offe, C. (1981) 'The Attribution of Public Status to Interest Groups: Observations on the West German Case', in S. Berger (ed.), *Organizing Interests in Western Europe: Pluralism, Corporatism and the Transformation of Politics* (Cambridge: Cambridge University Press): 123–58.

Olson, M. (1965) *The Logic of Collective Action* (Cambridge, MA: Harvard University Press).

Olson, M. (1971) *The Rise and Decline of Nations* (New Haven: Yale University Press).

Olsson, A. (2009) 'Euroscepticism Revisited – Regional Interest Representation in Brussels and the Link to Citizen Attitudes towards European Integration', paper prepared for delivery at the 11th Biennial Conference of the EU Studies Association, Los Angeles, 23–25 April.

Orzack, L. (1991) 'The General Systems Directive and the Liberal Professions', in L. Hurwitz and C. Lequesne (eds), *The State of the European Community* (Boulder, CO: Lynne Rienner): 137–51.

Orzack, L. (1992) 'International Authority and the Professions: The State beyond the Nation State', Jean Monnet Chair Papers, European Policy Unit at the European University Institute (Florence: EUI).

Pappi, F. and Henning, C. (1999) 'The Organization of Influence on the EC's Common Agricultural Policy: A Network Approach', *European Journal of Political Research*, 36: 257–81.

Parks, L. (2009a) 'In the Corridors and in the Streets: Evidence on EU-Level Campaigns by Social Movement Organisations', paper prepared for the conference on Bringing Civil Society in: The European Union and the Rise of Representative Democracy, European University Institute, Florence, 14 March.

Parks, L. (2009b) 'Improving Accountability in the European Union – The potential Role of NGOs', in S. Gustavsson, C. Karlsson and T. Persson (eds), *The Illusion of Accountability in the European Union* (London: Routledge): 155–69.

Pateman, C. (1970) *Participation and Democratic Theory* (Cambridge: Cambridge University Press).

Pedler, R. (1994) 'ETUC and the Pregnant Woman', in R. H. Pedler and M. P. C. M. van Schendelen (eds), *Lobbying the European Union: Companies, Trade Associations And Issue Groups* (Aldershot: Dartmouth): 241–58.

Persson, T. (2009) 'Civil Society Participation and Accountability', in S. Gustavsson, C. Karlsson and T. Persson (eds), *The Illusion of Accountability in the European Union* (London: Routledge): 141–54.

Phillips, A. (1995) *The Politics of Presence* (Oxford: Clarendon Press).

Phillips, L. (2009) 'Italian Prankster Spams EU Lobbyist Register', http://euobserver.com/9/27602, accessed on 27 August 2010.

Pitkin, H. (1967) *The Concept of Representation* (Berkeley: University of California Press).

Platform of European Social NGOs (2001) 'Democracy, Governance and European NGOs', http://ec.europa.eu/governance/social-ngos_en.pdf, p. 6, accessed on 14 July 2010.

Pochet, P. (2003) 'Subsidiarity, Social Dialogue and the Open Method of Co-Ordination: The Role of Trade Unions', in D. Foster and P. Scott (eds), *Trade Unions in Europe: Meeting the Challenge* (Brussels: P.I.E.-Peter Lang): 87–113.

Pointer, S. (2002) 'Promoting Consumer Confidence in e-Commerce: The "Brussels Regulation" – Real or Illusory Consumer Benefit? The Business Case', in R. Pedler (ed.), *Lobbying the European Union: Changes in the Arena* (Basingstoke: Macmillan): 35–56.

Pollack, M. (1997) 'Representing Diffuse Interests in EC Policy-Making', *Journal of European Public Policy*, 4 (4), December: 572–90.

Public Affairs News (2010) '"Revolving Doors" Cases Irk Transparency Groups', http://www.publicaffairsnews.com/no_cache/home/european-news/news-detail/newsarticle/revolving-door-cases-irk-transparency-groups/10/?tx_ttnews%5Bpointer%5D=8&cHash=d3282ae76a, accessed on 18 January 2011.

Quittkat, C. (2011) 'The European Commission's Online Consultations: A Success Story?' *Journal of Common Market Studies*, 49 (3): 653–74.

Quittkat, C. and Kotzian, P. (2011) 'Lobbying via Consultation – Territorial and Functional Interests in the Commission's Consultation Regime', *Journal of European Integration*, 33 (4).

Rhinard, M. (2002) 'The Democratic Legitimacy of the European Union Committee System', *Governance*, 15 (2): 185–210.

Richardson, J. and Coen, D. (2009) 'Institutionalizing and Managing Intermediation in the EU', in D. Coen and J. Richardson (eds), *Lobbying the European Union: Institutions, Actors and Arenas* (Oxford: Oxford University Press): 337–50.

Richardson, K. (1997) 'Introductory Foreword', in H. Wallace and A. Young (eds), *Participation and Policy Making in the European Union* (Oxford: Clarendon Press): xvii–xxiv.

Richardson, K. (2000) 'Big Business and the European Agenda', Sussex European Institute Working Papers 35, http://www.sussex.ac.uk/sei/1-4-10-1.html, accessed on 13 November 2010.

Riedel, R. (2010) 'Silesian Representations in Brussels – Objectives, Performance, Evaluations', paper presented at the International Political Science Association International conference Is There a European Model of Governance, Luxembourg, 18–20 March 2010.

Risse-Kappen, T. (1995) 'Structures of Governance and Transnational Relations: What Have we Learned?' in T. Risse-Kappen (eds), *Bringing Transnational Relations Back in: Non-State Actors, Domestic Structures and International Institutions* (Cambridge: Cambridge University Press): 3–36.

Roethig, O. (1994) 'Transnational Cooperation amongst Labour Groups', paper prepared for presentation at the Joint Sessions of the European Consortium for Political Research, Madrid, 17–22 April.

Roethig, O. (1995) 'ETUC and Trade Unions in Europe', in J. Greenwood (ed.), *European Casebook on Business Alliances* (Hemel Hempstead: Prentice-Hall): 271–82.

Ross, G. (1994) 'Inside the Delors Cabinet', *Journal of Common Market Studies*, 32 (4): 499–523.

Rucht, D. (1993) 'Think Globally, Act Locally? Needs, Forms and Problems of Cross-National Cooperation among Environmental Groups', in J. D. Lowe, P. D. Liefferink and A. P. J. Mol (eds), *European Integration and Environmental Policy* (London: Belhaven Press): 75–96.

Ruzza, C. (2000) 'Interests and Ideas in EU Level Environmental Policy: The Case of Tourism Policy', paper prepared for presentation at the XVIIIth World Congress of the International Political Science Association, Quebec City, 1–5 August.

Ruzza, C. (2011) 'Social Movements and the European Interest Intermediation of Public Interest Groups', *Journal of European Integration*, 33 (4).

Sabatier, P. (1988) 'An Advocacy Coalition Framework of Policy Change and the Role of Policy Oriented Learning Therein', *Policy Sciences* (21): 129–68.

Salisbury, R. H. (1969) 'An Exchange Theory of Interest Groups', *Midwest Journal of Political Science*, 13 (1): 1–32.

Sandholtz, W. and Zysman, J. (1989) '1992: Recasting the European Bargain', *World Politics*: 95–128.

Sargent, J. (1987) 'The Organisation of Business Interests for European Community Representation', in W. Grant and J. Sargent (eds), *Business and Politics in Britain* (Basingstoke: Macmillan): 213–238.

Saurugger, S. (2006) 'The Professionalisation of Interest Representation: A Legitimacy Problem for Civil Society in the EU?' in S. Smismans (ed.), *Civil Society and Legitimate European Governance* (Cheltenham: Edward Elgar): 260–76.

Saurugger, S. (2009) 'Analyzing Civil Society Organizations' Changing Structures in the EU. Lessons from the Social Movement and Party Politics Literature', paper prepared for the conference on 'Bringing Civil Society in: The European Union and the Rise of Representative Democracy', European University Institute, Florence, 14 March.

Saurugger, S. (2010) 'COREPER and National Governments', in D. Coen and J. Richardson (eds), *Lobbying the European Union: Institutions, Issues and Actors* (Oxford: Oxford University Press): 105–27.

Schneider, A (2003) 'Decentralization: Conceptualization and Measurement', *Studies in Comparative International Development*, Fall, 38 (3): 32–56.

Schultze, C. (2003) 'Cities and EU Governance: Policy-Takers or Policy-Makers', *Regional and Federal Studies*, 13 (1): 121–47.

Scotland Europa (2002) 'WWF Launches Campaign to Reform EU Fisheries Policy', 2002 Report (Fisheries), Issue 1 (Brussels: Scotland Europa).

Sidjanski, D. (1967) 'Pressure Groups and the European Community', *Government and Opposition*, 2 (3): 397–416.

Sietses, H. (2000) 'The European Round Table of Industrialists – An Assessment of Its Position', MSc Thesis, Erasmus University Rotterdam.

Sikkink, K. (2002) 'Restructuring World Politics: The Limits and Asymmetries of Soft Power', in S. Khagram, J. Riker and K. Sikkink (eds), *Reconstructing World Politics: Transnational Social Movements and Norms* (Minnesota: University of Minnesota Press): 301–17.

Slim, H. (2002) 'By What Authority? The Legitimacy and Accountability of Non-Governmental Organisations', *The Journal of Humanitarian Assistance*, http://www.jha.ac/articles/a082.htm, accessed on 13 November 2010.

Smismans, S. (2003) 'European Civil Society: Shaped by Discourses and Institutional Interests', *European Law Journal*, 9 (4): 482–504.

Smismans, S. (2005) 'Reflexive Law in Support of Directly Deliberative Polyarchy: Reflexive-Deliberative Polyarchy as a Normative Frame for the Open Method of Coordination', in O. De Schutter and S. Deakin (eds), *Social Rights and Market Forces: Is the Open Coordination of Employment and Social Policies the Future of Social Europe?* (Louvain-la-Neuve: Bruylant): 99–144.

Smismans, S. (2008) 'The European Social Dialogue in the Shadow of Hierarchy', *Journal of Public Policy*, 28 (1): 161–80.

Smismans, S. (2010) 'European Constitutionalism and the Democratic Design of European Governance: Rethinking Directly Deliberative Polyarchy and Reflexive Constitutionalism', in K. Tuori and S. Sankari (eds), *The Many Constitutions of Europe* (Aldershot: Ashgate): 169–94.

Smith, M. (2008) 'All Access Points Are Not Created Equal: Explaining the Fate of Diffuse Interests in the EU', *British Journal of Politics and International Relations* (10): 64–83.

Social Platform (2010) *How to Establish an Effective Dialogue between the EU and Civil Society Organisations* (Brussels: Social Platform).

Stern, A. (1994) *Lobbying in Europe After Maastricht: How to Keep Abreast and Wield Influence in the European Union* (Brussels: Club de Bruxelles).

Stichele-Somo, M. (2008) 'Financial Regulation in the European Union: Mapping EU Decision Making Structures on Financial Regulation and Supervision', http://www.eurodad.org/uploadedFiles/Whats_New/Reports/EUMapping_Financial_Regulation_FINAL.pdf, accessed on 12 November 2010.

Streeck, W. and Schmitter, P. C. (1985) *Private Interest Government: Beyond Market and State* (London: Sage).

Sudbery, I. (2003) 'Bridging the Legitimacy Gap in the EU: Can Civil Society Help to Bring the Union Closer to Its Citizens', *Collegium* (26), Spring: 75–95.

Sutcliffe, J. and Kovacev, M. (2005) 'Scottish Local Governments in the European Union: A Deepening Relationship within a Multi-Level Governance Setting', paper prepared for presentation at the Annual Meeting of the Canadian Political Science Association, University of Western Ontario, June.

Sutherland, P. (1992) 'The Internal Market After 1992: Meeting the Challenge', report to the European Commission by the High Level Group on the Operation of the Internal Market (Brussels: Commission of the European Communities).

Swianiewicz, P. (2002) *Consolidation or Fragmentation? The Size of Local Governments in Central and Eastern Europe* (LGI Books: Hungary).

Tanasescu, I. (2009) *The European Commission and Interest Groups* (Brussels: VUB Press).

Tarrow, S. (2006) *The New Transnational Activism* (Cambridge: Cambridge University Press).

Tatham, M. (2008) 'Going Solo: Direct Regional Representation in the EU', *Regional and Federal Studies*, 18 (5), October: 493–515.

Tenbücken, M. (2002) *Corporate Lobbying in the European Union* (Frankfurt: Peter Lang Press).

Thier, B. (2009) 'Implementing the ECTA Responsible Care Scheme in the European Chemical Land Transport Industry', presentation to the

European Chemical Transport Association Conference Barcelona, 13 February 2009, http://www.ecta.be/public/content/meetings/barcelona/docs/2.B.%20Thier.pdf, accessed on 17 January 2011.

Thomas, C. (2004) 'Cyberactivism and Corporations: New Strategies', in S. John and S. Thomson (eds), *New Activism and the Corporate Response* (Basingstoke: Palgrave Macmillan): 115–36.

Thomas, C. and Boyer, M. (2001) 'The American Interest Group Community in the European Union: Development, Make-Up and Operating Techniques', paper prepared for presentation at the 7th biennial conference of the European Community Studies Association, Madison/Wisconsin, 31 May–3 June 2001.

Timesonline (2011) 'I Did Not Know about Brothels or Slush Fund, VW Boss Tells Court', http://www.timesonline.co.uk/tol/news/world/europe/article3162451.ece, accessed on 17 January 2011.

Trade Association Forum (2006) *Commentary on the 2005 Benchmarking Study of Trade Associations* (London: Trade Association Forum).

Trade Union Congress (TUC) (1988) *Minutes of Congress 1988* (London: TUC).

Traxler, F. (1991) 'The Logic of Employers' Collective Action', in D. Sadowski and O. Jacobi (eds), *Employers' Associations in Europe: Policy and Organisation* (Baden-Baden: Nomos): 28–50.

Turner, L. (1995) 'The Europeanization of Labor: Structure before Action', paper prepared for presentation at the Fourth Biennial International Conference of the European Community Studies Association, Charleston, SC, 11–14 May.

Tyszkiewicz, Z. (1998) 'The European Social Dialogue, 1985–1998: A Personal View', in E. Gabaglio and R. Hoffman (eds), *The European Trade Union Yearbook 1998* (Brussels: ETUI): 35–47.

Tyszkiewicz, Z. (2001) 'National Members and Their EU Associations', in J. Greenwood (ed.), *The Effectiveness of EU Business Associations* (Basingstoke: Palgrave Macmillan): 171–81.

Van Apeldoorn, B. (2000) 'Transnational Class Agency and European Governance: The Case of the European Round Table of Industrialists', *New Political Economy*, 5 (2): 157–81.

Van Apeldoorn, B. (2001) 'The European Round Table of Industrialists: Still a Unique Player?' in J. Greenwood (ed.), *The Effectiveness of EU Business Associations* (Basingstoke: Palgrave Macmillan).

van Schendelen, M. P. C. M. (1998) 'Prologomena to EU Committees as Influential Policy Makers', in *EU Committees as Influential Policymakers* (Aldershot: Ashgate): 3–22.

Van Tulder, R. and Junne, G. (1988) *European Multinationals in Core Technologies* (New York: John Wiley).

Van der Storm, I. (2002) 'CASTer: Creating the Future in Steel Regions', R. Pedler (ed.), *European Union Lobbying: Changes in the Arena* (Basingstoke: Palgrave Macmillan): 229–56.

Van Waarden, F. (1991) 'Two Logics of Collective Action? Business Associations as Distinct from Trade Unions: the problems of associations of organisations', D. Sadowski and O. Jacobi (eds), *Employers Associations in Europe: Policy and Organization* (Baden-Baden: Nomos): 51–84.

Vogel, D. (1996) 'The Study of Business and Politics', *California Management Review*, 38 (3), Spring: 146–65.

Visser, J. and Ebbinghaus, B. (1992) 'Making the Most of Diversity? European Integration and Transnational Organization of Labour', in J. Greenwood, J. Grote and K. Ronit (eds), *Organized Interests and the European Community* (London: Sage): 206–37.

Wallace, H. (1997) 'Introduction', in H. Wallace and A. Young (eds), *Participation and Policy Making in the European Union* (Oxford: Clarendon Press): 1–16.

Wallace, H. and Young, A. (1997) 'Conclusions', in H. Wallace and A. Young (eds), *Participation and Policy Making in the European Union* (Oxford: Clarendon Press): 235–50.

Warleigh, A. (2000) 'The Hustle: Citizenship Practice, NGOs and "Policy Coalitions" in the European Union – The Cases of Auto Oil, Drinking Water and Unit Pricing', *Journal of European Public Policy*, 7 (2), June: 229–43.

Warleigh, A. (2001) 'Europeanizing Civil Society: NGOs as Agents of Political Socialization', *Journal of Common Market Studies*, November, 39 (4): 619–39.

Warleigh, A. (2003) *Democracy and the European Union* (London: Sage).

Watson, R. (2002) 'Knocking on the Parliament's Door', *E!Sharp*, February: 40–2.

Watson, R. and Shackleton, M. (2008, 2nd edn) 'Organized Interests and Lobbying', in J. Peterson and E. Bomberg (eds), *The European Union: How Does It Work?* (Oxford: Oxford University Press).

Weber, K. and Hallerberg, M. (2001) 'Explaining Variation in Institutional Integration in the European Union: Why Firms May Prefer European Solutions', *Journal of European Public Policy*, 8 (2), April: 171–91.

Webster, R. (1998) 'Coalition Formation and Collective Action: The Case of the Environmental G7', in M. Aspinwall and J. Greenwood (eds), *Collective Action in the European Union: Interests and the New Politics of Associability* (London: Routledge): 176–95.

Wendon, B. (1997) 'The Commission and Image-Venue Interaction in EU Social Policy', typescript, Anglia Polytechnic University.

Wessels, W. (1997) 'The Growth and Differentiation of Multi-Level Networks: A Corporatist Mega-Bureaucracy or an Open City?' in H. Wallace and R. Young (eds), *Participation and Policy Making in the European Union* (Oxford: Clarendon Press): 17–41.

White, D. (1997) 'Dealing with Trade Associations: A Two Way Process', in R. Bennett (ed.), *Trade Associations in Britain and Germany* (London: Anglo-German Foundation): 74–7.

Williams, G. (2005) 'Monomaniacs or Schizophrenics? Responsible Governance and the EU's Independent Agencies', *Political Studies*, 53 (1): 82–99.

Wilson, J. Q. (1995) *Political Organizations* (Princeton: Princeton University Press).

Wincott, D. (2004) 'Backing into the Future? Informality and the Proliferation of Governance Modes (and Policy Participants) in the EU', in T. Christiansen and S. Piattoni (eds), *Informal Governance in the European Union* (Cheltenham: Edward Elgar): 226–36.

Woll, C. (2006) 'Lobbying in the EU: From Sui Generis to a Comparative Perspective', *Journal of European Public Policy*, 14 (3), April: 456–69.

Woll, C. (2009) 'Trade Policy Lobbying in the European Union', in D. Coen and J. Richardson (eds), *Lobbying the European Union: Institutions, Actors and Issues* (Oxford: Oxford University Press): 277–97.

Wonka, A., Baumgartner, F., Mahoney, C. and Berkhout, J. (2010) 'Measuring the Size and Scope of the EU Interest Group Population', *European Union Politics*, 11 (3): 463–76.

Young, A. (1995) 'Participation and Policy Making in the European Community: Mediating between Competing Interests', paper prepared for presentation at the Fourth Biennial International Conference of the European Community Studies Association, Charleston, SC, 11–14 May.

Young, A. (1998) 'European Consumer Groups: Multiple Levels of Governance and Multiple Logics of Collective Action', in J. Greenwood and M. Aspinwall (eds), *Collective Action in the European Union: Interests and the New Politics of Associability* (London: Routledge): 149–75.

Young, A. R. (2010) 'The Politics of Regulation and the Internal Market', in K. E. Jørgensen, M. A. Pollack and B. Rosamond (eds), *Handbook of European Union Politics* (London: Sage): 373–94.

Young, A. and Wallace, H. (2000) *Regulatory Politics in the Enlarging European Union: Weighing Civic and Producer Interests* (Manchester: Manchester University Press).

Zadek, D. (2011) 'Corporate Europe Hypocrisy', http://risk-monger. blogactiv.eu/2010/05/25/corporate-europe-hypocrisy/, accessed on 17 January 2011.

Index

Access to Documents
   Regulation   32, 206, 208, 217
accountability   1–6, 22, 32
   citizen issues   136, 141, 173
   democratic legitimacy   200–11,
      218–23, 226
   lobbying   58, 63–4
   organized civil society   200–11,
      218–23, 226, 232, 235
advocacy   7, 15–17, 22, 93, 134–5,
      168, 171–4, 219, 225–6
Alhadeff, G.   130, 221–2
Alliance for a Competitive
      European Industry   75–6
ALTER-EU   59, 173–4
'alternative' perspectives   21, 81,
      156, 171, 203
AMCHAM-EU   73, 76, 78–9
Amnesty International   16, 136,
      140
Amsterdam Treaty   116, 145,
      159, 165, 167, 169–70, 193,
      209, 229
ANEC   48, 162–3
anti-globalization   8, 58, 171–2,
      203, 233–4
anti-racism   42, 116, 165–7
Assembly of European
      Regions   15, 190–1
associations   1–2, 9, 12–1, 22
   business *see separate entry*
   cross-sectoral   75–87, 99
   professional   60, 69, 96–100,
      103–6
   sector   86–92
   trade   10, 18–19, 23, 26, 48,
      54, 60, 69, 72, 88–92, 217
   see also individual associations

ATTAC   171, 174
Austria   76, 157, 187

Balme, R.   174, 192
Barroso, J. M.   61–2, 79, 113,
      136, 140, 154, 210, 222
Belgium   13, 45, 78, 83, 114, 176,
      187, 196
Bennett, R.   87, 90
Berkhout, J.   9, 11
Betts, P.   77, 79, 81, 83
BEUC   16, 48, 161–4
Birdlife International   155–7
Bouwen, P.   14, 29, 88, 233
Bouza Garcia, L.   8, 70, 135, 200,
      234
Branch, A.   49, 118
Browne, W.   71, 84
Brussels offices of the
      regions   176–7, 185–90, 198
business associations   16, 31, 63,
      67–75, 73, 86–92, 104, 107,
      147, 200–3, 232
   cross-sectoral   75–87, 76, 99
   direct company membership
      14, 18–20, 23, 67, 71–8,
      89–92, 147
Business Europe   14, 27–8, 49,
      51, 75–8, 83–6, 99, 118, 124,
      137, 220
business interests   65–9, 107–8
   single market   67, 80–2, 95–6,
      104–7
   see also business associations
Butt Philip, A.   12, 87, 147

Cabinets   36–7, 59–62, 151, 234
Caporaso, J.   14, 87

CASTer   180, 196
CEC   97, 99–100
CEE countries   46, 85, 124, 178–9
CEFIC   61, 88, 104, 147, 172
centre-local relations   177–9,
   181–5, 190–1
CEPLIS   15, 97, 100
Chabanet, D.   90, 174
Chalmers, A.   71, 192
channels of influence   23–7, 51–2
   'Brussels route'   25–6, 31–2
   inter-institutional mechanisms
   32–3, 45–7
   national route   27–31
   other EU-related structures
   47–8
   see also Commission; European
   Court of Justice; European
   Parliament; social dialogue
Cini, M.   36–7, *59*
citizen interests   128–30, *131,
   132–3,* 174–5
   consumers   128, *138,* 141, 145,
   148–9, 151, 158–64, 175
   development of   141–4
   environment   128, *131, 139,*
   140–2, *141,* 144–61, 164,
   174–5
   funding of NGOs   136–41, 144,
   150, *152,* 160–2, 165–8, 175
   organizational landscape   130–6
   social interests   164–71, 227
   social movements   171–5
Citizens Initiative   4, 28, 134–5, 217
Civil Society Contact Group   130,
   131, 135, 170, 221
codes of conduct   20, 38, *50,*
   54–8, 62–3, 102, 222–3, 226
Coen, D.   18, 91–2, 215, 234
Cohen, J.   223, 225
collective action   14, 44
   business   67–75, 88–90, 94, 107
   citizen issues   144, 161–2
   labour   110–11, 121–4

regions   178, 190–7
Commission   3, 5, 8, 24, 26, 28–9,
   32–40, 44, 47–9, 51–2
   business   70, 79–80, 84–91, 98,
   102–3, 122, 125
   citizen issues   129, 134–7,
   141–3, 147, 154–8, 163–4,
   168–70
   labour   111–13, 116–17, 119
   lobbying   55–9, 61–4
   organized civil society   199,
   206–15, 219–22, 226, 229–30,
   234
   regions   181, 184, 191–2, 196
Commissioners   36–8, 59–60, 62,
   69–70
   Cabinets of   36–7, 59–62, 151,
   234
Committee of The Regions   176–8,
   181, 183, 185, 187, 189, 191,
   196, 198
companies   20, 38, 118–19, 147,
   160, 163–4, 208, 212, 214,
   232
   direct membership associations
   14, 18–20, 23, 67, 71–8,
   89–92, 147
   see also firms; MNCs; SMEs
competencies, EU   7, 23, 26, 94–5,
   111, 142, 166–7, 178, 182,
   190, 196
   organized civil society
   199–200, 226–31, 235
Computer Implemented Inventions
   Directive   19, 41
CONECCS   9, 63, 217, 220, 222
Conference of Peripheral Maritime
   Regions   193, *194,* 231
consultation   2, 4, 9, 14, 32–9
   citizen issues   134, 140, 160
   labour   111–14, 118–19
   lobbying   57–8, 63
   organized civil society   206,
   209–16, 218–26, 230, 233–4

Consultative Council of Regional
  and Local Authorities   181,
  185, 191–2
consumer interests   3, 16, 41, 45,
  48
  business   68, 91
  citizen issues   128, *138,* 141,
    145, 148–9, 151, 158–64, 175
  organized civil society   204–5,
    210, 212–13, 220, 230
Consumer Programme   158, 161
Corporate Europe
  Observatory   58–61
Council of Europe   24, 28, 49–50,
  56, 113, 177, 184, 190–1
Council of European Municipalities
  and Regions   15, 190–1
Council of Ministers   25, 28, 30,
  40, 113, 176, 184, 187, 189,
  198
Council of the Bars and Law
  Societies of the EU   100,
  102–3, 105
Court of Auditors   47, 155
Court of First Instance   32, 51
CPME   95, 100, 102, 213
Crespy, A.   115, 172, 174
cross-border issues   66, 96, 99,
  102–4, 107–15, 120, 125–7,
  159–61, 183–5
cross-sectoral interests   14, 49–51,
  75–87, 99, *132, 132–3,* 147,
  157
Cullen, P.   42, 117, 130, 169
Curtin, D.   216, 223

Davignon, E.   70, 79, 84
decentralization   90, 156–7,
  177–9, 183, 198, 232
De Clerck-Sachsse, J.   135, 201
Defrenne case   43, 111, 168
de la Porte, C.   144, 225–6
deliberative democracy   64, 202,
  217, 223–6, 235
della Porta, D.   171–2

Delors, J.   49, 80–2, 113, 118,
  120, 227
democratic legitimacy   143, 200–6
  accountability   219–23
  consultation   209–16
  deliberative democracy   202,
    217, 223–6
  development of procedural
    initiatives   216–18
  group accreditation   218–23
  representativity   219–20
  transparency   206–11, 216,
    221–2
devolved authority   79, 177–80,
  179, 187–90, 193, 198
Directorates General   36–7
  Education and Culture   99, 113
  Employment and Social
    Affairs   99, 111–13, 117,
    120, 126–7, 130, 143–4,
    165–9, 185, 214–15, 229–30
  Enterprise and Industry   143,
    210
  Environment   39, 151, 155
  Regional Development   180,
    184
  SANCO   39, 159–60, 213–15
  Trade   39, 143, 225
Dølvik, J. E.   109, 124–7

economic agendas   113–17
Economic and Social
  Committee   121–2
Egan, M.   48, 86
Eising, R.   7, 12, 18, 48, 70, 90,
  200, 234
Environmental Fifth Action
  Programme   145, 147
environmental interests   6, 15–16,
  28, 37, 39, 46, 48
  business   107–8
  citizen issues   128, *131, 139,*
    140–2, *141,* 144–61, 164,
    174–5
  labour   113, 117

organized civil society 204–5, 218, 228
regions 178, 182, 189, 193
Equal Opportunities unit 169, 230
Eriksen, E. 223–4
Erne, R. 50, 112–16, 119, 123, 171–2
EU-level organization 121–6, 184–5
EU NGOs 140, *141*, 216, 221
EURATEX 7, 70
EURELECTRIC 70, 147
EU Research Framework Programmes 39, 91
EUROCADRES 97–100, 126
EUROCHAMBRES 14, 84–6
Eurocities 192–3, 231
Europa 59, 189, 207–9
European Anti-Poverty Network 116, 144
European Association of Craft, Small and Medium-Sized Enterprises 14, 49, 51, 84–7, 99, 104
European Association Statute 143, 222
European Business Test Panel 34, 212
European Centre of Employers and Enterprises 15, 49, 185
European Chemical Industry Association 61, 88, 104, 147, 172
European Citizen Action Service 15, 35, 134, 221
European Citizens Initiative 4, 28, 134–5, 217
European Confederation of Executive and Managerial Staff 97, 99–100
European Construction Forum 91–2
European Consumer Consultative Group 163, 220

European Consumers Consultative Group 213, 220
European Consumers Organisation 16, 48, 128, 161–4, 213, 220
European Council of the Liberal Professions 15, 97, 100
European Court of Justice 43–5, 52, 86, 96, 109–11, 114–15, 145, 155, 163, 168, 207, 230
European Economic and Social Committee 45–6, 98
European Environmental Bureau 142, 148, 151, 154–5, 157
European Food Safety Authority 47, 159
European Industry Federations 122, 124
European Investment Bank 46, 155, 180
European Lawyers' Union 100–1
European Metalworkers Federation 114, 123
European Monetary Union 22, 114
European Parliament 1, 4, 9, 11–12, 24–5, 35, 40–3, 52, 196
  citizen issues 130, 142, 156, 163, 169, 174
  labour 110, 113, 115, 120–2
  lobbying 55, 57–8, 62
  organized civil society 213, 219
European Partnership for Energy and the Environment 92, 147
European Public Affairs Directory 13, 18
European Public Services Union 122, 127
European Round Table of Industrialists 14, 69–70, 75, 77, 79–84, 147, 170, 172, 227–8, 230

European Services Forum   70, 76, 180
European Social Model   109, 120–1, 126
European Trade Union Confederation   15, 27, 48–50, 86, 97, 99, 109, 112–18, 120–7, 135
European Transparency Initiative   8, 16, 19–21, 29, 53, 57–62, 69, 136–7, 217, 226
European Transparency Register   8–9, 17, 25, 57–64, 128, 173, 178, 220–3, 234
European Union of Medical Specialists   100, 102
European Women's Lobby   17, 168–71, 229–31, 235
European Works Councils   118–19, 122
European Year against Racism   165–6
European Youth Forum   16, 137
Evetts, J.   103, 106
experts/expertise   37, 147, 150, 162, 189, 208, 210, 216–17

factionalism   16, 197, 201, 228, 232
'family' organizations/ networks   15, 46, *73,* 86, 130, *131,* 173–4
Fazi, E.   140, 147, 174
FEANI   100, 102, 106
Fielder, N.   70, 80, 83, 90
firms   48, 67–9, 79, 83, 87–92, 115
    large   14–20, 71–2, 74, 77, 86, 89–90, 228; as EU public affairs actors   48, 92–3, 228
    see also companies; MNCs; SMEs
Fraisse, L.   142–3
France   13, 18, 83, 94–6, 99, 114, 123–4, 196

free market   96, 126
Friends of the Earth   16, 35, 46, 113, 128, 142, 147, 150–1, 154–7, 173, 203, 210
funding of NGOs   4, 16–17, 22, 44, 48, *138–9*
    citizen issues   136–41, 144, 150, *152,* 160–2, 165–8, 175
    labour   124–6
    lobbying   58, 60–1
    organized civil society   201, 203, 206, 215, 229–30, 233
    regions   176–80

G10 group   15–16, 39, 46, 140, 150–4, *152–3,* 157, 161
GATS   70, 96, 107
Gehlen, C.   19, 41
gender issues   17, 44, 168–71, 229–31, 235
General Systems Directives   98, 105
Germany/Germanic countries   13, 18, 26, 30, 48, 83, 86, 92, 96, 111, 114–15, 118–20, 124, 145, 176–7, 187–9, 196
Gillies, D.   36, 40–1
globalization   8, 19, 21, 58, 64, 79, 81, 95, 171–2, 203, 233–4
Grande, E.   5, 70
Grant, W.   87–8, 91, 159
Graziano, L.   11, 156
Greece   179, 181, 191
Green-Cowles, M.   22, 78, 80–1, 91, 111
Greenpeace   16, 113, 128, 136, 140, 142, 150–1, 154, 156–7, 172–3, 203
Greenwood, J.   13, 49, 56, 69–71, 88–9, 91, 118, 177, 180, 188, 190, 219, 233
Greer, S.   18, 213, 215–16

group accreditation 5, 11, 56, 130, 218–23
Guiraudon, V. 166–7, 218
Gyllenhammer, P. 79, 84

Haas, E. 5, 199, 227
Hadden, J. 128, 150, 171–2, 233
Hall, I. 71, 213
Halpin, D. 56, 219, 225
Harlow, C. 38, 43–4, 163, 169, 206–7
Hart, D. 68, 228
Hayes-Renshaw, F. 28–9, 78
Helfferich, B. 169–70
high politics 21, 23, 27, 66, 82, 159, 228
Hooghe, L. 176, 179, 191–2, 197–8
Hüller, T. 214–15
Huysseune, M. 187, 190

IG Metall 115, 122
institutionalization 1–4, 125–30, 141–4, 154–7, 162–3, 168–75, 206, 233–4
integration 5, 7, 21–4, 26, 33, 43–4, 48
  business 65, 70, 79–81, 92, 94–6, 99, 104, 108
  citizen issues 129, 164–5, 167–8, 172
  labour 112, 114
  organized civil society 199, 206, 225, 227–31
  regions 190, 196–7
inter-institutional
  mechanisms 32–3, 45–7
International Union of Local Authorities 184, 191
Interregional Trade Union Councils 115, 123
INTERREG programmes 183, 192–3, 231
Ireland 35, 179, 181, 191
Italy 94, 176, 180, 188

Jans, T. 187, 190
Jarman, H. 39, 214
Joerges, C. 38, 223–4
John, P. 177, 180, 191, 197–8
Joint Technology Initiatives (JTI) 39–40

Kallas, S. 8, 11–12, 59–62, 64, 69, 137, 220
Kautto, P. 37, 90
Keating, M. 179, 181, 184, 191
Kendall, J. 142–3, 222
Kirchner, E. 87, 150, 163
Kohler, Koch, B. 4, 66, 201–2, 215, 224, 226
Kolb, F. 169–70
Kotzian, P. 210, 212–14
Kovacev, M. 176–7, 182

labour interests 109–13, 126–7
  economic agendas 113–17
  European organization 121–6
labour markets 49–50, 97, 101, 109–10, 113–16, 124–6, 142, 168–9, 230
  participative model 117–21
labour sectoral actors 122–3
Lahusen, C. 18, 20
Lange, P. 113, 231
Lehmann, W. 35, 41, 43
Lehmkuhl, D. 26–7
Leigh, C. 171–2
Levy, D. 67, 93, 232
'Liaison Group' 45–6
Lisbon Treaty 2, 24, 27–8, 44, 116–18, 135, 144–6, 204, 209–10
Long, T. 37, 68, 146–7, 149, 151, 154–6, 158, 228
Lörinczi, L. 37, 68, 146–7, 149, 151, 154, 158, 228
Lovecy, J. 95, 105
Lowery, D. 9, 11, 71
Lowi, T. 2, 66, 228, 232

McAdam, D. 12, 125
McAteer, M. 177, 197–8
McGown, M. 44–5
McLaughlin, A. M. 56, 87
Mahoney, C. 6, 20, 27, 93, 140,
    215, 232
Majone, G. 47, 205
majoritarian systems 6, 23, 51,
    121, 204, 224, 231
Mamadouh, V. 179, 187
Marks, G. 12, 125, 179, 182,
    187–8, 192, 197
Martin, A. 112, 125, 127
Marxism 65–6
Mattli, W. 80–1, 92
Mazey, S. 129, 150, 155, 168–70,
    230
MEPs 31, 35, 41–3, 55, 158, 164,
    213
Metcalfe, L. 176, 183
Milan European Summit
    (1985) 80, 82
MNCs 6, 19, 67–73, 79–80,
    83, 87, 92–3, 101,
    107–8, 111–12, 118,
    147–8
Moore, C. 187–9
Moravcsik, A. 181, 205
multi-level governance 1, 4, 68,
    176, 235, 197, 231

Nanz, P. 144, 225–6
Naurin, D. 33, 217
Neale, P. 103–4
neo-functionalism 7, 199, 226–9,
    235
Netherlands 13, 26–7, 45, 96,
    101, 114, 189–90
Neyer, J. 38, 223–4
Nokia 37, 90
Nollert, M. 80, 83, 90
non-group actors 17–21
Nordic countries 181, 190
Nugent, N. 3, 40

Olson, M. 72, 200
Open Method of
    Coordination 116, 144, 226
Orgalime 88, 148
organized civil society 199–200,
    231–5
    accountability 219–23
    consultation 206, 209–16,
        218–26, 230, 233–4
    deliberative democracy 223–6
    democratic legitimacy 200–6,
        209–16
    EU competencies 199–200,
        226–31, 235
    group accreditation 218–23
    integration 199, 206, 225,
        227–31
    procedural initiatives 216–18
    representativity 219–20
    transparency 206–11, 216,
        221–2
Orzack, L. 94, 105

Parks, L. 174, 233
participative labour market
    model 117–21
participatory democracy 1–3, 25,
    46, 58, 140–3, 201–5, 217–19,
    230–5
Permanent Forum of Civil
    Society 134, 221
Piattoni, S. 185, 224
Pitkin, H. 2, 203
pluralism 3–4, 18–22, 32–4, 39,
    47, 51–3, 201, 206–8, 214–16,
    231–4
Pointer, S. 29–30
Poland 135, 187
political systems 1–5, 22–3, 53–4,
    66, 93, 113, 202–7
    see also deliberative democracy;
        majoritarian systems; multi-
        level governance; participatory
        democracy

Pollack, M. 169, 230
Porter, M. 12, 147
Portugal 179, 181, 191
Posted Workers Directive 110,
    115, 127
Prakash, A. 67, 93, 232
Presidency 28, 30
Private Business Forum 85–6
procedural initiatives 216–18
professional associations 60, 69,
    96–100, 103–6
professional interests 65–9, 93–9,
    107–8
    EU sectoral 100–7
Public Affairs Practitioners 56–8

Qualified Majority Voting 24, 49,
    78, 82, 111, 114, 116, 145,
    160, 168–9
Quittkat, C. 35, 140, 210,
    212–15

race issues 42, 116, 165–7
Rawlings, R. 38, 44, 163, 169
regional governance 177–84
regulation 2, 21, 42, 45
    business 68, 72, 95, 106–7
    citizen issues 146, 151
    deregulation/re-regulation 26,
        72, 110, 126
    labour 110, 113, 126
    lobbying 8, 29, 53–64, 69, 137
    organized civil society 205–6,
        223, 232, 235
representativeness/
    representativity 46, 50–1,
        63, 98, 130, 134, 202,
        217–22, 226
Richardson, J. 150, 215, 230, 234
Richardson, K. 81, 92, 155, 168
Roethig, O. 120, 125
Rome Treaty 81, 141, 166–7, 180
Ronit, K. 70, 88
Ross, G. 112, 120, 125, 127

Ruzza, C. 113, 148, 173, 233
Salisbury, R. H. 75, 84
Sandholtz, W. 22, 70, 80
Saurugger, S. 30, 172, 202–3, 218
Schmidt, K. 59, 61–2
Schultze, C. 177, 193, 196
Scotland 176, 184, 189
Secretariat General 56, 61
sectoral interests 86–92, 100–7
Sikkink, K. 172, 223
Single European Act 81, 128, 227
single market 22, 49
    business 67, 80–2, 95–6, 104–7
    citizen issues 128, 145, 160,
        163, 167, 170
    labour 109, 111, 115, 118, 126
    organized civil society 227, 235
    regions 181–2, 196
SMEs 9, 14, 31, 42, 45, 75, 84–7
Smismans, S. 49, 130, 223, 225
Smith, J. 140, 147, 174
social dialogue 27, 49–51, 86,
    98–9, 110, 113, 116–18,
    121–2, 125–6, 130, 160
social interests 164–71, 227
social movements 21, 113, 128,
    150, 154, 156, 171–5, 233
Social Platform 15, 17, 27–8, 35,
    46, 130, 134, 140, 143, 164,
    220–1, 230
Society of European Affairs
    Practitioners 56–7
Spain 123, 156, 169, 176–7, 181,
    187–9, 196
Standing Committee of European
    Doctors 95, 100, 102, 213
Sudbery, I. 218–19
Sutcliffe, J. 176–7, 182
Switzerland 19, 156–7
systemic dependence 1–8, 21–2,
    35–7, 135–6, 203–4, 234–5

Takeover Directive 41, 113
Tanasescu, I. 211, 214–15

Technology Platforms   39–40
territorial interests   176–8, 196–8
  Brussels office   185–90
  collective action   178, 190–7
  EU-level organization   184–5
  regional governance   178–84
territorial representation
  offices   *186*, 187–90
Thatcher, M.   82, 120
Thomas, C.   78, 173
Trade Union Congress, UK   124–5
Trade Union Technical
  Bureau   125–6
transparency   2–6, 10–12, 20–2,
  30–4, 38–9, 44, 47, 209–11,
  216, 221–2, 233
  see also European Transparency
  Initiative; European
  Transparency Register
trans-regional networks   182,
  185, *194–5*, 197
Treaty on European Union   13,
  31, 129, 142, 145, 169–70,
  179, 206
Tyszkiewicz, Z.   77, 118, 121

UEAPME   14, 49, 51, 84–7, 99,
  104
UK   13, 18, 35, 72, 85, 92–6, 100,
  114, 120, 124–5, 154, 180,
  184, 189–90, 196, 200
UNICE   70, 121, 147
URBAN programmes   183, 192,
  231
US   18–19, 78–9, 91, 102

van Apeldoorn, B.   22, 80–3,
  228
van der Storm, I.   180, 196
van Waarden, F.   112, 121
variety of interests   8–11, *10*
Visser, J.   109, 124–7
Volkswagen   30, 119

Wallace, H.   29, 82, 125, 161–3
Warleigh, A.   156, 218, 223
watchdog organizations   56–7,
  147, 218, 226, 233
Watson, R.   12, 113
Wessels, W.   12, 92
White Paper on Governance   13,
  32–3, 58, 143, 176, 183–4,
  204–5, 217, 219–20, 234
Wilson, J. Q.   2, 91, 228
Woll, C.   7, 26, 70, 93, 200, 234
women's movement   17, 44,
  168–71, 229–31, 235
Wonka, A.   8–9, 18
Works Councils   112, 118–19,
  126
World Wide Fund for
  Nature   137, 142, 147–8,
  151, 154–7, 173
  European Policy Office   16, 37,
  68, 128, 146, 149

Young, A.   40, 82, 125, 145,
  160–3

Zadek, D.   140, 223
Zysman, J.   22, 70, 80